THE KINGSHIP OF JESUS

SOCIETY
OF BIBLICAL
LITERATURE

DISSERTATION SERIES

William Baird, Editor

Number 66
THE KINGSHIP OF JESUS
Composition and Theology in Mark 15

Frank J. Matera

Frank J. Matera

THE KINGSHIP OF JESUS

Composition and Theology
in Mark 15

SCHOLARS PRESS

Published by
Scholars Press
101 Salem Street
P.O. Box 2268
Chico, CA 95927

THE KINGSHIP OF JESUS
Composition and Theology in Mark 15

Frank J. Matera

Th.D., 1981
Union Theological Seminary
Richmond, Virginia

Advisor:
Paul J. Achtemeier

Library of Congress Cataloging in Publication Data

Matera, Frank J.
  The kingship of Jesus.

  (Dissertation series / Society of Biblical Literature ; no.
66) (ISSN 0145-2770)
  Originally presented as author's thesis (Th.D.—Union
Theological Seminary, 1981)
  Bibliography: p.
  1. Bible. N.T. Mark XV—Criticism, interpretation, etc.
2. Jesus Christ—Royal office—History of doctrines—Early
church, ca. 30-600. I. Title. II. Series: Dissertation series
(Society of Biblical Literature) ; no. 66.
BS2585.2.M29 1982   226'.306   82-708
ISBN 0-89130-564-5   AACR2

Printed in the U.S.A.

TABLE OF CONTENTS

ACKNOWLEDGMENTS

The research involved in writing a dissertation is a highly personal undertaking. But the finished product inevitably reflects the assistance of a wider community. At the conclusion of this dissertation I am especially conscious of the many people who have formed that community for me.

To Professor Paul J. Achtemeier, my Supervisor, I express gratitude for sure guidance and continual encouragement. It was he who first suggested that I center this study on Mark 15. From start to finish he has offered critical insights and has been an affirming presence.

To Professor James Luther Mays and to Professor Jack Dean Kingsbury, members of my Committee, I am grateful for a series of helpful suggestions and stimulating conversations on the Gospel of Mark. It was in their exegetical seminar that I first became interested in the Kingship of Jesus.

To Union Theological Seminary I am grateful for a number of generous fellowships which have allowed me to complete this work without financial anxiety. I shall always treasure many warm memories of its faculty, staff and students.

To the Library Staff of the Seminary, ever willing to be of assistance, I am deeply indebted. So many have helped in a quiet way.

To the people of Saint Patrick Parish and their Pastor, John McMahon, I extend thanks for making a stranger feel at home. To former parishioners and to friends who have encouraged this project I express my deepest appreciation.

Finally, to my family which has been a continual source of support and strength I dedicate this work as a sign of my love.

TABLE OF ABBREVIATIONS

AnBib	Analecta biblica
BETL	Bibliotheca ephemeridum theologicarum lovaniensium
Bib	Biblica
Bib Leb	Bibel und Leben
BJRL	Bulletin of the John Rylands University Library of Manchester
BKAT	Biblischer Kommentar: Altes Testament
BTB	Biblical Theology Bulletin
BZ	Biblische Zeitschrift
ConBNT	Coniectanea biblica, New Testament
CBQ	Catholic Biblical Quarterly
ConNT	Coniectanea neotestamentica
CTM	Concordia Theological Monthly
EvQ	Evangelical Quarterly
Et	Etudes
ETL	Ephemerides theologicae lovanienses
FRLANT	Forschungen zur Religion und Literatur des Alten und Neuen Testaments
HTR	Harvard Theological Review
Int	Interpretation
JBL	Journal of Biblical Literature
JSS	Journal of Semitic Studies
JTS	Journal of Theological Studies
LXX	Septuagint
MD	Maison-Dieu
MT	Massoretic Text
NICNT	New International Commentary on the New Testament
NRT	La nouvelle revue théologique
NovT	Novum Testamentum
NTAbh	Neutestamentliche Abhandlungen
NTS	New Testament Studies
PEQ	Palestine Exploration Quarterly
Rev Exp	Review and Expositor
RSR	Recherches de science religieuse (Paris)

RSV	Revised Standard Version
SANT	Studien zum Alten und Neuen Testament
SB	Stuttgarter Bibelstudien
SBL	Society of Biblical Literature
SBT	Studies in Biblical Theology
SJT	Scottist Journal of Theology
SNTSMS	Society for New Testament Studies Monograph Series
ST	Studia theologica
TDNT	Theological Dictionary of the New Testament
Theo	Theology
TTZ	Trierer theologische Zeitschrift
ZKT	Zeitscrift für katholische Theologie
ZNW	Zeitschrift für die neutestamentliche Wissenschaft
ZTK	Zeitschrift für Theologie und Kirche

INTRODUCTION

For the past sixty years, beginning with the form critics, the passion narrative has attracted the attention of a continuous stream of scholars.[1] The form critics concluded that the passion narrative was essentially different from the rest of the gospel material in its genesis and formation.[2] Dibelius was especially insistent upon this and wrote: "And that is exactly what differentiates the Passion story from the Gospel tradition as a whole, i.e., its early composition as a connected narrative."[3] What struck the form critics was the manner in which the passion narrative, unlike the first part of the gospel, read as a continuous narrative with references to time and place in which one event led logically into another. Karl L. Schmidt, who otherwise found numerous "seams" in the gospels, was especially struck by the character of this story which he termed "eine fortlaufende Erzählung."[4] The result of the form critics' work was to set the agenda for the following generation of scholars.

Not all critics accepted the conclusions of Schmidt, Dibelius and Bultmann. George Bertram, later followed by Gottfried Schille, seriously questioned the *Sitz im Leben* which Bultmann and Dibelius had suggested for the earliest narrative. Thus they emphasized the importance of the cult in the formation of the passion[5] rather than the need for a primitive historical account or a missionary sermon.[6] Nevertheless the basic premise remained; namely, that the passion narrative was qualitatively different from the rest of the gospel.

The rise of the redaction critics brought new insights into the gospels as a whole and into the literary activity of the individual evangelists in particular.[7] If, as the redaction critics maintained, the evangelists were more than collectors, then one could wonder about the formation and theology of the passion narrative. At what stage of development did the evangelists, especially Mark, receive either the passion narrative or traditions of that narrative? How active were the evangelists,

1

especially Mark, in forming the narrative or connecting it to
read as a continuous story?

One of the first attempts to attribute the passion narrative
to Markan redactional activity came from Johannes Schreiber.[8]
In his study of the crucifixion account, Schreiber claimed to
have identified two pre-Markan traditions, an historical report
and a Jewish, apocalyptic tradition.[9] Schreiber then showed how
the evangelist welded the two in order to form the present account. Although other authors sharply criticized Schreiber[10],
his work was significant because it integrated the passion theology into the entire gospel. No longer was the passion understood as representing a theology unaffected by the evangelist.
Rather, it was one with the redactor's total purpose.

A number of important works followed Schreiber. Peddinghaus
endeavored to prove that Ps. 22 was at the origin of a pre-Markan
passion narrative.[11] Linnemann claimed there was no such narrative but that Mark composed the first connected account from a
series of independent reports.[12] Ludger Schenke subjected Mk.
14:1-42 to an intensive investigation and concluded that this
part of the passion narrative, at least, derived from Mark's
redactional activity.[13] Wolfgang Schenk, on the other hand,
built on Schreiber's suggestion of two traditions in the crucifixion narrative and extended Schreiber's two sources into the
whole passion tradition.[14] Finally, Dormeyer, in his massive
work, after examining the entire narrative on the basis of vocabulary and syntax, arrived at still another source hypothesis that
was composed of three levels.[15]

The careful tradition history approach of these scholars has
not gone unchallenged. In his two-volume commentary on Mark,
Rudolf Pesch concludes that the disagreement among these authors
demands a new approach.[16] He has also disassociated himself from
the work of Kelber and a number of American scholars,[17] and instead proposes a traditional pre-Markan passion narrative. The
thesis of his commentary is that this narrative begins with Mk.
8:27, and that it originated in the Aramaic-speaking community
of Jerusalem.[18] In many ways, Pesch's work returns us to the
earlier position of Dibelius who was inclined to see a continuous
narrative in which "the force of the events is so great that
little room remains for an independent interpretation of the

happenings."[19]   On the other hand, the source hypotheses of
Schreiber, W. Schenk and Dormeyer are indebted to the spirit of
Bultmann, who was more inclined to describe the growth of the
narrative in terms of smaller traditions.[20]

However, Pesch's work, in its turn, has not gone unchallenged. Franz Neirynck has attempted to demonstrate that Markan
stylistic traits are common both to Pesch's alleged passion narrative and to the first half of the gospel.[21] Indeed, in his
earlier work, *Duality in Mark*, Neirynck argued effectively that
there is a certain homogeneity to Mark's style throughout the
gospel which he classifies under the rubric of duality.[22] The
importance of Neirynck's research is that source critics must
now ". . , reckon with the possibility that the composite expression reflects the author's own manner of writing."[23] In other
words, to employ pleonasm or redundancy as a criterion for source
criticism in Mark is a delicate task. Duplicate expressions may
betray diverse sources, but in Mark they need not. They may
simply be a characteristic of his style.

Finally, in recent years structural analysts have applied
their method to Mark's passion narrative.[24] Their concern, of
course, is not the traditions or sources of the narrative but
its so-called deep structure. Perhaps the most important contribution of such studies is their sensitivity to the manner in
which Mark's narrative forms a unity.

From this brief survey, it is apparent that the form critics' evaluation of the passion narrative has been seriously
questioned.[25] Scholars are more inclined than previously to see
Markan redactional activity in the passion narrative. Nevertheless, no one can read these several works without a certain
feeling of uneasiness. The number of source hypotheses is nearly
as numerous as the authors who have proposed them.

On the whole, Mk. 14 has fared better than Mk. 15. In
chapter 14, stories such as the anointing at Bethany, the last
supper, the agony in the garden and Peter's denial seem to have
enjoyed a prior existence.[26] Consequently, it has been easier
to highlight Markan redactional activity there than in chapter
15. Moreover, the presence of the crucifixion narrative in
chapter 15 has centered attention upon this smaller unit rather
than on the entire chapter. Finally, even scholars who admit

that Mark is responsible for the majority of chapter 14 are not
so inclined to see that same activity in chapter 15.[27]

In light of this, our study intends to investigate chapter
15 as a unit in order to investigate its composition and its
theological theme. In terms of composition, we are interested
in determining the extent of Markan editorial activity. Is
Mark as active in this chapter as in earlier sections of the
gospel? Or, is he working with a connected narrative which he
has left essentially untouched?

Many of the works listed above suggest that the evangelist
was not working with a single passion narrative but with a variety of sources. However, the disagreement among their authors
shows how difficult it is to make a precise determination of
sources, especially in terms of specific verses, half verses,
etc. Moreover, if Neirynck is correct when he sees a homogeneity
in Markan style throughout the gospel, then the final redactor
has already rewritten many of his sources. In that case the
assignment of verses and half verses to the tradition or to the
redactor, so as to account for the entire chapter, is a risky
enterprise to say the least.

This study will not attempt yet another tradition history
of the passion narrative. Rather we propose to investigate to
what extent the evangelist has connected and arranged the blocks
of material present in chapter 15. In other words, can we detect such Markan editorial techniques so as to conclude that
Mark is responsible for arranging and structuring the narrative
as we find it today? Thus the first part of our investigation
will be a compositional analysis.

In a second section we shall build upon the results of this
compositional analysis in order to elucidate the theme and theology of Mk. 15. We shall argue that by carefully arranging
the material available to him, the second evangelist sought to
develop a royal theme. More specifically, Mark has employed the
six-fold use of the title "King" (15:2,9,12,18,26,32) and a
series of three mockeries (15:16-20a; 27-32; 35-36) to highlight
a royal theology which climaxes with the centurion's confession (15:39).

However, inasmuch as the redactor does not apply the title
"King" to Jesus prior to chapter 15, it will be necessary for us

to explain how he has prepared for the royal theology of this chapter. Therefore, beginning with the material in this chapter, expecially the three mockeries, we shall endeavor to work our way back into the gospel. In this manner we will show that the results of our second section confirm what we have learned from the first: that is, Mark is responsible for the composition and arrangement of chapter 15. He has composed this chapter in terms of a royal theme for which he has prepared the reader in the first part of his gospel. Thus we seek to demonstrate a unity between composition and theology. Mark has composed this chapter in light of a royal motif which we can find in the material which prefaces the passion as well as in chapter 15.[28]

CHAPTER I

JESUS, PILATE, BARABBAS

In this chapter we shall examine two scenes, the hearing before Pilate (15:1-5) and the release of Barabbas (15:6-15). These seemingly simple accounts present a number of complicated questions. What relationship is there between the hearing before Pilate and the trial before the Sanhedrin? Is one modeled upon the other or are they otherwise interdependent? Does Mark envision a second, morning trial in 15:1 or is he recalling the reader's attention to the night trial? How do we explain the sudden and seemingly unprepared for question of 15:2? Is it a part of the original tradition or was it introduced later? Finally, what is the relationship between the hearing before Pilate and the Barabbas incident? Are we dealing with one or two traditions? To answer these questions we shall begin with a detailed examination of the hearing before Pilate and conclude with a similar study of the release of Barabbas. The primary focus of our work will be to determine to what extent Mark has or has not been redactionally active.

I. THE HEARING BEFORE PILATE

Commentators have long noticed the parallel between the hearing before Pilate and the trial before the Sanhedrin.[1] In both episodes the entire Sanhedrin gathers together (14:55; 15:1) to hear or bring charges against Jesus (14:56-59; 15:3). Jesus, however, does not respond (14:61a; 15:5), so that both the high priest and Pilate must question him further (14:60,61b; 15:2,4). Nonetheless, there are significant differences between the two scenes. In the first, the high priest poses the climactic question ("Are you the Christ, the Son of the Blessed?") only after the accusations have been brought forth. But in the Roman hearing, Pilate immediately asks Jesus if he is the King of the Jews. Finally, the reactions of the high priest and of Pilate are totally different. In the first story the high priest tears his garment in anger[2] (14:63) while in the second the governor

7

stands amazed (15:5). The result of these similarities and
differences is that commentators have not been able to agree
upon the relationship between these two accounts. Braumann
judges that the trial before the Sanhedrin is somehow modeled
upon the hearing before Pilate[3], while Schneider and Genest[4]
maintain that the opposite is also possible.

A close examination of Mk. 15:1-5 reveals that v.1 is an
introductory verse for which Mark is primarily responsible.
Verses 3-5 represent an older tradition which he has inherited
and reworked. Finally, Mark has positioned v.2 between the introduction and older tradition forming the present pericope.
Inasmuch as Mark is responsible for the trial narrative[5] in
chapter 14, we shall argue that the redactor has molded both of
these accounts simultaneously. However, as in earlier doublets,
he was not concerned to form a perfect parallel. We now begin
a closer examination of the story.

The Introductory Verse

A morning trial? Our first task is to determine how Mark
understood *symboulion poiēsantes* in v.1. Does the phrase refer
to a second trial held in the morning before the Sanhedrin or
does it recall the night trial? Commentators have often ap-
proached this question with an agenda that endeavors to synchro-
nize the synoptics. Therefore, in light of Lk. 22:66, which
presents an early morning trial, they have argued that Mk. 15:1
represents the remnant of an early morning trial.[6] In that case
it would be doubtful that we are dealing with Markan material
in 15:1. However, others have tried to avoid the difficulty of
a second, morning trial by choosing the textual variant
hetoimasantes.[7]

The reading *symboulion poiēsantes* is supported by A B W Ψ
0250 f[1,13] and means "hold a consultation," while *symboulion
hetoimasantes* finds witnesses in ℵ C L 892 and translates "form
a plan, decide, consult, plot."[8] Clearly the latter avoids the
difficulty of a second, morning trial by suggesting that after
the night trial the Sanhedrin formed a plan in the morning by
which they delivered Jesus to Pilate. Matthew has followed this
interpretation by choosing an expression which means approximately the same, *symboulion elabon*, Mt. 27:1. However, in Mark,

the best witnesses support *poiēsantes*, while the reading of
hetoimasantes appears to be a later attempt at clarification.

Nonetheless, the more difficult reading does not necessarily
mean that Mark intended his readers to understand a second
trial. If we translate the aorist participle *poiēsantes* as expressing action antecedent to the main verb *apēnegkan* then we
may render the verse as follows: "And immediately, early in
the morning, after they had held a consultation (14:55-64), the
chief priests . . . after they had bound Jesus led him away and
handed him over to Pilate."[9] In this translation *prōi* does not
refer to when the consultation was held, but to when they delivered Jesus to Pilate. On the other hand the RSV gives the
impression of a morning trial when it reads: "And as soon as
it was morning the chief priests, . . . held a consultation; and
they bound Jesus and led him away and delivered him to Pilate."[10]
However, if our suggestion is accepted, then in 15:1 Mark is
resuming the narrative which the mockery (14:65) and Peter's
denial (15:66-72) interrupted. Thus 15:1 is not the remnant of
a morning trial but Mark's manner of recalling the night trial.

It is clear that Mt. 27:1 does not refer to a second trial
but serves as the ". . . definitive conclusion to the trial
scene as well as a coherent staging point for the insertion of
the special material about the fate of Judas."[11] In Mark, however, the definitive action against Jesus was taken in 14:64
katekrinan auton enochon einai thanatou. Consequently, Mark,
who has already closed the trial in 14:64, merely needs to remind the reader of that trial in 15:1 while Matthew, who has
not yet formally closed the trial in 26:66, uses 27:1 as the formal closing of his account.

Finally we note that if 15:1 refers to the night trial,
then this reference forms a loose bracket with the trial proper
(14:55-65) around Peter's denial (14:66-72). In that case, we
have a double bracket whereby Peter's denial brackets the trial,
and the trial brackets the denial.[12]

                    Peter's denial (14:54)
                       trial (14:55-65)
                    Peter's denial (14:66-72)
                       trial recapitulated (15:1)

If our study has been correct, then we have a first indication that 15:1 is not the remnant of a primitive narrative but

is attributable to Mark's own redactional activity. However,
we must investigate v.1 further and see if we can identify other
traces of the redactor's hand.

    A further investigation. Commentators have often noted the
overloaded character of v.1.[13] The use of two main verbs
apēnegkan and *paredōkan* adds to a sentence already heavy with
participles, *poiēsantes, dēsantes*. However, it is the listing
of the Jewish leaders which contributes most to the overloaded
character of the sentence. Not only does Mark name the three
categories which compose the Sanhedrin (priests, elders,
scribes), but he also adds the Sanhedrin (*kai holon to synedrion*)
as though it were a separate body.[14]

    It is the priests, however, that Mark seems to emphasize.
The elders and scribes accompany them (*meta tōn presbyterōn kai
grammateōn*) just as in 15:31 the priests mock Jesus with the
scribes (*meta tōn grammateōn*). Indeed, throughout chapter 15
the priests are the principal villains. They accuse Jesus
(15:4), they deliver him to Pilate out of jealousy (15:10), and
they arouse the crowd (15:11) to ask for Barabbas.

    The manner in which Mark highlights the priests and the
redundancy of listing all the members of the Sanhedrin, and then
the Sanhedrin, leads us to suspect that he is combining traditions. The suspicion seems justified when we note that in 14:53b
and 14:55, the list of leaders, when combined, is almost identical to that in 15:1.[15] Thus we suggest that Mark has inserted the
list of 14:53b, *pantes hoi archiereis kai hoi presbyteroi kai
hoi grammateis*, into the list of 14:55, *hoi de archiereis kai
holon to synedrion*, by means of the preposition *meta* to form
15:1.

    The probability that the list of leaders in 15:1 derives
from these verses is increased if we accept the suggestion, presented above, that Mark is not recounting a new trial but is
merely reminding the reader of what has already happened in chapter 14. In that case, the listing of the opponents from that
chapter helps to recapitulate what has taken place as well as to
point forward to what is yet to come. Later we shall argue that
Mark employs this technique of combining traditions to form a
transitional or introductory verse when we discuss the list of

women in 15:40. There we shall see that 15:40 is a conflation of 15:47 and 16:1.

Besides the overloaded character of 15:1 there are other signs that Mark is responsible for this verse. *Kai euthys* is a Markan expression found approximately twenty-three times within the gospel. And in five instances (1:12, 29; 6:45; 8:10; 14:43) the expression is employed, as it is here, to begin a new section. The use of *prōi* with *kai euthys*, however, is unique and will be considered below.

Symboulion, on the other hand, occurs only one other time in Mark; namely, 3:6. However, commentators have noted the redactional nature and importance of this verse.[16] In 3:6 the Pharisees and Herodians devise the first plot against Jesus. That theme is resumed in 11:18 and 12:12 (without the use of *symboulion*). Thus it would seem that the plot begun in 3:6 comes to its climax in 15:1 and must be attributed to the evangelist.

Similar to *symboulion* in theological importance is *paredōkan*. Mark employs the word three times (15:1,10,15) in the scenes we are considering, and in v.15 it forms a neat bracket with v.1: *kai paredōkan Pilatō . . . kai paredōken ton Iēsoun.*[17] The religious leaders hand Jesus over to Pilate, who hands him over to the soldiers. Between these two incidents occur the hearing before Pilate and the release of Barabbas.

Moreover, the handing over of Jesus is the conclusion of a long chain that began with John the Baptist (1:14), continued with the choice of Judas (3:19), was predicted by Jesus (10:33), and finally was carried out by Judas (14:10,11,41,42,44) according to Jesus' further prediction (14:18) and despite his warning (14:21).

Finally, we mention two other Markan characteristics, the omission of the particle, i.e., asyndeton, before *dēsantes*, and the use of *holon*. Mark's omission of the particle has been noticed by many authors and in this case Matthew corrects it.[18] On the other hand, the evangelist frequently employs *holon* in generalizing expressions (1:28,33,39; 6:55; 8:36; 12:30,33,44; 14:9, 55; 15:1,16,33).[19]

Time in chapter 15. As we mentioned, *prōi* with *kai euthys* occurs only in this verse. However, we believe that, in this instance, the usage is explainable as Markan since Mark seems to have constructed a crucifixion day in this chapter (15:1,25, 33,34,42).

The passion chronology remains a disputed point among Markan students. Although there are numerous time indicators beginning with chapter 11, no one has been able to arrange them into a satisfying scheme.[20] Scholars who support a schema of seven days[21] are faced with the objection that the first day has an end (11:11) but no specific beginning, just as the third day has a beginning (11:20) but no specific end. Moreover, the problem is complicated by the chronology of 14:1,12. Does the redactor intend us to count one or two days between these verses?[22] Thus Neirynck notes that a schema of seven or eight days in Mark 11-16 is "plus que douteux";[23] and Achtemeier writes that " . . . the 'last week' of Jesus in Jerusalem must remain a general designation . . . not an exact chronological definition."[24]

In the passion narrative (11-16), however, two days do have a clearly marked beginning and end, the day of the temple cleansing (11:12-19) and the day of crucifixion (15:1-42). Moreover, both are reckoned according to the Roman mode of time (midnight to midnight) rather than to the Jewish (sunset to sunset).[25] This precise chronology in chapter 15, as compared to the rest of the passion narrative, leads us to suspect that in 15:1, *prōi* is not part of an older tradition that the evangelist inherited, but a part of his redactional purpose to frame this chapter in a specific manner.

The investigation of this first verse has been a lengthy but necessary exercise. We can now suggest, however, that 15:1 is not the remnant of an earlier tradition but the redactional work of Mark. His reference to the night trial, the list of Jewish leaders, the vocabulary, the redundancy, the pleonasm and the time scheme, all support our thesis. By this verse the evangelist effects a transition from the important events of chapter 14 and prepares for his crucifixion day in chapter 15.

Pilate's Question

The appearance of Pilate's question comes suddenly and un-
expectedly.[26] It breaks the flow of the narrative between v.1
and vv.3-5, and it occurs before Pilate has had an opportunity
to hear the charges brought against Jesus. Luke evidently understood this difficulty because he announces the charges to Pilate
(23:2) before Pilate asks Jesus the question, "Are you the King
of the Jews?" Matthew has followed Mark except that he has inserted the tradition about Judas' death (27:3-10) between the
introductory verse (27:1-2/Mk. 15:1) and the question 27:11/
Mk. 15:2). Moreover, Matthew prepares for the question more
carefully by describing the situation between Jesus and Pilate
in forensic language.[27] The effect of Matthew's interlude, and
the more formal language, is to relieve the abruptness present
in Mark's narrative. In John, the Jews do not explain the exact
charges to Pilate (18:30), but the extended introduction to
Pilate's question again relieves the tension which arises from
the abruptness of Mark's narrative.

The unanticipated nature of this question (which the other
evangelists have avoided or relieved) has led commentators to
suggest that v.2 has been inserted into vv.1, 3-5.[28] Others,
however, have wondered why the redactor would have inserted the
question in such an awkward place rather than after 15:5.[29]
Moreover, if there were an earlier account consisting of vv.1,
3-5 (in which v.2 was later inserted), then that account did not
give a reason for Jesus' death.[30]

We have argued that 15:1 belongs to Mark's redactional activity. Consequently, we do not agree that 15:2 was "inserted"
into an earlier tradition composed of vv.1,3-5. Rather, we suggest that Mark has formed the question of 15:2 in light of 15:26,
the inscription on the cross.[31]

The historic present[32] (*legei*) which Mark employs and which
Matthew and Luke alter to *ephē* seems to be one indication of the
author's hand as well as the use of the compound *epērōtaō*.[33]
Thus the placement of the question in this apparently awkward
position seems to be Mark's manner of announcing what will be
an important element for chapter 15, namely, the kingship of
Jesus (15:2,9,12,18,26,32).[34]

The form of Pilate's question, *sy ei*, recalls a number of similar formulations in the gospel.

1:11 *sy ei ho huois mou*

3:11 *sy ei ho huios tou theou*

8:29 *sy ei ho Christos*

14:61 *sy ei ho Christos ho huios tou eulogētou*

Eduard Norden maintains that *sy ei* is a Semitic formula comparable to *egō eimi*, and the examples which he cites show that its function is often to reveal or manifest the deity.[35] In Mark it is striking that the formula is used only in relationship to titles such as "Son of God," "Christ" and "King."

All of the evangelists are aware of the *sy ei* formula and employ it. Matthew, Luke and John follow Mark's usage in the hearing before Pilate (Mt. 27:11; Lk. 23:3; Jn. 18:33). In the scene before the Sanhedrin, Matthew and Luke again follow Mark (Mt. 25:63; Lk. 22:67). However, in this case they remove the ambiguity in Mk. 14:61, which might allow the reader to understand the high priest's question as a sarcastic statement rather than a question, by recasting the phrase to read,[36] *ei sy ei ho Christos*. In the confession at Caesarea Philippi only Matthew (16:16) follows Mark in the formulation, while in the baptismal scene it is Luke (3:22) who follows the second evangelist. Finally, the cry of the unclean spirits (Mk 3:11) finds a parallel in Lk. 4:41 but not in Matthew.

However, it is only Mark and Luke who are consistent in their usage, so that they alone employ the formula with some sort of title.[37] We suggest that this is not coincidental, but rather that Mark intends his readers to relate "King of the Jews" to the other titles made in conjunction with *sy ei*, namely, "Son of God" and "Christ." In that case the placement, and perhaps the origin of the question, belongs to the redactor.

The Silence of Jesus

On the basis of our analysis thus far, we suggest that vv.1 and 2 were not originally a part of vv.3-5, but rather have been introduced by the redactor. On the other hand, vv.3-5 appear to be based on an earlier tradition which Mark has reworked, and now form a doublet with 14:60-61a.[38]

15:4a *ho de Pilatos palin epērōta auton legōn*

14:60   *kai anastas ho archiereus eis meson epērōtēsen ton*
                                          Iēsoun legōn
15:4b   *ouk apokrinē ouden*
14:60b *ouk apokrinē ouden*
15:4c   *ide posa sou katēgorousin*
14:60c *ti houtoi sou katamarturousin*
15:5a   *ho de Iēsous ouketi ouden apekrithē*
14:61a *ho de esiōpa kai ouk apekrinato ouden*

As the verses now stand, however, Mark has reworked them so
that the question of v.2 has been fully integrated into the
structure. Thus we notice the remarkable manner in which vv.3-5
interlock and bracket each other, and the way in which v.2 now
fits into the pattern.[39]

    2 *epērōtēsen auton ho Pilatos . . .*

        3 *kai katēgoroun autou . . .*

    4a *ho de Pilatos palin epērōta auton*
                4b *ouk apokrinē ouden*
        4c *ide posa sou katēgorousin*
                5a *ouketi ouden apekrithē*
    5b *hōste thaumazein ton Pilaton*

In this arrangement Pilate's question (2,4a) brackets the
priests' accusations (3), and the priests' accusations (3,4c)
bracket Pilate's question (4a). Moreover, the last accusation
(4c) is bracketed by the double negatives (4b,5a), and the whole
episode is bracketed by references to Pilate (2,5b). Finally,
the allusion to Pilate's amazement is repeated in 15:44. Later
we shall show that the redactor has inserted 15:44 into the
burial scene. This double reference to Pilate's amazement[40]
leads us to suspect that the redactor has also been at work here.

    In brief, these bracketing techniques, plus the use of
polla (3), *ide* (4), *palin* (4) and the double negatives (4,5),
which Matthew has avoided, suggest that Mark has reshaped an
earlier tradition.[41]

    We can summarize our investigation of Mk. 15:1-5 by saying
that the evangelist has reworked an older tradition which related
Jesus' silence before his accusers[42] and used this tradition in
the hearing before Pilate and the trial before the Sanhedrin.
To this tradition he joined v.2 in order to recall a series of
earlier titles and to prepare for an important theme. Finally,

he introduced the material, and the entire chapter, with the extended introduction of v.1. The result is that the redactor has
constructed a "trial" scene before Pilate to parallel the trial
in chapter 14. However, whereas the first trial ended with a
climactic confession (14:62), this scene begins with an ambiguous and unexpected confession (15:2) which will grow in inten-
sity. Moreover, whereas the first trial ends with a specific
condemnation (14:64), the second does not.

The placement of Pilate's question and Jesus' response at
the beginning of the hearing is purposeful. In the first trial,
the confession provided a climax to the trial and to the chapter.
Here it is less dramatic because its purpose is to establish a
theme. By rendering Jesus' answer in an ambiguous manner, Mark
not only allows the narrative to continue, but he also presents
a problem which must be resolved. In what sense is this man the
King of the Jews?

The presence of two scenes similar in nature and structure,
but not perfectly parallel, can be found in the feeding stories
(6:34-44; 8:1-9), in the healing stories (7:32-37; 8:22-26), and
in the accounts of Jesus' prophetic knowledge (11:1-6; 14:12-16),
as well as the two "trials."[43] We suggest that Mark has redacted
both of these scenes simultaneously from earlier traditions because he intends to draw a parallel between them.

II. THE RELEASE OF BARABBAS

Above we concluded that vv.1-5 do not form a pre-Markan
pericope but that they are the result of the author's editorial
work. We must now examine the relationship between the Barabbas
incident and the opening verses. Was the Barabbas story originally connected to the account found in vv.3-5 or was it joined
to that tradition at a later date?

The release of Barabbas begins with what appears to be an
extended introduction (15:6-8). The arrival of the crowd upon
the scene is just as sudden and unexpected as was Pilate's question. Indeed, when we read v.6 for the first time, our natural
inclination is to refer the pronoun *autois* to the religious
leaders who have been in discussion with Pilate (15:3). When we
reach v.8, however, it is quite clear that Mark intends us to

understand the pronoun of v.6 as referring to the people in the
crowd, since he makes the identification in v.8 and in the re-
mainder of the narrative (15:9,11,12,14,15) where *autois* clearly
refers to the crowd. Matthew, by contrast, has eliminated any
possibility of difficulty by avoiding the pronoun and by immediately identifying the actors as the crowd (27:15).

The main purpose of v.8 is the introduction and identification of the crowd. It substantially repeats the information of
v.6 except that now we are told that the pronoun in v.6 refers
to the crowd (*ochlos*). The use of *archomai* plus the infinitive[44]
in v.8 suggests that the redactor may be at work. And indeed,
when we examine the structure of vv.6-8, they disclose a type
of bracketing arrangement whereby the reference to Barabbas in
v.7 is enclosed by the references to "ask" in vv.6 and 8.

> v.6 *apelyen autois hena desmion ho parētounto*
>
> v.7 *Barabbas*
>
> v.8 *ho ochlos arxato aiteisthai kathōs epoiei autois*

These stylistic traits and the belabored introduction suggest
that the redactor has created a transition between the scene
before Pilate and the release of Barabbas. At an earlier stage,
the story may have consisted of vv.6,9,11-15a. Mark would have
extended the introduction with vv.7-8 in order to introduce
Barabbas and to clarify that the *autois* in v.6 refers to the
crowd. Verse 10, as we shall discuss below, is a parenthetical
expression introduced in order to lessen the guilt of the crowd,
whereas v.15b forms a loose bracket with v.1 through the use of
paradidomai and so probably belongs to the redactor.

The original tradition which Mark inherited seems to have
cast the crowd in a negative light. Elsewhere in the gospel,
however, the evangelist does not portray the crowd in such a manner. Rather, great crowds follow Jesus (2:4,13; 3:9,20; 4:1;
5:21,24) and are amazed at his teaching and miracles (9:15;
11:18). Moreover, the fact that the leaders fear the crowd
(11:32; 12:12) implies the favorable attitude of the crowd toward Jesus. Only once does the crowd show hostility toward him,
and that is in the garden of Gethsemane when " . . . Judas came
. . . and with him a crowd with swords and clubs, from the chief
priests and the scribes and the elders" (14:43). In this instance, however, Mark diverges from his usual practice of

referring to the crowd with the definite article,[45] so that the
crowd with Judas is distinct from "the" crowd which customarily
followed Jesus. Thus the negative picture of the crowd here
sharply contrasts with Mark's portrait in the rest of the gospel
and leads us to suspect that he is dealing with a traditional
story that he has inherited.

Nonetheless, even here the redactor attempts to soften the
judgment of the traditional story upon the crowd. Verse 10 appears to be a parenthetical expression[46] which Mark has introduced in order to shift the onus of guilt from the crowd to
the priests. He has accomplished this by what scholars have
termed his *gar* explanatory clauses.[47] By such expressions Mark
injects an added insight into the narrative. Here he seems to
be saying that although the crowd will soon call for Jesus'
death (15:13,14), it should be clear to the reader that the
crowd which acts in that way is a crowd incited by the priests.

The connecting links between this incident and the hearing
before Pilate are three: the title, "King of the Jews", which
occurs in 15:2,9,12; the role of the priests in 15:1,3,10,11;
and the action of "handing over" Jesus which comes in 15:1,10,
15. In every instance, however, the connecting links between
the two stories are the result of some sort of Markan editorial
activity.

First, the title, "King of the Jews," which is so prominent
in this incident, seems to have been introduced in 15:2 because
of the Barabbas story as well as the charge of 15:26. Second,
the role of the priests, which is so prominent in 15:1-5, has
been introduced in 15:10 to remove some of the onus from the
crowd and to strengthen 15:11 which, for Mark's purposes, did
not sufficiently emphasize the guilt of the priests. Finally,
the *paradidomai* also goes back to Mark. We find it in his *gar*
explanatory clause (15:10) and in 15:1,15. The last two instances form a bracket around the entire scene (15:1-15). Therefore, we suggest that the release of Barabbas was not originally
connected with the silence of Jesus. Rather the redactor has
brought together two traditions by an extended introduction
(15:6-8), by the emphasis placed upon the role of the priests
(15:10), by the title, "King of the Jews" (15:2), and by the
brackets formed by "handing over" (15:1,15).

The result of Mark's editorial work is that the trial scene
(vv.1-15) is now a unity in which there is a dialogue between
Pilate and the priests, or Pilate and the crowd inspired by the
priests.[48]

    1) Priests *hand over* Jesus to Pilate
        2) Pilate questions Jesus
    3) Priests accuse Jesus
        4) Pilate questions Jesus
        5) and marvels
  6-8) Crowd approaches Pilate
        9) Pilate questions crowd
      10) and knows priests' jealousy
  11) Crowd aroused by priests
    12) Pilate questions crowd aroused by priests
  13) Crowd aroused by priests "crucify him"
   14a) Pilate questions crowd aroused by priests
14b) Crowd aroused by priests "crucify him"
   15) Pilate *hands over* Jesus

The story, then, is not a comparison between Jesus and Barabbas,
but a growing accusation against the priests who have handed
over Jesus to Pilate and will mock him as King when he is on the
cross (15:32). Even the role of the crowd is secondary in comparison to the priests. Although the crowd calls for Jesus'
crucifixion, it does so under the spell of the priests and then
disappears from the narrative. It is not the crowd which mocks
Jesus at the cross, but the passersby (15:29) and the bystanders.

The lack of emphasis on Barabbas in Mark is underlined when
we see how Matthew, intent on such an emphasis, has had to alter
the Markan narrative. The first evangelist insists on pairing
Jesus and Barabbas in order to stress the choice between the
two.[49] Where Mark speaks only of Barabbas (15:9,11) Matthew
draws out the choice between Jesus and Barabbas (27:17,20).
Moreover, he introduces the brief interlude in which Pilate's
wife pleads on behalf of Jesus (27:19). In this way he heightens
the innocence of Jesus *vis à vis* Barabbas.

The result of Mark's redactional activity is that he has
fashioned a narrative which proceeds as a dialogue between Pilate
and the priests, or the crowd inspired by the priests. The
point of the dialogue is to accent the guilt of the priests.

The building blocks for the narrative have been set in place by
the evangelist who has inherited two stories, the silence of
Jesus (15:3-5) and the release of Barabbas (15:6,9,11-15a).
By an extended introduction to the second story, Mark has brought
the two together. Moreover, he has conferred a unity upon the
section in three ways. First, he has introduced the question
in 15:2 with the title, "King of the Jews." Second, he has
highlighted the guilt of the priests by his *gar* explanatory
clause in v.10. Third, he has bracketed the scene by the use
of *paradidomai* in 15:1,15. The result is a "trial" scene composed of different traditions which alternates between Pilate
(15:2,4-5,9-10,12,14a,15) and the priests or the crowd inspired
by the priests (15:1,3,6-8,11,13,14b). However, unlike the
trial before the Sanhedrin there is no formal condemnation in
the hearing before Pilate. We suggest that the reason for this
is found in Mark's polemic against the priests. They have already condemned Jesus in 14:64. Therefore, neither Pilate nor
the crowd needs to condemn Jesus in a formal way a second time.
The primary villains remain the priests.

CHAPTER II

THE MOCKERY OF JESUS

In this chapter we propose to investigate three scenes in
which mockery is the main motif: Mk. 15:16-20a; 27-32; 35-36.
Our purpose is to determine the relationship of these scenes to
the larger narrative as well as the compositional character of
each pericope. We wish to know how integral each story is to
the whole, and what traces, if any, there are of Markan redactional activity. To answer these questions it will be helpful to
study how each pericope has been fitted into the wider narrative.

I. MOCKERY BY THE ROMAN SOLDIERS

Commentators have often noticed that this scene appears to
have been inserted into the existing narrative.[1] The primary
reason is that *hina staurōthē* (15:15b) finds a natural continuation in 15:20b, *kai exagousin auton hina staurōsōsin auton*.
Moreover, the reference to crucifixion in both verses serves as
a framing device for the mockery story. As we have already indicated, the use of such a device is a favorite Markan technique
and a sign that the redactor is at work.

However, there are also other reasons for suspecting that
Mark inserted this story. A comparison with the other gospels,
for example, suggests the free-floating character of this material. This can be seen in Matthew, who has followed Mark closely
and yet feels a need to tie the pericope more tightly with what
has preceded by identifying the soldiers as belonging to the
governor (*tou hēgemonos*, 27:27).[2] Moreover, Matthew's use of
tote (27:27) to introduce the story has the effect of making it
one more incident in a long progression of events and so draws
the reader's attention away from the inserted character of the
material.

John also knows a mockery scene (19:2-3) which has remarkable parallels to Mark's and may be dependent upon it as the
following linguistic contacts, taken from Jn. 19:2-3, show:
plexantes stephanon . . . akanthōn . . . porphyroun . . . chaire

21

. . . *Basileus tōn Ioudaiōn.*[3] Moreover, John's usage of
rapismata (19:3) recalls still another mockery scene in Mark,
namely, that which occurs after the trial before the Sanhedrin
(14:65). Inasmuch as John does not have a parallel to that incident, it is possible that he is combining elements from both
mockeries in the present story. For us, however, the most important point is that John has chosen to place his scene within
the hearing before Pilate rather than after it as Mark does. By
shifting the position of the story, he shows the free-floating
character of the material which each evangelist employed to his
own purpose.

Luke also has a mockery scene, although it is questionable
that it is dependent upon Mark.[4] In the third gospel, the story
occurs within the Herod incident (23:11). However, here it is
Herod and his soldiers who mock Jesus rather than the Romans.
There is no salutation of Jesus as King nor any royal apparel.
Rather, Jesus' persecutors place an *esthēta lampran* upon him, the
same apparel that the divine messenger to Cornelius wears in
Acts 10:30. Although Luke is probably not dependent upon Mark
(the only linguistic contact is *empaizas*), it is significant
that, like John, the third evangelist has placed the mockery
scene in a new setting.

Our survey has shown that the mockery tradition was rather
widespread and free-floating. Matthew and Mark place the mockery
after the hearing before Pilate; John and Luke place it within
the context of the hearing before Pilate. Moreover, Luke knows
a version in which Jesus' kingship is not the issue, or he has
so redacted the story as to eliminate any question of kingship.
When we consider that even in the present Markan structure the
scene could have been placed after 15:5 without much difficulty,
it becomes more apparent that Mk. 15:16-20a was inserted in its
present setting by the evangelist.

If Mark, as we have argued, is responsible for the placement
of this story, we may also ask if he has shaped and formed the
tradition in any way. There are a number of stylistic traits
which suggest that he has. First, Mark has recounted the initial
part of the episode in the historic present (*sygkalousin, endidyskousin, perititheasin*). Second, the title, "King of the Jews,"

is introduced by the Markan *archomai* plus the infinitive. Third, there is an example of pleonasm in Mark's usage of *tithentes ta gonata* and *prosekynoun autō*, a pleonasm[5] which Matthew has eliminated by the participle *gonupetēsantes* (27:29). Finally, the *esō tēs aulēs*, eliminated by Matthew, seems to refer the reader to 14:54 (*esō eis tēn aulēn*) and 14:66 (*en tē aulē̩*) as though Mark were trying to draw a parallel between what happened after the trial before the Sanhedrin, and what occurred after the hearing before Pilate.[6] These stylistic traits suggest that in some way the redactor has been at work.

Many commentators believe that v.19a is an intrusion into the narrative inasmuch as this incident of cruelty disrupts a scene in which mockery is the motif.[7] In favor of this view we notice that *eneptyon* occurs not only in this verse but also in the third passion prediction (10:34) and in the mockery after the night trial (14:65). In other words, it appears that the redactor has introduced this verse and this word in order to recall earlier material.

Another sign of intrusion into the narrative is the awkward placement of v.19b, the mock worship of the king. A comparison with Matthew shows that the first evangelist recognized this and reordered Mark's account.[8]

Matthew	*Mark*
robing	robing
crowning	crowning
scepter	
genuflection	acclamation
acclamation	striking with reed
spitting	spitting
striking with reed	genuflection

As the chart indicates, in Matthew the cruelties are arranged in an ascending order (spitting, striking) and the genuflection is transferred to a more logical position, i.e., before the acclamation. Thus Matthew gives order to Mark's clumsy insertion.

We would like to urge, however, that it is precisely the "clumsy" character of the Markan account which suggests the redactor's hand and discloses his purpose. First, a close examination reveals that Mark has inserted the cruelties (19a) within a loose bracket, between the salutation "King of the Jews"

and the homage rendered to the king in v.19b. Second, the
placement of this homage (after the cruelties), plus the use of
prosekynoun, results in an ironic scene; that is, after the
soldiers have made sport of Jesus, they unwittingly pay homage
to him as King. In Matthew, however, this irony has been lost
since the soldiers make sport of Jesus after they have paid
him homage. In other words, the final note in Mark, is homage,
whereas the final note in Matthew is cruelty. If we simplify
the chart, the result is as follows:

Matthew	*Mark*
genuflection	acclamation
acclamation	cruelty
cruelty	genuflection

Thus while Matthew may have a more logical order, the "clumsy"
arrangement of Mark results in a more ironic situation; that is,
the one the soldiers abuse is the one to whom they pay homage.

Finally, there is still further artistry in this scene in-
sofar as it is bracketed by *kai endidyskousin auton porphyran*
(15:17) and *exedysan auton tēn porphyran* (15:20a). The double
mention of the royal garment, before and after the mockery,
emphasizes the title, "King of the Jews," which Mark introduces
by *archomai* plus the infinitive.

We conclude that this scene has received its shape and form
from the redactor. The stylistic traits indicate that Mark has
rewritten an earlier tradition and inserted it into the narrative. The result is that he has given this pericope linguistic
contact with other stories (10:34; 14:65) and added irony to an
already ironic situation. Moreover, there is further contact inasmuch as *enepaizan* in 15:20a points to the third passion prediction (10:34) and to the second mockery (15:31). Thus, by
his linguistic contacts, Mark seems to place the priests in the
same category of mockers as the heathens, since, like the Gentiles (15:19-20), the priests spit upon (14:65) and mock (15:31)
Jesus.

II. MOCKERY AT THE CROSS

The second mockery (15:27-32) is a highly stylized account
which involves three distinct groups: the passersby who

blaspheme, the priests and scribes who mock (*empaizontes*) and
the thieves who deride (*ōneidizon*) Jesus. As usual there is
a close parallel between Matthew and Mark. Luke, however, has
reworked the story so that the mockers now consist of the
leaders (*archontes*) who mock (*exemyktērizon*), soldiers who jeer
(*enepaizan*) and a thief who blasphemes (23:35-39). Not only
has the third evangelist added the account of the repentant
thief (23:40-43) but he has also placed the charge (*epigraphē*)
against Jesus after the mockery by the soldiers (23:38). Moreover, the soldiers' mockery (23:36-37) is a parallel of Mark's
third mockery (15:36). Thus it appears that Luke has synthe-
sized two mockery scenes in this single account.[9] There is no
comparable mockery scene in John.

Once more we note that Mark seems to have inserted the
episode into its present position. In this instance, the bracketing verses are 25,26 (the third hour)[10] and 33 (the sixth
hour). Thus, the derision of the crucified occurs between the
third and the sixth hours.

Mark has employed this technique of inserting an incident
in order to account for the passage of time in at least one
other place, the death of John the Baptist and the mission of
the disciples. In that instance, the redactor told the story of
the Baptist's death (6:14-29) between the time that Jesus sent
his disciples on mission (6:7-13) and their return (6:30). The
use of the present pericope in order to mark the passage of time
upon the cross, therefore, appears thoroughly Markan.

Neither Matthew nor Luke report the third hour, although
both note the sixth and ninth. Moreover, Matthew introduces
this mockery with *tote* (27:38), the same word that he employed
in the first. The result is that neither his nor Luke's account
has the quality of inserted material to the same extent that
Mark's has.

Why Matthew and Luke have eliminated the third hour is
puzzling. However, the answer may lie in Mark's conception of
a crucifixion day. Earlier we pointed out that there are only
two days clearly marked out as beginning and ending in the
second evangelist's passion narrative, the day of the temple
cleansing (11:12-19) and this day. Moreover, while Mark is
aware of the Jewish mode of reckoning days (14:12,15:42), he

seems to be counting days according to the Roman system.[11] Consequently, in the crucifixion day, the primary function of the
three hour schema is to record the hours of Jesus' last day.
If this is so, then the concept of a crucifixion day may explain
the omission of the third hour in Matthew and Luke in the following way.

In Matthew *prōias de genomenēs* (27:1) refers more to the
conclusion of the night trial than it does to the beginning of
the crucifixion day. Likewise, *kai hōs egeneto hēmera* in Lk.
22:66 is more intent upon setting the trial during the day than
it is in marking the beginning of a crucifixion day. Mk. 15:1,
however, has a different function. As we have already shown,
according to Mark, the definitive judgment was made in 14:64.
Therefore, the purpose of *euthys prōi* is to point forward to the
crucifixion day. We urge that it is this crucifixion day which
has influenced Mark's schema of three hours,[12] a schema into
which he was able to insert the second mockery. Matthew and
Luke, less intent upon describing such a crucifixion day, have
omitted the third hour.

There is a further clue that vv.27-32 have been inserted
into the narrative. It is the tension which arises between the
crucifixion of Jesus (15:25) and the crucifixion of the two
thieves (15:27). The latter crucifixion is described in the
historic present as though that crucifixion were contemporaneous
with the crucifixion of Jesus. But in 15:25 the aorist shows[13]
that Jesus' crucifixion has already occurred. Matthew has relieved the tension by replacing Mark's *kai* with *tote* (27:38)
just as he did in the first mockery. In this manner he introduces the mockery as the next event in a progression of events.
Mark's *kai*, however, leaves the impression that his mockery
scene has been inserted into the narrative.

Luke has placed the narrative in a slightly different setting by repeating it after the division of Jesus' garments
(23:34). Mark could have done the same and placed the mockery
between 15:24 and 15:25. In that way he would have avoided the
tension described above. Of course Mark has not done so, and
we simply point to the possibility as a way of calling attention
to the inserted nature of the present pericope.

If we are correct when we insist upon the inserted nature
of this material, can we detect any traces of Markan activity
within the story itself? We should like to point to three
elements which we believe betray such activity.

The first is a technique that we have already highlighted
in the first mockery, the use of brackets. In this instance
Mark surrounds his material with *syn autō staurousin* (15:27) and
synestaurōmenoi syn autō (15:32). The historic present in 15:27
suggests that this verse has been edited by the redactor. Verse
32b, which introduces a third group of mockers (who have no part
in the dialogue), may have been added in accordance with Mark's
preference for threes.[14]

Second, the dialogue of the mockery is highly stylized so
that the words of the passersby run smoothly into the derision
of the priests and scribes.[15] While the ridicule of the passersby
concludes with the challenge to Jesus to save himself, the
mockery of the priests and scribes begins with the taunt that
he cannot. Finally, both mockeries, that of the passersby and
that of the priests and scribes, conclude with the same taunt,
"come down from the cross." The effect of this continuous dialogue is to form a sort of bracket around the priests and scribes
(15:31) as well as to connect their mockery even more tightly
with that of the passersby.

It would appear that Mark had some share in the formation
of this dialogue since nearly every element refers to his wider
theology. First, *ho kataluōn ton naon kai oikodomōn en trison
hēmerais* echoes the trial, *egō katalysō ton naon touton ton
cheiropoiēton kai dia triōn hemērōn allon acheiropoiēton
oikidomēsō* (14:58). Second, the challenge to descend from the
cross, *katabatō nyn apo tou staurou* may recall Jesus' command to
take up the cross *kai aratō ton stauron autou* (8:34), as well
as the Lord's ascent to Jerusalem *anabainontes eis Ierosolyma*
(10:32), for the express purpose of suffering. Third, the challenge that the crucified should save himself, *sōson seauton . . .
allous esōsen, eauton ou dynatai sōsai*, contradicts Jesus' own
injunction of 8:35 that whoever tries to save his life will lose
it, and whoever loses his life will save it. Moreover, the
word *dynatai* may allude to the disciples complaint in 10:26,

kai tis dynatai sōthēnai, as well as Jesus' reply, *panta gar dynata para tǭ theǭ* (10:27). Finally, the emphasis on "seeing" in order to believe may well refer to the quotation from Isaiah in the parable chapter, *hina blepontes blepōsin kai mē idōsin* (4:12), as well as the Pharisees' request for a sign in 8:11-13. Thus, in every instance the dialogue of the mockery is thoroughly Markan.

What can we say of the title, "the Christ, the King of Israel," which occurs within this dialogue? The use of the royal title is interesting here since "King of Israel" has replaced "the King of the Jews," and for the first time we encounter the title in apposition with another title,"Christ." Has Mark brought the titles together?

Christos occurs seven times[16] in Mark (1:1; 8:29; 9:41; 12:35; 13:21; 14:61; 15:32). Three times the evangelist uses the title by itself (8:29; 9:41; 13:21) and four times with another title (1:1; 12:35; 14:61; 15:32). In two of these occurrences the title apposed to *Christos* is "Son of God" (1:1)[17] or its surrogate "Son of the Blessed" (14:61). In one instance Mark brings the title in apposition to "Son of David" (12:35), whereas in the last case it stands in apposition to "King of Israel." At no point does *Christos* explain another title. Rather, for Mark *Christos* is always explained by other titles. Inasmuch as *Christos*, not "King," is the title which runs through the gospel, we suspect that in the present instance Mark has introduced "King of Israel" as a further definition of *Christos*. In that case the mockery may have once dealt only with the title *Christos* and later the redactor interjected "King of Israel" as a further definition, namely Jesus is "the Christ" as "the King of Israel."

The third and final place where we point to Markan redaction is the introduction of the scribes in 15:31, *meta tōn grammateōn*. As in 15:1,3,10,11, the main actors in 15:31 are the priests. Once more the scribes appear in a secondary position, and Mark introduces them in the same manner he did in 15:1, *meta tōn presbyterōn kai grammateōn*.

The introduction of the scribes at this juncture seems to refer to earlier portions of the gospel where Mark presented the

scribes as especially interested in the messianic question.
Thus it is the scribes who say that Elijah must come first (9:11)
and it is the scribes' doctrine of the Messiah which Jesus com-
bats in the question of David's son (12:35-37). Therefore, it
is appropriate that at the cross Mark introduces them as being
with the priests and ridiculing Jesus. For the scribes, Jesus
cannot be the Messiah because he is not David's royal descendant
in the tradition of a powerful King of Israel.

The second mockery scene, like the first, displays Markan
redaction. We have seen that Mark is responsible for the placement of the episode and for the shaping of the story. We can
now propose that Mark inherited a mockery tradition and that he
enclosed it by references to the thieves at the beginning and
at the end. Moreover, Mark has been active in the development
of the dialogue as well as the introduction of the scribes into
the narrative. Finally, for the first time the title "King"
comes to a certain fullness. "King of Israel" has replaced "King
of the Jews," and Mark has set it in apposition to *Christos*.
The one mocked as "the King of the Jews" in 15:16-20a is now
mocked as "the Messiah, the King of Israel."

III. THE ELIJAH MOCKERY

The third mockery (15:35-36) occurs immediately before the
death of Jesus. Once more Matthew has followed Mark. Luke is
aware of the incident but, as we have already noted, he has
placed it within the mockery at the cross (23:36). John may also
have been aware of the story or a similar tradition if we can
judge by word contacts such as *oxous* and *spoggon* (19:29).[18] However, in John there is no mockery, only the fulfillment of the
scripture (19:28-30). The fact that all the evangelists know
an incident which concerns the *oxous* is remarkable. Moreover,
it is significant that both Luke and John have employed it in
different ways. This freedom points to free-floating material
which each evangelist has used for his own purpose.

An examination of where Mark has situated the verses reveals that once more he has enclosed them in brackets. In this
case the bracketing words are *eboēsen ho Iēsous phōnē megalē*
(15:34) and *apheis phōnēn megalēn* (15:37). Matthew has similar

bracketing words, *aneboēsen ho Iēsous phōnē megalē* (27:46) and
palin kraxas phōnē megalē (27:50). However, a significant clarification has occurred in Matthew's account. In Mark it is not
clear whether Jesus uttered one or two cries. Certainly it is
possible to interpret 15:37 as a second, wordless cry, and by
the addition of *palin* Matthew has done just that. However,
given Mark's penchant for the insertion of material, it is also
possible to understand the aorist participle, *apheis*, as referring to the same cry uttered in 15:34. In other words, just as
in 15:1 Mark recalled the reader's attention to the trial, after
it has been interrupted by the denial scene, so here he recalls
the reader's attention to the cry in 15:34 which was interrupted
by the third mockery.

As we have said, the incident with the *oxous* does not appear to have been tied to a particular context. Luke makes no
reference to Elijah and places the story within the second
mockery (23:35-36). John has completely transformed the incident or knows a tradition which has. The free-floating character of this material, and the brackets to which we have
pointed, lead us to suspect that Mark is responsible for the
present setting of the story. Therefore, once more we ask if
the material contains any traces of his redactional activity.

When we compare these verses to Matthew, it is obvious that
the first evangelist has clarified some of Mark's ambiguity.
For example, Matthew makes it clear that the person who ran for
the sour wine was one of the bystanders, and that the crowd,
rather than the bystander, says *aphes idōmen*. In Mark, the
identity of the bystander (*tis*) is anonymous, and the bystander
is the one who utters *aphete idōmen*. To conjecture that the
bystander was a Jew, since only he could understand the Elijah
theology, or to conjecture that he was a Roman because he would
have the *posca* is to confuse historical and literary judgments.[19]
The text simply does not say who the bystander was. Rather, as
others have suggested, it appears that Mark has combined two
traditions here.[20] So we urge that Mark has inserted *dramon
de tis [kai] gemisas spoggon oxous peritheis kalamō eptizen
auton legōn* within *ide Ēlian phōnei* and *aphete idōmen ei erchetai
Elias kathelein auton.*

By inserting one piece of material into another, Mark employs his bracketing technique once more in a mockery scene.
Here he surrounds the tradition about the drink by references
to Elijah at the beginning and end. Earlier we noted that he
bracketed the first mockery by references to the thieves crucified with Jesus. This technique, plus the number of participles (six), the omission of the particle before *gemisas*, and
the use of *ide* suggest that the evangelist is at work.

Now that we have investigated the incident, we wish to return once more to the inserted nature of this material and view
it in still another light. A comparison with Matthew reveals
that Matthew has tied this mockery to the second mockery through
the catchword *sōsōn* (27:49). Mark, however, does not refer to
an earlier scene. Rather he employs *kathelein* (15:36) a word
for lowering somebody from the cross. The fact that Matthew has
altered Mark discloses more than theology; it reveals the independent nature of the tradition that Mark has inherited and inserted. That is, there does not appear to have been a prior
relationship between the second and the third mockery until
Mark brought them together.[21] Matthew has united them somewhat
through the catchword *sōsōn* while Mark has preferred to keep the
traditional word *kathelein*.

Still another clue that these verses represent an earlier
tradition which Mark has inserted comes from the words of Ps.
22 quoted in 15:34. If we set aside the historical question of
Jesus' *ipsissima vox*, it is difficult to understand how a Greek
reader could see a connection between *Elōi and Elia*.[22] The
reading of D Θ 059 565 seems to have realized the problem and
so altered the text ". . . to the parallel in Matthew (27:46)."[23]
Matthew probably also saw the difficulty and employed the Hebrew
Eli so that there would be a clear word play between *Eli* and
Elia. However the fact that Mark's text contains this tension
speaks strongly in favor of divergent traditions which have been
brought together, in this case the words of Ps. 22 and the call
for Elijah. Therefore, once more we confirm our hypothesis that
Mark has inserted this mockery as he has the first two.

In Mk. 9:11-13 Peter, James and John ask why the scribes
say that Elijah must come first. Jesus replies that Elijah

does come first in order to restore all things (9:12a). Then
a passion prediction concerning the Son of Man interrupts the
dialogue (9:12b). Finally, in v.13 Jesus tells the disciples
that Elijah has already come. The interesting aspect of this
section is that the Elijah material, *Ēlias men elthōn* (9:12a)
and *Ēlias elēlythen* (9:13) brackets the Son-of-Man prediction
(9:12b) just as the Elijah material brackets the episode of
the sour wine in the mockery we have just studied.

We allude to this incident for two reasons. First, Mark
seems to be using the same techniques in chapters 9 and 15,
bracketing and inserting material. Second, the fact that the
bystanders ridicule Jesus for calling Elijah is somehow related
to the words after the Transfiguration. In the latter scene
Jesus has already told the disciples that Elijah has come. Thus
it is clear to the reader that Elijah cannot come to save Jesus
from the cross because he has already come in the person of John
the Baptist.

IV. A FURTHER MOCKERY

There is yet another mockery scene (14:65) within the passion. Although it does not occur in chapter 15, we intend to
examine it in order to see if it bears any resemblance to what
we have studied thus far.

Once more Matthew follows Mark even as to the placement of
the scene. In both gospels the mockery happens after the trial
before the Sanhedrin, and before Peter's denial. In Luke (where
Peter's denial precedes the trial), the incident takes place
before the trial and after the denial. Whether Luke is dependent upon Mark is difficult to say.[24] In favor of contact are
common verbs such as *perikalypsantes*, *prophēteuson* (22:64) while
differences such as *enepaizon autǭ derontes* (22:63) indicate
that he may have had access to still another tradition. In
either case, it is important for us that Luke has placed the
mockery in a new position causing us to suspect the free-floating
character of the material.

If we read the Markan account in context, it is the members
of the Sanhedrin who spit at Jesus, blindfold him, strike and
taunt him as a prophet. Only later do the servants hit him.

In Luke, however, those who mock Jesus are not the members of the Sanhedrin but the ones in charge of him before he is brought to trial.

In Matthew the scene begins as the first two mockeries did, with *tote*. In this way the evangelist is able to gain some distance from the trial. However, he too has the members of the Sanhedrin striking Jesus.

The different placement of the scene in Luke and the horror of the Sanhedrin striking Jesus again leads us to suspect that this mockery, like the first three, was once a free-floating piece of tradition. Matthew and Mark have made the members of the Sanhedrin the villains whereas Luke has charged the atrocities to those responsible for guarding Jesus. The point to notice is that in Mark we discover who the mockers are from the context and not from an expressed subject. Only at the very end is an expressed subject mentioned, *hoi hypēretai*, and clearly it does not refer to the first part of the mockery.

Although the mockery is not bracketed, as are the other three, there is no doubt that it could be lifted from the narrative without any difficulty. In fact, if it were not in the narrative, there would be an even clearer insertion of the trial (14:55-64) within the denial scene (14:54, 66-72). Thus we believe that this scene, like the others, was inserted by Mark.

We suggest that the evangelist was active in this scene as he was in the others. The *kai ērchanto* at the beginning of v.65 acts very much like an attachment formula.[25] In this instance, it introduces the infinitive *emptyein* which recalls the third passion prediction (10:34) and points forward to the first mockery (15:19).

The use of *prophēteuson*, however, is strange since the trial concerns Jesus' messiahship and not his claim to be a prophet. This makes us suspect that Mark has inherited a tradition to which he has added an introduction and then inserted it into the present setting. Thus this mockery manifests much the same redactional activity as the other three. In four instances Mark has inherited, molded and inserted scenes of mockery into the narrative.

V. CONCLUSION

Now that we have examined the mockery scenes we wish to summarize our results. First, we have noted that each of the scenes in chapter 15 has been inserted into its present position by the redactor. Bracketing words such as "crucify," "third" and "sixth" hours, "great cry," all serve to fit the particular scene into its wider context.

Second, each scene reveals a significant amount of Markan redactional activity. By far the most common technique was to bracket or enclose the material. Thus the first scene is bracketed by the reference to the purple robe; the second by the reference to those crucified with Jesus; and the third by the reference to Elijah.

Third, in each scene Jesus' opponents mock him as a messianic pretender. The soldiers mock him as the King of the Jews, the priests and scribes deride him as the King of Israel, who cannot save himself, and the bystanders mock him as the Messiah whom Elijah will not aid.

Together these mockeries form a remarkable structural element in the formation of chapter 15. Each scene is separated from the other by an intervening pericope so that we arrive at the following structure.

	trial	
(crucify)	MOCKERY	(crucify)
	crucifixion	
(3rd hour)	MOCKERY	(6th hour)
	darkness	
(great cry)	MOCKERY	(great cry)
	death	

We are not claiming that this is the structure of chapter 15. But we are urging that Mark has used the mockeries in order to build up the passion narrative of chapter 15. However, we have not yet answered the question, was there a narrative into which he simply inserted these scenes, or is he also responsible for the setting of the three mockeries? We shall turn to this question in the next chapter when we examine the crucifixion narrative, the death of Jesus, and the burial scene.

CHAPTER III

CRUCIFIXION, DEATH, BURIAL

In the last chapter we studied the three mockery scenes
and concluded that in each instance they were inserted into
their present setting. Inasmuch as we have already considered
verses 1-15, it remains for us to examine the material which
surrounds the mockery scenes in order to complete our compositional analysis. Accordingly, we have classified these verses
under the headings of Crucifixion (20b-26), Death (33-34, 37-39)
and Burial (40-47).

Once more our purpose is to determine whether or not there
is Markan redactional activity in these sections. As we mentioned at the close of the previous chapter, we are especially
interested to discover whether the material which now surrounds
the mockery scenes was part of an earlier connected narrative
or whether the redactor has also been at work here. Consequently,
we shall be attentive to how these sections have been constructed
and what relationship they bear to the wider chapter.

I. CRUCIFIXION

The Search for an Earlier Narrative

In his commentary on Mk. 15:21-32, Nineham writes:

> This section is generally agreed to comprise a brief
> foundation story, no doubt derived from the primitive
> Passion narrative, and various items of tradition
> which had generally attached themselves to it.
> Scholars differ a good deal about precisely which
> verses belong to the primitive narrative, though
> there is general agreement that vv.21 (or v.20b)
> to 24a were among them.[1]

We have quoted Nineham at length because he expresses a view
which continues to be highly regarded, i.e., that there is a
primitive, historical narrative embedded in the crucifixion account. What Nineham claims for vv.21-32 is especially apt for
the section we are studying. The simplicity of the language and
syntax, the detached nature of the material and the frequent
use of the historic present have led many commentators to conclude

that these verses are the remnant of a primitive account. However, as Nineham notes, scholars " . . . differ a good deal about
precisely which verses belong to the primitive narrative."[2]

The impetus to view the crucifixion narrative as containing
some type of historical narrative comes in large measure from
Bultmann, who wrote: "In Mark's Gospel there is a legendary
editing of what is manifestly an ancient historical narrative to
which we may trace back vv.20b-24a."[3] As in so many other instances, Bultmann's insight was a determining influence upon a
whole series of scholars. Thus Finegan spoke of an "historische
Basis" which remained in vv.22,24a,26,37,40f.[4] Taylor said of
vv. 21-41 that " . . . one gains the impression of a comparatively brief foundation story, which has attracted to itself
various items of tradition."[5] In Taylor's opinion vv.21-24,26
came from a non-Semitic source which he labeled "A" while v.25
was part of the Semitic or "B" source.[6] Cranfield called attention to the disparate nature of vv.21-41 and wrote that they
gave the impression " . . . of being rather the result of the
piecing together of a number or eye-witness testimonies."[7] Indeed, even in the most recent commentaries and studies there
remains a strong conviction that embedded somewhere in these
verses there is the vestige of a primitive account. Schweizer
sees " . . . a very simple account of the crucifixion in vv.20b-
24a which, obviously, is very old."[8] Schneider claims that behind vv.20b-41 stands " . . . die älteste Erzählung von der
Kreuzigung und dem Tode Jesu. Sie war der Kristallisationspunkt
für die gesamte Passionsüberlieferung."[9] Finally, Gnilka[10] concludes that the historical kernel is found in vv.20b-22,24-27,40.

Since the publication of Schreiber's *Theologie des Vertrauens* there has appeared yet another approach to the crucifixion narrative.[11] After an analysis of style, vocabulary and
syntax Schreiber proposed that there were two crucifixion traditions embedded within the present narrative. The first,
15:20b-22a,24,27 " . . . ist offenbar ein alter Geschichts-
bericht, der aus persönlichen und theologisch-apologetischen
Gründen tradiert wurde."[12] Besides this historical report
Schreiber identified a second apocalyptic account in vv.25,26,
29a,32c,33,34a,37,38 which he said " . . . verkündet den Tod

Jesu mit Hilfe alttestamentlicher jüdisch-apokalyptischer Vor-
stellungen."[13] Of course Taylor had already spoken of two
sources in the passion narrative but Schreiber was the first to
view these sources (which differed from Taylor's) as competing
theological traditions.

Wolfgang Schenk based much of his work upon Schreiber's
analysis of two crucifixion traditions. Like Schreiber he isolated an historical, Simon tradition in 15:20b-22a,23a?, 24,27,
29b? and an apocalyptic tradition in 15:25,26,29ac,30,33,34a,37,
38,39.[14] Moreover, he extended these two traditions back to
chapter 11.

The work and approach of Dormeyer was similar to that of
Schreiber and Schenk inasmuch as he also set a premium upon the
analysis of vocabulary, style, and syntax. However, his analysis
of the material led him to entirely different results. Dormeyer
assigned 15:21,22a,23,24a,26,27,31a,32c,34ab,37,38,40 to the oldest
redaction of Mark which he labeled "T." Verses 31b and 32a, he
maintained, came from a second redactor which he called "Rs,"
while the remaining material (22b,24b,25,29,30,32b,33,34c,35,36,
39,41) originated with the final redactor of the passion, "Rmk."[15]

Unlike Schreiber and Schenk, Dormeyer speaks neither of an
apocalyptic source nor an historical report which derives from
the eye witness of Simon. Rather, he interprets his oldest tradition (T) in terms of the typology of the suffering Just One
which, he maintains, finds its *Sitz im Leben* in the catechesis
of the Hellenistic, Jewish-Christian community. "Rs" introduces
dialogue into the earlier narrative and shows that Jesus fulfills
the Old Testament titles of Prophet, Rabbi, Son of David, King
of Israel, and Son of the Most High, through his death and resurrection. Like "T" this second redaction served a catechetical
purpose. "Rmk" widened the Christology of the passion by introducing the Son of Man material so that Jesus' behavior became
a model for Christians to imitate in the period between Jesus'
death and the second coming.[16]

The work of Eta Linnemann stands apart from the three authors mentioned above. She is especially critical of Schreiber's
text, literary and style critique as well as his use of word
statistics.[17] As an alternative she proposes her own de-compo-
sitional analysis whereby she endeavors to establish the

primitive coherence ("ursprünglichen Zusammenhang") of the story
behind the present text.[18] She believes that she can isolate
such an original connection in the hour schema of the crucifixion narrative.[19] According to her this original nucleus comprised vv.22a,24a,25a,33,34a,37,38. To this a Christian scribe
supplemented scriptural references, vv.23,24b,27,34b. Finally,
Mark added his own redactional work which we find in vv.26,29b,
30b,31a,32,39.[20]

Criteria for Isolating Earlier Narratives

As disparate as these authors and approaches are, they
share many criteria in making their judgments of what constituted
the original sources for the crucifixion narrative. Thus, those
authors who would agree with Bultmann's position that there is
"an ancient historical narrative"[21] behind the present text
point to the simplicity of this account written with the frequent
use of *kai* parataxis and the historic present.[22] Indeed,
Schreiber and Schenk even use the historic present as a criterion
for reconstructing their Simon tradition.

Again, authors have continually employed the doublets within the narrative in order to separate sources. For Schreiber
and Schenk the double mention of the crucifixion (15:24,25),
the double reference to the drink (15:23,36), the two great
cries (15:34,37), and the similarity of the mockeries (15:29f.,
31f.), signal the use of originally diverse sources.[23]

For many authors, especially Dormeyer,[24] the employment of
word statistics has become a criterion for distinguishing layers
of tradition.

Finally, Mark's three hour schema has served as still another clue for discovering sources.[25] Bultmann attributed the
hours to Markan redaction.[26] But in recent years as authors
discerned more than one source in the passion narrative, they
saw the three hour schema as a natural crystallization point for
such material.

We can summarize by saying that the extensive use of the
historic present, apparent doublets, word statistics and the
three hour schema have aided Markan students in their quest for
a primitive crucifixion narrative and for sources of the passion

narrative. In our investigation of vv.20b-26 we shall keep
these criteria in mind as we attempt to determine the nature of
this material.

Analysis of Mk. 15:20b-26
     We have already noted that these verses occur after the
mockery by the soldiers and before the mockery by the passersby,
priests, scribes and criminals. Matthew has kept the same setting for his parallel account. In Luke and John, however, the
crucifixion begins immediately after the hearing before Pilate
since both authors have transferred the first mockery scene to
another setting.
     It is important to note what emphasis this positioning has
upon the narrative. Read in isolation, vv.20b-26 do not mention
who crucified Jesus. In context, however, it is clear that the
Roman soldiers crucified Jesus after they had mocked him. In
Lk. 23:26-34, however, we find a different situation. It is
not until 23:36, a different pericope, that the Roman soldiers
are mentioned for the first time. In fact, reading Lk. 23:24-25
we have the distinct impression that Pilate delivered Jesus over
to the Jews for crucifixion.
     We are not arguing that Luke believed that the Jews physi-
cally crucified Jesus. But we are saying that by the simple
positioning of the material, specifically the mockery, each evangelist was able to add theological nuances to the narrative he
composed. Thus, in the case of Luke, the omission of the Roman
mockery before the crucifixion seems to result in a theological
statement that the Jews, rather than the Romans, crucified Jesus.
     In terms of the general order of events, Matthew and Mark
are in agreement except for the fact that Matthew has omitted
the reference to Alexander and Rufus and to the third hour.
Luke has dropped the same details plus the Hebrew name, Golgotha,
the incident of the wine, and the inscription on the cross (which
he reserves for 23:38). He has introduced special material
about the women of Jerusalem and placed the first mention of
the thieves in a more logical setting.

MT.	MK.	LK.
Jesus led out	Jesus led out	Jesus led out
Simon	Simon	Simon
------	Alex & Rufus	------
------	------	Women of Jer.
Golgotha	Golgotha	------
wine	wine	------
crucified	crucified	crucified
------	------	criminals
garments	garments	garments
------	third hour	------
inscription	inscription	------

On the basis of vocabulary Taylor judges that in this
section Luke is following and editing a non-Markan source.[27]
He hardly considers the possibility that Luke may have edited
Mark for theological reasons.[28] We feel that except for the
special material concerning the women of Jerusalem, Luke's arrangement can be explained by such theological editing. Thus,
he eliminated the names of Simon's sons because they were no
longer known to his community. The omission of the wine avoids
a doublet, and the early introduction of the criminals adds to
the logic of the account.

The main point of our comparison, however, is to highlight
the loose character of the Markan construction, which lends itself to the insertion of new material as well as to the arrangement and omission of old material. Unlike the pericopes that
we have studied thus far, these verses give the impression of
having been strung together in an almost arbitrary fashion. It
is little wonder that those searching for a primitive narrative
have been able to arrange these verses into so many different
accounts. The very disconnected character of the verses lends
itself to such an enterprise so that one can nearly always arrive
at a new and better construction as Matthew and Luke did.

Besides the loosely constructed character of Mk. 15:20b-26,
there is also a remarkable similarity in sentence structure which
we have outlined below.

20b	*kai*	hist. pres.	obj. *hina* and subj. obj.
21	*kai*	hist. pres.	obj. *hina* and subj. obj.
22	*kai*	hist. pres.	obj.
23a	*kai*	imperf.	obj.
23b	subject *de*		aor.

24a	*kai*	hist. pres.	obj.
24b	*kai*	hist. pres.	obj.
25a	imperf.	*de*	pred. nom.
25b	*kai*	aor.	obj.
26	*kai*	imperf.	pred. nom.

When we compare this section with the parallels, we note
that Matthew and Luke have eliminated all vestiges of the historic present. Moreover, in four instances, Matthew has given
greater coherence to Mark's account by avoiding the second
evangelist's frequent *kai* parataxis (Mk. 15:21/Mt. 27:32; Mk.
15:23/Mt. 27:34; Mk. 15:24a/Mt. 27:35a; Mk. 15:24b/Mt. 27:35b).
The result is that although Matthew follows Mark's order rather
closely, he has tightened up the narrative and given it a greater
sense of coherence. If Mark had inherited a similar "loose"
narrative, we wonder if he would not have done much the same.
In other words, if this is the remnant of an old historic tradition, it is difficult to comprehend why the tradition was not
molded into a more coherent unit. We suspect the explanation is
that Mark has assembled diverse traditions in a simple manner
and has employed the historic present to give the narrative a
certain vividness.

The Historic Present

Commentators have long noted that the historic present
" . . . is very frequent in Mark's narrative, comparatively rare
in Matthew's, and extremely rare in Luke's."[29] Hawkins gives a
list of 151 historic presents in Mark.[30] Of this number seven-
ty-one are some form of *legō*, and twenty-four employ a form of
erchomai or its compound. Mark's usage does not reveal any rigid
patterns,[31] but there are some general rules. For example,
Mark frequently begins a pericope with some form of *erchomai*.[32]
Second, no section is ever written exclusively in the historic
present;[33] there is always an aorist, imperfect, perfect, or
combination of these within the pericope. The historic present
gives vividness to the account, the imperfect supplies movement,
and the aorist or perfect summarizes and gives a sense of conclusion. Finally, except for a few instances of *legō* (Mk. 3:34;
11:33), the gospel *never* uses the historic present to conclude
a pericope or section.

To explain the usage more positively we may say that Mark
employs the historic present as a sort of introductory tense;
that is, the historic present introduces or begins important
action whereas one of the past tenses concludes or summarizes
the activity.   Therefore, we usually find the historic present
within the first part of the narrative and some form of the
past tense in the second part.[34]   An examination of the pericopes
listed below tends to confirm this use of the historic present
(pericopes that use *legō* or *erchomai* exclusively have not been
included).

> 1:12,13 (temptation), 3:13-19 (choosing of Twelve),
> 4:35-41 (storm at sea), 5:21-24,35-43 (Jairus' daughter),
> 6:7-13, 30 (mission of the Twelve), 6:45-46 (dismissal
> of the crowd), 7:31-37 (deaf and dumb man), 8:1-9
> (feeding), 8:22-26 (blind man), 9:2-8 (transfiguration),
> 10:46-52 (Bartimaeus), 11:1-11 (entry to Jerusalem), 12:
> 13-17 (taxes), 14:12-16 (preparation of last supper),
> 14:32-42 (Gethsemane), 14:43-50 (arrest), 14:51-52
> (flight of young man), 14:53-64 (trial), 15:16-20a
> (mockery), 16:1-8 (empty tomb).

We have made these remarks about the historic present for two
reasons. First, some commentators have cited the use of this
tense as one criterion for judging these verses of the crucifixion account as part of a primitive narrative.[35]   Second, others
such as Schreiber and Schenk, have employed the tense change as
their criterion for isolating sources.[36]

Contrary to these opinions, we urge that the historic present in 15:20b-26 has been employed in a manner consistent with
the rest of Mark's gospel and should be attributed to the redactor.   That is, the evangelist has marshalled a series of historic presents in these verses in order to add vividness to the
account and to introduce the second mockery (15:27-32).   That
this is the case is plain from the character and nature of vv.
20b-26.   Unlike the other sections of chapter 15, these verses
hardly form a tightly knit pericope.   Rather they represent
traditions and reminiscences loosely strung together.

An example similar to vv.20b-26 occurs in the first mockery
(15:16-20a).   In vv.16-17 we find a series of three historic
presents.   Once more the function of these verses is to prepare
for the mockery proper which occurs in vv.18-20a.   As Zerwick
notes,[37] there is a parallel between vv.16-17 and 20b-26.   In

each instance the historic present prepares for the mockery
which follows. Thus we conclude that the historic present is
not the key to a literary source nor the remnant of an eyewit-
ness account. Rather, it is the redactor's stylistic technique
for introducing action and adding vividness to his account.

The Problem of Doublets

A second reason that many critics have spoken of diverse
traditions in the crucifixion narrative is the presence of doublets. In the section that we are considering, for example, commentators have consistently flagged vv.24 and 25 as such. In
v.24 Mark says *kai staurousin* and then seems needlessly to repeat the remark in v.25, *kai estaurōsan auton*. Matthew has
avoided the repetition by altering *estaurōsan* to *etēroun* (27:36).
Moreover, the variant readings in Mark show attempts to eliminate the repetition in at least two ways. First, D has substituted *ephylasson* for *estaurōsan* in Mk. 15:25. Second, φ pc sy[p]
sa[pt] have interpreted Mark's *kai* as *hote*. The effect of this
latter change is to keep the double mention of the crucifixion
but to make the second reference an explanation of the first
rather than a mere repetition (it was the third hour *when* they
crucified him).[38]

Contrary to the view that vv.24 and 25 represent two
sources, we suggest that in the present instance we have a classic case of Markan duality;[39] that is, Mark is making a double
statement of the same event, repeating and developing the motif
in a second statement. This technique is similar to that in
vv.31-32 where the mockery of the priests and scribes seems to
repeat that of the passersby (vv.29-30), and to that in vv.34
and 37 where there is a double mention of the great cry. In each
case, however, we discover that the second statement is not
merely repetitive; it adds a detail which clarifies the first.
Thus, at the mention of the second cry we are told that Jesus
died. In the mockery of the priests and scribes there is the
added notice that although Jesus saved others he cannot save
himself. Finally v.25, the second reference to the crucifixion,
informs us that it was the third hour when they crucified Jesus
and that at that hour he was crucified as the "King of the Jews"
(15:26).

We suggest that such apparent doublets are not a safe guide for separating sources. Rather they manifest Mark's penchant for duality and, like the historic present, the doublet of vv.24 and 25 points more to Markan style than it does to diverse traditions.

Once we have recognized that vv.24 and 25 are not necessarily from different sources but a manifestation of Markan style, we begin to suspect that the third hour is also redactional in nature and not the remnant of a three hour schema. The mention of the third hour is Mark's way of making the crucifixion more precise as well as marking the time of a crucifixion day; there is no need to attribute it to an earlier source.

Mark's penchant for duality also manifests itself in the manner he repeats words and recalls earlier phrases. Thus we can point to the double mention of *topos* in v.22, *epigraphē* and its cognate *epigegrammenē* in v.26,[40] and *arē* in vv.21,24. The last example is especially instructive since the phrase *tis ti arē* in v.24 is clearly not a part of Ps. 22 as recorded either by the Masoretic text or by the Septuagint. Matthew has dropped the enigmatic phrase and the Western reading of Mark would do the same. However, when we see *tis ti arē* against *hina arē ton stauron autou* in v.21 there is a probable explanation for its presence. By the second use of *arē* the redactor draws our attention to the first occurrence and contrasts those who "take up" the cross of the Crucified One with those who "take" his garments. These examples of repetition, redundancy and duality point to Markan style rather than separate sources.

Finally, we highlight two other elements of Markan style found in v.22 and throughout the gospel. The first is the use of *pherein* in the sense of bring rather than carry,[41] a usage corrected by both Matthew and Luke. The second is Mark's formula for translation,[42] *ho estin methermēneuomenon* 15:22; 15:34. The simpler *ho estin* occurs in 3:17; 7:11; 7:34; 12:42; 15:16. These stylistic traits are just one more indication that the redactor is at work.

Conclusion

At this point it will be helpful to summarize what we have been saying and to draw some general conclusions. First, we

have noted that the historic present and the doublet of vv.24
and 25 are not sufficient criteria for discerning different
sources within the crucifixion narrative. The historic present
has been employed in Mark's customary manner to introduce material, and vv.24 and 25 manifest the evangelist's penchant for
duality. Second, within these verses there are still other
stylistic traits which point to Markan activity.

Therefore, we suggest that instead of a primitive narrative
or a present historic tradition, we have a series of loosely
connected phrases which Mark has assembled. He connects a number of traditions and historical remembrances (Simon, the place
of crucifixion, the wine, the garments, the inscription) by
the use of *kai* and relates them in the historic present for the
sake of vividness. In this fashion the entire section serves
as a preface for the second mockery. In other words, we do not
believe that Mark was working with a connected narrative but
rather with a series of traditions and details which he has assembled. He framed these verses to serve as a connecting link
between the first and second mockeries, and as an extended introduction to the mockery of Jesus on the cross.

Finally, we must ask why Mark chose to place the inscription "King of the Jews" at the end of this section. That the
inscription could have been positioned elsewhere is clear from
Luke's account, which situates it within the second mockery
(23:38). In Mark, however, the inscription comes at the closing
of the crucifixion account (15:26), just before the mockery.
Moreover, Mark has closely associated it with the third hour
(15:25), so that Jesus is proclaimed King at the moment of his
crucifixion. We suggest that in its present position, v.26 enjoys a double function. First, it publicly announces that Jesus
was crucified as "the King of the Jews" (15:20b-26). Second,
it stresses that Jesus will be mocked and ridiculed (15:27-32)
in his capacity as King.

For Mark the inscription is a theological statement as
well as an historical fact. Matthew says that the inscription
was *epanō tēs kephalēs autou* (27:37). Luke writes *ēn de kai
epigraphē ep' autō* (23:38) and John refers to it as a *titlon*
(19:19). However, Mark simply mentions the inscription without

explaining its placement upon the cross. We suggest that the
reason is his view of the inscription as a theological proclamation as well as an historical fact.

II. DEATH

In this section we shall examine the verses which enclose
the third mockery (15:33-34,37-39). Once more our purpose is
to determine whether they represent an already existing framework into which the third mockery was inserted, or whether Mark
shaped them to form a frame into which he then inserted the
mockery (15:35-36).

A comparison with Matthew shows that he follows Mark
closely; his major contribution is the addition of the natural
and supernatural events which accompany the death of Jesus
(27:51-53). Matthew has situated these signs between the tearing of the temple curtain and the centurion's confession. As
usual, Luke has done more rewriting and has arranged the material in a new fashion.[43] The mockery (without the mention of
Elijah) has been transferred to 23:36-37; the tearing of the
temple curtain has been placed before the great cry; and Ps. 22
has been replaced by Ps. 31. Finally, at the conclusion of
Luke's account the people return home beating their breasts.

MT.	MK.	LK.
6th to 9th hour	6th to 9th hour	6th to 9th hour
------	------	curtain
Ps. 22	Ps. 22	Ps. 31
mockery	mockery	------
cry	cry	------
death	death	death
curtain	curtain	------
signs	------	------
Son of God	Son of God	Just Man
------	------	People repent

Once more we can observe that the type of material before
us is such that new traditions can easily be inserted and old
material dropped or given a new arrangement. Moreover, the
tearing of the temple curtain, as well as the Elijah mockery,
appears to have been inserted into its present position. By
the artful employment of *exepneusen*[44] in vv.37 and 39, the
evangelist manages to provide a frame for the tearing of the

temple curtain. Matthew, however, has substituted *aphēken to
pneuma* (27:50) for *exepneusen* in Mk. 15:37 and then refers to
the earthquake (27:54) instead of Jesus' death (cf. Mk. 15:39)
as the reason for the centurion's confession. In this way he
has dismantled the framing effect that results from Mark's
double mention of Jesus' death.

Mark effects a second, less noticeable framing of material
when he inserts the centurion's confession between two references to seeing, *idōn de ho kentyriōn* (15:39) and *gynaikes apo
makrothen theōrousai* (15:40). Beginning in v.32 and continuing
in vv.36,39,40,47 two words for seeing (*idōn, theoreō*) function
as catchwords for Mark. The unacceptable faith of the mockers
who must see in order to believe (15:32,36) passes to the faith
of the centurion who believes because he sees the death of
Jesus (15:39). His confession is followed by the notice of the
women who look on from a distance. Thus, besides the mockery
and the tearing of the temple curtain, it appears that Mark has
constructed a very loose bracket using the catchwords *idōn* and
theoreō around the centurion's confession. We can outline the
composition of this section as follows:

		(34)	*phōnȩ mēgalȩ*
		(35-36)	[mockery]
		(37)	*phōnēn megalēn*
		(37)	*exepneusen*
		(38)	[temple curtain]
(39)	*idōn* . . . .*exepneusen*		
(39)	[confession]		
(40-41)	*theōrousai*		
(42-46)	[burial]		
(47)	*etheōroun*		

In light of Mark's theological concerns it would seem that
we can attribute vv.38,39 to him. Verse 38 deals with the
temple theme and clearly refers to 14:58, 15:29, and the material
of chapters 11-13. The word for tear, *eschisthē*, also occurs in
the baptismal scene (1:10). There the heavens are torn so that
the Spirit can descend, and a voice from heaven declares that
Jesus is the only Son (*ho huios mou ho agapētos*). Finally,
within v.38 there is a case of pleonasm caused by the pairing of

eis dyo with *ap'anōthen*, a redundancy which Matthew eliminates.[45]
These three reasons (theological theme, use of *eschisthē*,
pleonasm) convince us that v.38 should be attributed to the
redactor.

We make the same claim for v.39 because of the role which
"Son of God" plays in the rest of the gospel. Prior to v.39
the Father has proclaimed Jesus as his Son at two significant
moments, the Baptism (1:11) and the Transfiguration (9:7).
Therefore, it appears that the confession of the centurion belongs to the structure of the gospel[46] and that we are on firm
ground when we assign this verse to the redactor.

If we examine v.33 (the sixth hour) we discover that this
verse has also been shaped by Mark. In 15:33 he employs
ginomai in a construction of the genitive absolute in order to
express time. Mark resorts to this construction in nine instances: 1:32; 4:35; 6:2,21,35,47; 14:17; 15:33,42. In eight
of these, the evangelist marks the beginning of a new pericope
by the construction. Therefore, we suggest that Mark is responsible for the hour schema which begins this section. It
is a part of his crucifixion day.

Conclusion

We have argued that once more Mark has inserted material
and bracketed it by key words such as "die" and "see." Moreover, he has introduced this section by his second reference to
the three hour schema. The first reference to the hours (15:25)
frames one side of the second mockery (15:27-32) and this reference (15:33) completes the frame. However, perhaps the most
important result of our analysis is that vv.33-34 and vv.37-39
form a frame around the Elijah mockery (15:35-36), and appear
to have been shaped by Mark. Therefore, we make a judgment
here similar to that made for vv.20b-26; that is, this section
does not represent a narrative that Mark inherited but a series
of traditions which he shaped and formed.

                              III. BURIAL

In this final section our task will be to examine the
burial story and determine what literary connection it has with
what we have studied thus far.[47] At first it may seem strange

that we have included vv.40-41 in this section rather than in
the last. It is important to remember, however, that the manner
in which we are dividing this chapter for the sake of compositional analysis is not necessarily the fashion in which we would
arrange it for the purpose of an outline. Therefore, while
Mk. 15:40-41 may have more kinship with the story of Jesus'
death than with the burial story, in terms of the way the narrative was composed, it belongs to the latter.

Finally, as we shall see, the burial account in Mark is
related more to the total content of chapter 15 than it is to
chapter 16. Senior acknowledges this when he writes:

> For Matthew, more than for Mark, 27:55-56, represents
> a terminal point in the Passion narrative. . . . The
> burial account becomes simply a preparation for the
> resurrection motifs that will dominate the rest of the
> Gospel.[48]

By contrast Mark's burial story contains explicit references
to chapter 15 and for that reason we examine it as the final
episode of the passion narrative.

The Lists of Women

The point we intend to investigate concerns the relationship between the lists of women in 15:40; 15:47 and 16:1. Is
there a traditional list among these? Are two or all of the
lists traditional? The answer to this question is crucial for
our understanding of how the burial story relates to what precedes it.

According to the best witnesses[49] the lists read as follows:

15:40 *Maria hē Magdalēnē kai*
      Maria hē Iakōbou tou mikrou kai Iōsētos mētēr kai Salōmē
15:47 *Maria hē Magdalēnē kai*
      Maria hē Iōsētos
16:1 *Maria hē Magdalēnē kai*
      Maria hē tou[50] *Iakōbou kai Salōmē*

At this point the problems which beset the critic are numerous.
First, there is the discrepancy in the lists. In 15:47, James
the Less disappears whereas in 16:1, Joses is absent and James
is no longer referred to as "the Less." Second, there is a
question of translation which involves determining the proper

relationship between the second Mary and James and Joses. Is
she the mother, the wife or the daughter of these men?

   The majority of translations render 15:40 as does the
Revised Standard Version, " . . . Mary the mother of James the
younger and of Joses." Lohmeyer[51] and Finegan,[52] however, would
translate it as " . . . Mary the wife of James the younger and
mother of Joses." Pesch suspects that the reading of B and Ψ
interprets the text correctly and arrives at a list of four
women: Mary Magdalene, Mary the mother (or wife?) of James the
Less, (Mary) the mother of Joses (cf. 15:47), and Salome.[53]

   Blinzler argues that the identification of a woman by both
her husband and her son does not otherwise occur in Mark and
so militates against such a translation here.[54] In this case
the genitive article must govern all the words up to and including *mētēr*. Against Pesch's opinion speaks the spread of
the witnesses (ℵ [corr] D L [Δ] Θ) and the fact that throughout
the gospel the evangelist has a preference for listing groups of
people in two's and three's.[55] Accordingly, we choose to read
the second Mary as the mother of both James the Less and Joses.

   Verses 15:47 and 16:1 present us with a strange problem of
translation, because if they are read in isolation, our first
inclination is to interpret the second Mary in 15:47 as either
the wife or the daughter of Joses.[56] In fact certain witnesses
(W f[13]) foresaw the difficulty and added *mētēr* after Joses.

   The same situation arises in 16:1. If we read the text in
isolation the translation would be that the second Mary is
either the wife or the daughter of James.[57] It is only in the
light of 15:40 that the relationship between Mary and Joses
(15:47), and Mary and James (16:1), is clarified. That is, we
interpret both of these Marys as being the same person, the
mother of Joses and James. Do these problems of translation
give us any clue as to the tradition of the texts? What is
the relationship between the second Mary in 15:47 and 16:1, and
James and Joses? Is there a primitive list?

   With Schenke and Broer, we believe that part of the solution
lies in determining the relationship between 15:42-47 and
16:1-8. Were the stories originally a unity or were they separate legends later joined together? After examining both

stories, Schenke and Broer conclude that the two stories were
not originally connected.[58]

In favor of an original unity is the chronology (sabbath),
the women, their knowledge of the grave's location, the stone
and the anointing. However, Schenke argues that these elements
are not conclusive.[59] The chronology, for example, is plainly
dependent upon the wider passion story and so cannot serve as a
decisive argument. The knowledge of the grave's location and
the mention of the stone are the type of details that attach
themselves to a grave legend. The anointing is double-edged; it
also argues against an original unity since 15:46 presupposes
that Jesus' body was buried with dignity. According to this
account, Joseph even had time to purchase a new linen cloth.
If the two pericopes were originally a unity, then why was there
need for the women to anoint the body in 16:1? The second
anointing presupposes that there was not a proper burial, an
assumption which is hardly the case. Thus there is a tension between 15:46 and 16:1.

On the other hand, if the two stories were originally separate, as Schenke and Broer believe, then the discrepancy in
the lists of 15:47 and 16:1 can be explained. Each story would
have had its own list[60] and the second Mary would not necessarily be the same person in both lists.

Furthermore, if we observe these two lists, we see that
when combined they form the list of 15:40. We propose that Mark
joined these lists in order to clarify the relationship of the
second Mary to James and Joses[61] and to provide a transition
from the death to the burial scene. In other words, just as the
evangelist combined 14:53b and 14:55a to form 15:1, so he has
joined 15:47 and 16:1 to form 15:40. The introduction of
"mother" in 15:40 would then unite the two Marys by showing a
common relationship to James and Joses. The addition of "the
Less" to James' name was probably made in order to distinguish
him from the son of Zebedee. Moreover, as Senior points out,
"this may have been the signal that justified Matthew's use of
'mother of the Sons of Zebedee' in place of Mark's Salome."[62]
We conclude that 15:47 and 16:1 were originally separate lists
that Mark inherited, and that from them he created a new list;
namely, 15:40.

The Redactor's Hand

If the list of 15:40 is redactional in nature, we must inquire whether there are any other clues to Markan activity in
15:40-41. We suggest that a comparison of these verses with
Mt. 27:55-56 reveals such a clue.

Mt. 27:55-56	Mk. 15:40-41
Women at a distance	Women at a distance
who followed and served	----------
M. M., Mary, Mother of Zeb.	M. M., Mary, Salome
----------	who followed and served
----------	and many others

A close reading of the two texts discloses that Matthew has done
more than give a new arrangement of Mark; he has clarified the
exposition of the second evangelist. In the Markan text there
is a confusion over the relative pronoun *hai* in v.41. Does it
refer to the three women only, or does it include the women of
v.40 as well? Some witnesses, C A L W Δ, attempt to clarify
the text by introducing *kai* which has the effect of referring
the pronoun to all the women. Matthew, by giving the text a
new arrangement, has made it obvious that it was all the women,
including the three, who followed and served Jesus.

What we find interesting is that the ambiguity of Mark
seems to result from an insertion of the three women into the
narrative. If we remove their names the text reads smoothly
and there is no confusion. The evident insertion of these names
indicates that once more we have uncovered the redactor's hand.

We conclude that the burial story has been attached to the
passion narrative by vv.40-41, and that these verses are redactional in nature. With 15:47 they form a frame around the burial
story. Mark would have received the burial story with the list
of 15:47 already attached to it. Thus all that he needed to do
was preface this account with 15:40-41 in order to complete the
frame.[63] In this way not only was the burial legend inserted
between the two references to the women watching, it was also
related to the mockery and death scene by the catchword "see."
We must now inquire whether there is redactional activity within
the burial account itself.

Pilate's Amazement

The burial legends of Matthew, Mark and Luke display a high degree of agreement.[64] All mention the role of Joseph, the nature of the grave and the presence of the women. However, it is clear that the tradition which Matthew and Luke received from Mark was in the process of growth.[65] This is especially so for the chronology (Matthew and Luke eliminate the reference to the preparation day), and the character of Joseph (Matthew makes him a disciple; Luke calls him a good and just man). Moreover, these gospels no longer found Mark's scene between Pilate and the centurion meaningful for their purposes and so eliminated it. However, it is precisely these verses of Mark that we shall now consider.

Commentators have noted that there is a rough transition from v.45 to 46.[66] In reading these verses one almost has the impression that the participles *agorasas* and *kathelōn* refer to Pilate rather than to Joseph. Certain witnesses (D Θ Σ 565) saw the difficulty and introduced *ho de Iōsēph* in order to effect a smoother transition. However, when we read v.46 immediately after v.43 the transition seems perfectly natural. This has led many exegetes to conclude that vv.44-45 are a later insertion into an earlier account of the burial.[67]

Broer has analysed the vocabulary of this passage[68] and claims that it is Markan in nature. However, his argument is no more conclusive than any argument from such statistics. This is especially the case here since *ethaumasen* has been employed in its classical construction[69] and *palai*, a *hapax* for Mark, has been used instead of *ēdē*. For us, a more convincing argument is the structure of the verses.

When we analyze vv.44-45 we discover that Mark is once more bracketing and framing material. The technique begins in v.43b.

$$\underset{\,}{ē}tēsato\ to\ sōma\ .\ .\ .$$
$$.\ .\ .\ ei\ ēdē\ tethnēken\ .\ .\ .$$
$$.\ .\ .\ ton\ kentyriōna\ .\ .\ .$$
$$.\ .\ .\ ei\ palai\ apethanen\ .\ .\ .$$
$$.\ .\ .\ edōrēsato\ to\ ptōma\ .\ .\ .$$

As the construction stands, the centurion is bracketed by two references concerning Jesus' death as well as a request and the

and the fulfillment of the request, for Jesus' body.[70] We have
continually met this bracketing and framing technique in Mark so
that we are on firm ground in seeing his hand at work here.

Moreover, the use of different words to express the same
basic thought (*soma-ptōma*, *ēdē-palai*) is a technique which the
evangelist employs at other points in his gospel. Thus in
8:18-21 he uses two different words for basket (*kophinous* and
spyridōn) in order to join the two feeding stories which employ
the same words (*kophinōn* in 6:43, *spyridas* in 8:8). And in the
request of James and John (10:35-40), he employs two different
words for left (*aristerōn* and *euōnymōn*). Later, in the second
mockery, he uses the latter of these and seems to draw a parallel
between the seats of honor requested by James and John, and the
crosses occupied by the thieves. We suggest that in the present
instance Mark's purpose for employing *ptōma* is to draw a deliberate parallel between the death of Jesus and the death of the
Baptist in 6:29 where the same word is found. These are the only
two instances of the word in the gospel. Moreover, just as
John was placed in a grave (*ethēkan auto en mnēmeiǫ*, 6:29) so
was Jesus (*ethēken auton en mnēmeiǫ*, 15:46).

Furthermore, if, as we have argued, Mark introduced these
verses, then he has managed to relate this story to the hearing
before Pilate by the repetition of *thaumazō* (15:5,44), as well
as to the crucifixion by the second appearance of the centurion
(15:39,44). Therefore, the purpose of these verses may not be,
as some have argued,[71] apologetic (a proof by the double mention
of the death that Jesus really died), but a way of referring
this story to what has preceded it. More specifically, the
burial scene becomes, through the reference to Pilate's wonder
and the centurion's report, the burial of the King of the Jews
and the royal burial of the Son of God. Even this scene, then,
as edited by Mark, has been drawn into the royal orbit.

Still another clue to the independent character of this
narrative is the tension that arises between the chronology (it
was already evening of the preparation day) and Joseph's action
of buying a linen cloth.[72] If it were merely preparation day,
there would be no problem. However, when the evangelist insists
that it was *ēdē opsias* a tension arises. Not only was it

preparation day, it would appear that the Sabbath had begun.[73]
If, however, the time notice belongs to the evangelist, then
the tension can be explained. The primitive account probably
began *epei ēn paraskeuē elthon Iōsēph*. Mark would have introduced the reference to evening in order to complete his crucifixion day, and then translated the meaning of preparation day
for his readers.[74] Thus he was careful to preserve the old
story, but in the process of giving it a new setting and com-
pleting the time scheme, he caused the tension between the time
of day and Joseph's commercial activity.

        Finally, we need to mention the ambiguity surrounding the
word *bouleutēs* (15:43). Was Joseph a member of the Sanhedrin
or of a local council? If the answer is the former, then we
confront still another tension since 15:1 makes it clear that
all condemned Jesus. Today many commentators leave the question
open and indicate that Joseph need not have been a member of
the Sanhedrin.[75] However, this historical solution does not
solve the literary problem inasmuch as Mark does not identify
to what council Joseph did belong. To that extent 15:43 does
clash with 15:1. The most likely explanation is that Mark has
assembled diverse traditions and in the process left unresolved
the tension that resulted from such a process.

Conclusion

        Our analysis has shown that vv.40-41 appear to derive from
the evangelist's redactional activity and that he has employed
them to frame the burial legend and attach it to the passion
narrative. Originally the legend did not have a time indication
(evening), but Mark introduced it to complete the crucifixion
day. Finally, he inserted vv.44-45 in order to refer the story
to what had already occurred. By mentioning the centurion and
Pilate one more time, Mark recalls the trial of the King of the
Jews and the death of the Son of God. Moreover, Pilate's amazement serves as a final bracket so that the amazement of Pilate
at the silence of the King of the Jews and at the death of the
Son of God begins and ends Mark's crucifixion day.

CHAPTER IV

COMPOSITION AND THEME

In this chapter we propose to summarize what we have said
thus far and then to draw some conclusions concerning the composition and the theme of Mark 15.

I. COMPOSITION

We have mentioned over and over again that Mark has composed this chapter in terms of a crucifixion day. Verses 1 and
42 mark the limits of this day which has been divided into three-
hour periods (15:25,33,34). Thus our first and simplest chart
is as follows:

(1) morning (25) third (33) sixth (34) ninth (42) evening

According to Mark this day begins and ends with a scene before
Pilate, and in each scene Pilate is amazed (15:5,44). Thus,
Mark has framed the chapter by a time scheme as well as by two
scenes before Pilate.

Within chapter 15, Mark has inserted three mockeries
(15:16-20a, 27-32, 35-36) and in each instance he has bracketed
them. He has enclosed the first by references to leading Jesus
out for crucifixion, the second by references to the third and
sixth hours, and the last by the great cry.

led out to be crucified [16 - 20a] led out to be crucified
                  third hour [27 - 32] sixth hour
                  great cry [35 - 36] great cry

Moreover, we have determined that in each of these scenes Mark
has enclosed material within still other brackets. The first
mockery refers to the purple robe at the beginning (15:17) and
at the end (15:20a). The second mockery mentions those who
were crucified with Jesus at the beginning (15:27) and at the
end (15:32). Finally, the third mockery begins (15:35) and
ends (15:36b) with Elijah.

```
        purple robe [king of the Jews] purple robe
          thieves [ King of Israel ] thieves
          Elijah [      drink      ] Elijah
```

Between the second and third mockeries we examined a series
of redundant, loosely connected verses narrated in the historic
present. These verses concluded with the reference to the third
hour and the inscription "King of the Jews." We interpreted
these verses as an extended preface to the second mockery. According to our analysis, the evangelist connected and arranged
these verses.

Next we investigated the material that surrounded the third
mockery and once more we noted that it betrayed Markan redactional activity. Not only did these verses bracket the third
mockery by the reference to the great cry, we discovered that
they also included material which had been bracketed (the tearing
of the temple curtain, the centurion's confession). Again we
made the judgment that the redactor had arranged these verses.

```
                                      (37) death
                                      (38) [curtain]
        (39a) seeing.....................    death
        (39b) [confession]
        (40)  seeing
```

We pointed out that this section and the burial story were
connected by the frequent references to seeing which began in
v.32, continued in vv.36,39, and were concluded in vv.40,47.
Moreover, we showed that the burial account, which was framed
by the references to the women watching, also contained inserted
material.

```
        (32) let us see
        (36) let us see
        (39) seeing
        (40) women seeing from a distance
             (43b) Joseph asks for body
                   (44a) if already dead (amazed)........15:5

                        (44b) centurion.................15:39

                   (44c) if already dead
             (45)  Joseph granted body.................. 6:29
        (47) women seeing
```

Finally, we noted that Mark has also bracketed the first
fifteen verses of this chapter. In 15:1 the Jews *hand over*

Jesus to Pilate, and in 15:15 Pilate *hands over* Jesus to be
crucified. However, we concluded that originally these fifteen
verses were not a unity. The extended introduction to the
Barabbas incident (15:6-8) revealed that the story once had
another setting. Only Mark's insertion (15:8) told us that the
autois in v.6 referred to the crowd and not to the priests.
Moreover, we discovered that within the extended introduction
there is the Markan technique of bracketing.

> (6) whom they *asked* for
> (7) Barabbas
> (8) began to *ask*

Thus we suggested that these verses formed Mark's transition
from the hearing before Pilate to the release of Barabbas.

However, we judged that even vv.1-5 were not an original
unity, as the awkward placement of Pilate's question manifested.
Rather, we urged that Mark was responsible for the introduction
(15:1) to the entire chapter and for the placement of Pilate's
question (15:2). We saw vv.3-5 as a doublet of 14:60-61a and
argued that the redactor had reworked an older tradition which
told of Jesus' silence. Thus he brought together this earlier
tradition and Pilate's question in the following way:

> (2) And Pilate *asked* him
>> (3) and they *accused* him
> (4a)Pilate *asked* him again
>>>> (4b).............*answered nothing*
>> (4c)how much they *accuse*
>>>> (5a).............*answered nothing*

We concluded that vv.3-5 and vv.6,9,11-15a represented separate
traditions and that Mark joined them together by the extended
introduction found in vv.6-8. Furthermore, he placed v.2 in
its present setting and gave the fifteen verses a unity by
bracketing them with references to handing over Jesus (15:2,15b).
We may represent this construction in the following manner:

> (1) Markan introduction (handed over)
>> (2) Pilate's question
>>> (3-5) tradition of Jesus' silence
> (6-8) Extended Markan introduction
>>> (9-15) tradition of Barabbas (handed over)

We can now draw some conclusions from our study. First, a
number of traditions were available to Mark: the silence of
Jesus before his accusers, the release of Barabbas, a series of
mockeries, the burial of Jesus. Besides these larger traditions
he also had access to smaller bits of information such as: the
role of Simon, the place of crucifixion, the charge against
Jesus, the use of Ps. 22 in the passion apologetic.

Second, Mark assembled these traditions into a coherent
narrative just as he had assembled other elements of tradition
in the first part of his gospel. His primary technique was to
insert and bracket material, and then to arrange the whole in
terms of a crucifixion day.

Third, we cannot exclude the possibility that Mark had
some kind of passion tradition before him, but it does appear
that *the present form* of the passion narrative, as we find it in
the second gospel, is very much the result of Mark's redactional
activity. Like all authors, Mark was constrained by the logic
of the events (hearing, crucifixion, death, burial), but within
that logic of events he effected an arrangement of material
which reflected more than an historical report. Mark was responsible for the theological arrangement of the present narrative.

Fourth, the three mockeries appear to have played an important role for Mark. By placing them after the hearing before
Pilate, after the crucifixion, and after the great cry, the redactor employs them as a means of emphasizing what has just
taken place. Thus, immediately after Jesus is accused and rejected as "King of the Jews" (15:1-15), the soldiers mock him as
"King of the Jews" (15:16-20a). Next Jesus is crucified as
"King of the Jews" (15:20b-26) and the priests and scribes mock
him as the "Messiah, the King of Israel," who cannot save himself (15:27-32). Finally, Jesus cries out as a forsaken Messiah
King (15:34) only to be mocked by the bystanders as a false
messiah to whom Elijah will not come. Our study implies that
this arrangement is purposeful and is the work of the redactor.
Mark has utilized these mockeries as vehicles for confirming
and emphasizing the kingship of Jesus and, as we shall see, a
means of preparing for the centurion's climactic confession
(15:39).

II.   THEME

In our analysis of Mark 15, we concluded that the evangelist
composed this chapter in much the same manner that he did the
first part of the gospel; that is, Mark inherited traditions
which he arranged and allowed to speak for themselves.[1] It is
now incumbent upon us to ask if Mark had a controlling theme by
which he juxtaposed these traditions and held them together.
On the basis of our investigation, we propose that the overall
theme of chapter 15 is the "Kingship of Jesus," a motif which
Mark develops through the six-fold use of "King" (15:2,9,12,18,
26,32) and the three mockery scenes.[2]

We argued, in light of its sudden and unanticipated appearance, that Mark was responsible for v.2 which links his own introduction (15:1) and a tradition about the silence of Jesus
(15:3-5). This verse announces the theme of the chapter, a
theme which comes to public proclamation in the charge against
Jesus (15:26). Taken together, vv.2 and 26 form a loose bracket
around the hearing before Pilate, the Barabbas incident, and the
soldiers' mockery.

We maintained that the story of Barabbas (15:6-16) and the
soldiers' mockery (15:16-20a) were probably independent traditions
that Mark inherited. In view of the title "King," it becomes
clear why he appropriated them; both pericopes already contained
the royal title. Thus, using the theme of kingship as his guide,
Mark constructed this portion of the narrative by framing these
stories with vv.2 and 26 so that Jesus is accused as King (15:2),
rejected as King (15:9,12), mocked as King (15:18), and crucified
and publicly proclaimed as King (15:26).[3]

We believe that the charge against Jesus is historically
founded.[4] Nonetheless, for Mark and his community, it has taken
on profound theological significance. This can be seen in the
redactor's employment of *epigraphē*.[5] Luke says that the inscription was above him (*ep' autǭ*, 23:38). Matthew writes that the
charge (*aitian*) was placed above his head (*epanō tēs kephalēs*,
27:37), and John converts the inscription into a full blown
title (*titlon*, 19:19) written in Hebrew, Greek and Latin. Mark,
however, simply mentions that there was an inscription without
noting its placement on the cross. It is as though the *epigraphē*

is a theological statement rather than simply a physical object.[6]

In our investigation of the second mockery (15:27-32), we pointed out that the dialogue of the priests and scribes (15:31-32) was a stylized continuation of the dialogue in vv.29-30. Moreover, the dialogue of this mockery shows many affinities to Markan language and theology found in the rest of the gospel. This led us to conclude that Mark was probably responsible for reshaping the dialogue and perhaps for joining the titles "Messiah" and "King of Israel."[7]

It is clear that Mark intended the entire scene to be read as a royal mockery. The thieves at Jesus' right and left recall the request of James and John for seats at Jesus' right and left when he will be enthroned in his glory (10:35-40).[8] And the title, "the Christ, the King of Israel," continues the theme begun in v.2 and publicly proclaimed in v.26.

Mark pursued the theme in the third mockery (15:35-36) where the bystanders ridicule Jesus as calling for Elijah.[9] In light of the second mockery it is evident that they, like the priests and scribes, ridicule Jesus in his capacity as a royal figure.[10] They mock the great cry (15:34) as a desperate call by a false Messiah King for Elijah's help. In other words, just as the priests and scribes mock the Messiah King because he cannot save himself so the bystanders ridicule him because Elijah will not deliver him from the cross.

Mark drew a contrast between the manner in which the bystanders respond to the great cry (mockery) and the reaction of the centurion (confession). While the former mock Jesus as a false Messiah King for whom Elijah will not come, the latter confesses him for what he truly is, God's Son. In light of the six-fold use of "King" in chapter 15 it would appear that Mark understood sonship in terms of Old Testament messianism, i.e., the King is God's royal son.[11] So the centurion's confession, made in the context of Jesus' death, gives theological meaning to the six-fold use of the title "King" and provides the dramatic climax of chapter 15.

Finally, we noted that Mark developed the burial scene so that it refers the reader to the hearing before Pilate and the

centurion's confession. When Pilate learns that Jesus had already died, he marvels (15:44), just as he marveled at the silence of the King of the Jews before his accusers (15:5). Moreover, Pilate learns that Jesus has died from the centurion who
proclaimed the King of the Jews to be the Son of God. Thus the
final scene recalls the first where the royal theme was introduced, and the presence of the centurion reminds the reader that
the dead King of the Jews is the royal Son of God, the King of
Israel. In this manner the final act becomes a royal burial
scene.

     We summarize by saying that chapter 15 moves inexorably to
the death of Jesus and the centurion's confession through a
series of incidents which continually point to the kingship of
Jesus. First, Jesus is accused as King (15:2), rejected as
King (15:9,12) and mocked as King (15:18). Second, Jesus is
crucified as King (15:26) and mocked as King of Israel (15:32).
Third, Jesus cries out as a forsaken Messiah King (15:34), is
mocked as a Messiah King for whom Elijah will not come, and is
confessed as the King he truly is, God's royal Son (15:39).
Finally, in 15:44, a highly redactional verse, Mark makes the
burial scene a royal burial by reminding the reader of the
opening scene (15:2) and the centurion's confession (15:39). In
every instance then, Mark unfolds the royal theme as he presses
on to his story's climax, the death of Jesus and the centurion's
confession.

                    III. GOSPEL AND THEME

     If, as we have maintained, Mark composed chapter 15 around
the motif of kingship, two questions confront us. First, in
what sense did Mark understand Jesus' kingship? Second, how
does he manifest this in the rest of the gospel? These questions
are especially urgent since the title "King," applied to Jesus,
does not occur before this chapter.

     On first reading, one is tempted to argue that although
the title occurs six times in this chapter it is of little importance to Mark. Rather, it appears that "King of the Jews"
is the political charge which the Christian community now rejects. As evidence one could point out that Jesus' answer to

Pilate's question is ambiguous when compared with his affirmative reply before the high priest. Moreover, the title "King"
always comes on the lips of Jesus' opponents: Pilate (15:2,9,
12), the soldiers (15:18), the priests and scribes (15:32).

It is true that Jesus' response to Pilate is ambiguous when
compared with his answer before the Sanhedrin. However, the
fact that Pilate continues to use the title in the very next
scene (15:9,12) indicates that, within the Markan framework,
the reader should accept Jesus' response as affirmative in some
fashion.[12]

If Mark intended to disavow the title he was free to place
an explicit denial upon Jesus' lips. Such a denial would have
formed a sharp and artful contrast with Jesus' answer to the
high priest. More importantly, it would have indicated that
the title "King" in the rest of the chapter was not a title that
Mark attributed to Jesus. In other words, the continued use
of "King," after Jesus explicitly rejected it, would have been
a sure sign that Mark also refused to attribute "King of the
Jews," or "King of Israel" to Jesus.

Since Mark persisted with the title, without having Jesus
explicitly denying it, we suggest that there is some aspect of
it he wishes to affirm. That is to say, in some manner (understood by the evangelist and his community) Jesus *is* King of
the Jews and King of Israel.[13]   But since Mark did not embrace
the title with an unambiguous "I am," neither should the reader.

Second, it is not sufficient to argue that because Jesus'
enemies call him "King," Mark did not esteem the title. Donald
Juel has shown that irony is one of the most prominent features
of the passion narrative.[14]   For example, at the very moment
that Jesus is being mocked as a prophet (14:65), one of his
prophecies (Peter's denial, 14:30) is being fulfilled.[15]   Pilate
(15:9,12) and the soldiers (15:18) unwittingly call Jesus "King
of the Jews" just as the priests and scribes name him "the Christ,
the King of Israel" (15:32), and in each instance the title is
ironically true. The irony of this chapter reveals that in some
fashion Jesus is a royal figure.[16]   However, the fact that his
opponents employ the title in ridicule betrays that they and
Mark have different expectations.[17]   There is a tension between

the way Mark would have the reader comprehend Jesus' kingship
and the notion of kingship which the mockers espouse.

We suspect that the needs of Mark's community may explain
some of this tension. Inasmuch as Mark did not compose the rest
of the gospel as an historical report, it is reasonable to assume
that neither did he redact the passion narrative primarily for
historical information. The passion narrative is a theological
document just as the first part of the gospel is. More specifically, Mark wrote for the needs of a community. It is with this
community in mind, then, that we must also read this chapter.

In the first mockery (15:16-20a), for example, the objection to Jesus' messiahship seems to be that the Romans ridiculed
him as a messianic pretender. If the leaders of Jerusalem delivered Jesus to Pilate (15:1), if the crowds refused to accept
him as King (15:13,14), and if the soldiers mocked Jesus as a
pretender, then how can the members of Mark's community claim
that Jesus was the Messiah King?

In the second mockery (15:27-32), the rejection revolves
around salvation and the temple. Jesus has not fulfilled the
traditional expectations for Israel's King in regard to either.
Instead of being the temple's protector, he has become its de-
stroyer;[18] instead of being the Savior, he needs to be saved.
How can the members of Mark's community call Jesus the Messiah
King if he has not fulfilled the traditional expectations of
the Messiah, the King of Israel?

Finally, Jesus cannot be the Messiah King because in his
hour of need he cried for Elijah and the prophet did not come to
his aid. How can the members of Mark's community call Jesus the
Messiah King if Elijah did not come to his rescue? In other
words, the thrust of this account is not simply the mocking of
Jesus, it is also the mocking of a Christian community which has
placed its faith in a crucified Messiah King.[19]

As the conclusion of a gospel that begins with the affirmation that Jesus is the Messiah (1:1), this chapter represents
Mark's final teaching on that subject for the sake of his community.[20] And, as we shall see, the response of the centurion
represents the proper confession of Jesus' kingship which Mark's
community can make because it, like the centurion, stands on

the other side of Jesus' death and the tearing of the temple
curtain.

In the following chapters we intend to pursue the theme of
kingship in three ways. First, in the second mockery Mark
raises the question of Jesus' Davidic kingship through the use
of the title, "King of Israel." In chapters 11-12 he raises
the same issue as well as the temple theme.[21] Consequently,
we shall read these chapters in order to grasp how he handles
the royal theme there and what relationship it has to chapter 15.

Second, we shall return to the hearing before Pilate, the
first mockery and the burial scene. The language of these sections is reminiscent of the third passion prediction (10:33,34)[22]
and the death of John the Baptist (6:14-29). By these linguistic
contacts it appears that Mark is reminding the reader that
Jesus suffers in his capacity as the Son of Man just as John the
Baptist suffered in his role as Elijah, the precursor (9:11-13).
Consequently, we shall examine the Son-of-Man material in Mark
in order to ascertain if it supports the royal motif of chapter
15.

Finally, we shall investigate the relationship between the
great cry of Ps. 22, the Elijah Mockery, the tearing of the
temple curtain, the death of Jesus and the centurion's confession. More specifically, we shall show that these diverse traditions climax the royal theme of chapter 15 and of the gospel.

We intend to demonstrate that there is a continuity between
the theme of kingship in this chapter and the rest of the gospel.
Mark has carefully prepared for the six-fold use of the title
"King" and the three mockeries of chapter 15. For the careful
reader the appearance of the royal motif in chapter 15 is neither
unexpected nor unanticipated. Thus, just as the first part of
this study laid the foundation for the second, so the second
part will confirm the first. That is, Mark is responsible for
the composition of chapter 15, and he has composed this chapter
in light of a royal theme for which he has carefully prepared
in the first part of his gospel.

CHAPTER V

IN WHAT SENSE A KING?

I. CHAPTERS 11-12

Chapters 11-12 are crucial for the second gospel since they
mark the end of Jesus' journey to Jerusalem and the beginning
of his temple ministry. The third passion prediction taught us
that Jerusalem is Jesus' goal; but the city's opposition was
already announced during the Galilean ministry. In 3:22 the
scribes came from Jerusalem and accused Jesus of casting out
demons by the prince of demons. In 7:1-5 scribes again arrived
from Jerusalem and complained that Jesus did not follow the
traditions of the elders. Thus, even before Jesus enters the
city the reader knows that it will be the place of his death.

Within chapters 11-12 references to the city and temple
abound. On three occasions (11:11,15,27) Jesus enters Jerusalem.
The first time he inspects the temple, the second time he
cleanses it, and the third time he undertakes an extended
teaching ministry within it. But never does Jesus spend the
night in Jerusalem. Rather he retreats to Bethany (11:11) which
is outside the city (11:19).

The period Jesus spends in Jerusalem appears to cover three
days, but as we remarked earlier there are difficulties with
such a time scheme.[1] There is no beginning to the first day
(11:1?), nor any closing of the third day (12:44?, 14:1?,
14:17?). Only the second day has a clear beginning (11:12) and
end (11:19).

Perhaps more important than chronology is the reaction of
the Jerusalem leaders to Jesus. Twice (11:18, 12:12) they seek
(*ezētoun*) to kill him. The theme of seeking is an important one
for Mark. The crowds seek Jesus (1:37), his mother and brothers
seek him (3:32), the Pharisees seek a sign (8:11), the authorities seek his life (11:18; 12:12; 14:1; 14:55) and the women
seek his body at the empty tomb (16:6). Thus the seeking to
destroy Jesus, which occurs in these chapters, is part of a
larger theme.

67

Another important reaction of the authorities comes in
12:34b, after the scribe's question about the greatest commandment. When Jesus has responded to all of his opponents Mark
says, "And after that no one dared to ask him any question."
On the one hand, the time of questions has ended[2] until the
trial when Jesus will openly disclose his messiahship (14:61-
62). On the other hand, the verse sets apart the first three
questions and prepares for the climactic question about David's
son which Jesus, not his opponents, will ask.[3] By highlighting
Jesus' question, Mark has shown that in some manner it will
clarify[4] all that has taken place in chapters 11-12. The
question of David, raised by Bartimaeus and by the triumphal
entry, will find its resolution.

Finally, Mark has framed chapters 11-12 in three different
ways. First, he suggests that the chapters should be read under
the rubric of the Son-of-David question by placing references
to David at the beginning and end of the section.[5] Thus, as
Jesus enters Jerusalem the acclamation of 11:10 anticipates the
coming Kingdom of David and recalls the cries of Bartimaeus
(10:47-48). Then, when Jesus has disposed of all his opponents,
he climaxes his teaching in the temple with his own question
concerning David's son.

A second framing occurs with the double quotation of Ps.
118. At the conclusion of both the royal approach (11:1-11)
and the parable of the vineyard (12:1-12), Mark has employed
the psalm to interpret what has taken place. In the first instance, the crowds greet Jesus as the one who brings David's
Kingdom (11:9b-10) whereas in the second, Jesus points to the
only son as the rejected stone which has become the cornerstone.
Inasmuch as Ps. 118 is the only scripture in this gospel perfectly quoted from either the Masoretic text or the Septuagint,
its importance for Mark, his community, and the gospel should
not be underestimated.[6] Moreover, he alluded to it in at least
one other place and perhaps even in a second. First, in the
passion prediction of 8:31, the use of *apodokimazō* appears to
refer to Ps. 118:22 (LXX 117:22) where the Septuagint employs
the same word. Second, in 9:12, another passion saying, the
reference seems to be to the same psalm;[7] however, here the

1) a monarch will
dah when Israel
ted on the throne
r *the (commander's)*
(3) [and] the *feet*
til the Messiah of
of David; for to
the Covenant of
lasting generations,
the Law with the mem-
. . .] is the syna-
]
atriarchal Blessing[24]

not cease from
from his children's
ah comes, to whom
ons shall obey.
49:10 Targum Onkelos

rom the house of
orah from his seed,
ah shall come, the
of him shall nations

49:10 Targum Jonathan[25]

ited saw a relationship
9:10-11, then it also un-
e Messianic king.
nificant number of allu-
this pericope. The royal
n fulfills the Davidic
cepter belongs; he comes

we have studied, there
s. 118. In 11:9b-10, Ps.
ith a Christian acclama-
r father David that is
of "hosanna." Matthew,
ation so that in every
y welcomed, not merely as
ion but, as the messianic
rdance with the declared
esus the Son of David
of the couplet. Luke
in the name of the Lord"

evangelist, or his tradition, employed *exoudeneō*. The same word
is found in Acts 4:11 which is a quotation from Ps. 118:22.
Thus *exoudeneō* and *apodokimazō* appear to be synonyms for the
same underlying Hebrew, *māᵓas*.[8] Since the psalm enjoys such a
prominent role in the gospel it is probable that the evangelist
intended a reference to it in 9:12 as well as 8:31.

Finally, Mark has framed this material by two references
to the Mount of Olives (11:1; 13:3). In the Old Testament, the
Mount of Olives was a place of worship (II Sam. 15:30-32). In
Zech. 14:4 the prophet presents the Mount as a location of
eschatological judgment.[9] On the basis of this citation, it
appears that there existed a tradition that the Messiah would
come from this place. Both in *Antiquities* (XX, 8,6) and the
Jewish Wars (II, 13,5) Josephus referred to the false prophet,
"the Egyptian" (cf. Acts 21:38), as mounting his messianic as-
sault upon Jerusalem from this site in order to destroy the
Romans. The tradition is also alive in Acts 1:6 where the apos-
tles, while on the Mount of Olives, ask the Risen Lord if he
will establish the Kingdom of Israel at this time. Inasmuch as
these verses occur in places that some scholars see as redactional,[10] Mark may have employed the double reference to the
Mount of Olives to highlight the messianic character of this
section.

In recent years a number of authors have examined these
chapters in light of the temple theme.[11] Our purpose, however,
is to view them from another vantage point, namely, Jesus' royal
messiahship. We shall endeavor to show that in addition to
the temple theme, Mark has also sustained a royal theme between
the triumphal entry and the question about David's son. The
appearance of this motif is not at all surprising in view of the
passion narrative and especially the second mockery. There,
the passersby and religious authorities ridicule Jesus as the
temple-destroyer and the Messiah, the King of Israel. Here Mark
has prepared for both themes that will dominate that scene. He
will show Jesus as breaking with the old temple and pointing to
the new. He will raise the question of royal messiahship and
indicate in what ways old titles have become inadequate and
must be reinterpreted.

II. THE KING APPROACHES

The so-called triumphal entry is fraught
On the one hand, there is a royal approach to
temple that is seen in allusions to Zech. 9:9;
I Kg. 1:38-40; II Kg. 9:13. On the other hand
is muted and anticlimactic. The temple rather
Jesus' destination,[13] and when he arrives he si
situation and returns to Bethany (11:11). No c
within the city or temple; all activity takes p

By contrast, in Matthew allusions become e
makes Zech 9:9 one of his formula quotations an
throws the city into an upheaval (*eseisthē*, 21:
also clearer than Mark. As Jesus descends the
Mount of Olives, his disciples greet him as ". .
comes in the name of the Lord!" (19:38). Thus,
argued that this is not a triumphal or messianic
meier cautions that "we must be careful to read
Mark wrote it, not as we know it from other gosp

The tradition Mark received ended with the
v.10. On the other hand, vv.1 and 11 probably f
tional framing for the pericope. The overloaded
v.1 suggests that the evangelist has been at work
graphically, Bethphage is closer to Jerusalem tha
and yet the present order seems to contradict thi
Bethany and the Mount of Olives play such an impo
this section, Mark has most likely added them. I
entrance into the temple, his exit into Bethany, f
glance are also redactional inasmuch as they are a
wider framing of the section in which the Lord ent
three times (11:11,15,27) and then retreats to Bet
19).[16] For the rest it appears that we are dealin
traditional story.[17]

The story is reminiscent of the royal enthron
Solomon (I Kg. 1:38-40) and Jehu (II Kg. 9:13).[18]
Solomon rides David's mule to Gihon where Zadok and
the people shout "Long live the King." In the secc
people take off their garments and proclaim "Jehu i
Neither reference has formed the present story but
the intimations of kingship which are present.

[The explanation of this is that]
[not] be wanting to the tribe of Ju
rules, (2) [and] a (descendant) sea
will [not] be wanting to David. F
staff is the Covenant of kingship,
are [the Thou]sands of Israel. Un
Righteousness comes, the Branch (4
him and to his seed has been given
the kingship of his people for eve
because (5) he has kept [. . .]
bers of the Community. For (6) [
gogue of the men [of mockery . .
                          4 Q P

The transmission of dominion shall
the house of Judah, nor the scribe
children, forever, until the Messi
the Kingdom belongs, and whom nati
                          Gen.

Kings and rulers shall not cease
Judah, nor scribes who teach the
until the time when the King Mess
youngest of his sons, and because
melt away.
                          Gen.

Therefore, if the tradition Mark inher
between the triumphal entry and Gen. 4
derstood Jesus' entrance as that of th

We summarize by saying that a sig
sions point to the royal character of
figure who comes on the *pōlon dedemen*
promises. He is the one to whom the s
to claim it as a humble king.

Besides the scriptural allusions
is also the explicit quotation from P
118 (LXX 117:26a) has been combined w
tion,[26] ("Blessed is the Kingdom of o
coming!") and inserted between shouts
Luke and John have altered the acclam
instance Jesus " . . . can be publicl
a pilgrim engaged on a prophetic miss
King whose coming takes place in acco
will of God."[27] Thus Matthew calls
(21:9) and eliminates the second par
names him " . . . the King who comes

(19:38), and John makes clear that the one who comes is " . . . even the King of Israel!" (12:13). In Mark, the acclamation is one of messianic fervor[28], but the only identification of Jesus is as *ho erchomenos*. Despite both the royal imagery of 11:1-10 and the cries of Bartimaeus (10:47-48), Mark calls Jesus neither King nor Son of David.

The interpretation of the acclamation is dependent upon the two members of the couplet. As is often the case in Mark, the second member tends to expand upon and to clarify the first. Thus the coming Kingdom of our Father David defines the Coming One. The one who comes in the name of the Lord brings that Kingdom. Inasmuch as Bartimaeus has just called Jesus the Son of David (10:47-48), the implication by association is that Jesus comes as the Son of David and accompanying his arrival is the coming Kingdom of David.

The problem is that in 11:1-11 Jesus approaches Jerusalem as a royal figure who fulfills the prophecies of Zech. 9:9 and Gen. 49:10. The crowds even acclaim him as in some manner inaugurating the Kingdom of David. Yet Mark has not applied either "King" or "Son of David" to Jesus. Moreover, all of this activity takes place before Jesus enters the temple of Jerusalem. On the basis of this, some have suggested that the scene should be read as anti-Jerusalem or anti-Davidic.[29] But is such an interpretation necessary?

The tension between such a blatantly royal tradition and its anticlimactic, redactional setting is purposeful. Through it Mark did not deny the Davidic promises; rather he showed that they cannot yet be publicly proclaimed. It is no accident that in this pericope Mark has not announced Jesus as the King of Israel and that so much is done by allusion as if to create a sense of ambiguity. The reason is that the redactor has carefully reserved the title "King" for Chapter 15 when it will be impossible to misunderstand the character of Jesus' kingship.[30]

In chapter 15, the accusations of the priests, the inscription on the cross and the mockeries will proclaim what the triumphal entry could not, Jesus is the Messiah, the King of Israel. To proclaim this publicly in the triumphal entry would have invited misunderstanding, the same misunderstanding the priests

and scribes display in the second mockery. For them kingship
consists in the power to save oneself as well as others (15:31).
However, it is precisely this kingship which Mark rejected.
Therefore, in the triumphal entry, he announced Jesus as King
only by allusion. The explicit title will be reserved for
chapter 15 when the passion has begun. Then there can be no
mistaking the nature of Jesus' kingship. The King of Israel is
a crucified Messiah.

As Mark's community reads this story, it understands what
the historical actors could not. The *Kyrios*[31] of 11:3 is the
one Isaiah prophesied at the beginning of the gospel (1:3), and
the one that David must call Lord (12:37), i.e., the Messiah
King.[32] Likewise, the Coming One of the acclamation is the one
John announced as more powerful than himself (1:7-8), namely,
the Messiah King who will baptize in the Holy Spirit. The
Coming One[33] will return in his capacity as the eschatological
Son of Man who will come in the glory of his Father with his
angels (8:38). He will come upon the clouds with power and
glory (13:26), and will be seated at the right hand of the
power (14:62). Thus, in this pericope, *Kyrios* and *ho erchomenos*
serve as surrogates for the royal title which cannot be publicly
revealed until the passion has begun.

The triumphal entry prepares for the royal theme of Chapter
15. Jesus comes as King but cannot be explicitly proclaimed as
such until the passion. Then, in ironic fashion, accusation,
inscription and mockery will proclaim that to which the entry
could only allude. For Mark, kingship cannot be disassociated
from the cross.

III. THE REJECTED STONE

In the parable of the vineyard, Mark continued the process
of clarifying in what sense Jesus is King. It is not our inten-
tion to give a full exegesis of this parable.[34] Rather, we
shall limit our agenda to two points. First, we wish to highlight the connection Mark made between the *huion agapēton* (12:6)
of the parable and the only Son of the Baptism (1:11) and
Transfiguration (9:7). Second, we shall emphasize the relationship between the only Son of these accounts (1:11; 9:7; 12:6)

and the rejected stone (12:10) found in the scriptural citation
from Ps. 118:22 which concludes the parable. In this manner
we hope to demonstrate that Mark identified the only Son of the
parable as a rejected, royal figure.

The parable of the vineyard occurs immediately after a
section in which the priests, the scribes and the elders question Jesus' authority (11:27-33). Jesus' immediate response is
to raise the question of John's baptism (11:30), but because the
leaders refuse to respond, Jesus does not answer their query
(11:33). It is at this point that Mark introduces the parable
in which Jesus, contrary to what has just been said, appears to
give an answer.

Although Mark designated this pericope as a parable, it is
evident that there is a difference between the teaching here
and the parables found in 3:23-27, 4:1-34; 13:28-29. In 12:1-
11 Jesus' teaching is clearly allegorical as can be seen from
the reaction of the religious leaders who seek to seize him
because they know the parable is directed at them (12:12).

Scholars disagree as to whether or not the original parable
spoken by Jesus was an allegory.[35] Influenced by the work of
Jülicher, many are hesitant to attribute allegorical speech to
Jesus.[36] Although we do not intend to enter into that debate,
we wish to emphasize that in its present form this parable is
an allegory for Mark.[37] The wicked husbandmen are the religious
leaders, the servants are the prophets and the only Son is
Jesus. But how did Mark understand this only Son?

The Only Son

Huion agapēton only occurs two other times in Mark, the
Baptism (1:11) and the Transfiguration (9:7).

1:11 *Sy ei ho huios mou ho agapētos en soi eudokēsa*

9:7 *Houtos estin ho huios mou ho agapētos akouete autou*

In both instances there is no explicit Old Testament quotation,
only a number of possible allusions (Gen. 22:2; Ps. 2:7; Isa.
42:1).

Gen. 22:2 *ton huion sou ton agapēton, hon agapēsas*

Ps. 2:7   *Huios mou ei sy*

Isa. 42:1 *Iakōb ho pais mou, antilēmpsomai autou*
          Israēl ho ekleltos mou, prosedexato auton hē
          psychē mou

Jeremias is the strongest proponent for the position that the background of 1:11 is the servant text of Isa. 42:1. He argues that behind the present *huios* there once stood the *pais* of Isa. 42:1. In this regard he points to Mt. 12:18 *idou ho pais mou hon hēretisa ho agapētos mou eis hon eudokēsen hē psychē mou* as a strong parallel to Mark's baptismal scene.[38] He suggests that the change from *pais* to *huios* occurred because the former designation was offensive to the Gentile church as not expressing " . . . the full significance of the majesty of the glorified Lord."[39] Thus, *huios theou* replaced *pais* even in the Hellenistic Jewish Christian church. Finally, since Jeremias understands the reference as originating in the Hebrew text, the lack of linguistic contact between Mk. 1:11 and the Septuagint of Isa. 42:1 does not present an insurmountable obstacle for him.

Jeremias' arguments have not been convincing. *cEbed* is the Hebrew term employed in Isa. 42:1. I. Howard Marshall points out that of its 807 occurrences in the Masoretic text only once is it translated by *huios* (Deut. 32:43), and here the Septuagint follows a Hebrew manuscript from Cave four at Qumran rather than the Masoretic text.[40] Moreover, the Septuagint uses *pais* as a translation of *bēn* only in Prov. 4:1; 20:7. Therefore, it seems strange that an original *pais* would have been replaced by *huios*.

Morna Hooker has demonstrated that *ho agapētos* (Mk. 1:11; 9:7) does not appear in any Greek version of Isa. 42:1 known to us and that it is never used in the Septuagint to translate the Hebrew root *bāhar* which is found in Isa. 42:1.[41] Moreover, in the Septuagint we find *prosdexato auton hē psychē mou* while in Mk. 1:11 we read *en soi eudokēsa*.[42] Therefore, on two counts (*huios* and *agapētos*) Mk. 1:11 does not appear to depend on either the Masoretic text or the Septuagint, and on a third (*en soi eudokēsa*) there is significant divergence from the Septuagint.

Moreover, if Matthew understood the baptismal formula of his gospel as reflecting a servant Christology, it is strange that he did not bring it into agreement with his quotation of 12:18-21. Although his baptismal formula differs from Mark's

(*houtos estin ho huios mou*, 3:17), he still refers to Jesus as
huios rather than *pais*.[43]

We suggest that the primary background for the Baptism and
Transfiguration is Ps. 2:7. There is a change in the word order
between the psalm and the baptismal formula. But as Marshall
notes, the placement of *sy ei* at the beginning of the quotation
rather than at the end (as in the psalm) puts the emphasis upon
the naming of Jesus as God's Son rather than upon the choice of
the addressee to be the son.[44] The phrase, *en soi eudokēsa*
could refer to a number of passages as Hooker points out.[45]
However, in this case it seems appropriate to remain in the
realm of royal, Davidic imagery and to accept Schweizer's suggestion that this is an allusion to II Sam. 22:20.[46] There
David speaks in his capacity as king and tells how the Lord
delivered him " . . . because he delighted in me."

Agapētos, which finds an echo in Gen. 22:2, need not be
regarded as a separate title or synonym for *ho eklektos* (Isa.
42:1). Here the word is probably used in the sense of "only"
as the parable of the vineyard seems to imply.[47] Thus the
Genesis allusion is a way of underscoring the uniqueness of the
father-son relationship. Just as Isaac was Abraham's only son,
so Jesus is the only Son of the Father.

An indirect testimony that the primary background of the
baptismal account is the royal theology of Ps. 2 can be found in
Lk. 3:22, and the witness of the church Fathers. The Western
reading of Lk. 3:22 changes the text into an unambiguous reference to Ps. 2:7. Thus we have an indication that some witnesses
understood the scene exclusively in terms of the psalm.[48] Moreover, as Lindars points out, many patristic references to the
Baptism quote only Ps. 2:7.[49] Thus Justin writes:

> . . . a voice out of the heavens spoke the words which
> had been uttered by David, when he, in the person of
> Christ, spoke what was later to be said to Christ by
> the Father: "Thou are my Son; this day have I begot-
> ten Thee."
> *Dialogue with Trypho* 88[50]

> It is narrated in the Memoirs of the Apostles that
> as soon as Jesus came out of the River Jordan and a
> voice said to Him: "Thou art My Son, this day I have
> begotten Thee, . . ."
> *Dialogue with Trypho* 103[51]

If the servant was the primary background for the Baptism and
Transfiguration, it is strange that someone such as Justin did
not develop the allusion.

We do not eliminate the possibility that there is also an
allusion to Isa. 42:1.[52] As Lövestam notes, Ps. 2:7 and Isa.
42:1 were joined in the Midrash on the Psalms.[53] However, we
are urging that the primary background for the Baptism and
Transfiguration is Ps. 2 and its royal imagery. At both of
these events the Father announces Jesus as his royal Son.

As the royal Son, Jesus is also the inheritor of the Davidic
promises. This is clear from the association of Ps. 2 with Ps.
89 and II Sam. 7 in Heb. I:5-6. From this string of scriptural
texts, it appears that Ps. 2 was associated with the Davidic
promises at an early stage.[54] Thus the presence of the psalm
at the Baptism and Transfiguration points to Jesus as the royal
Messiah.

From this study it is clear that if Mark has drawn a relationship between the only Son of the parable and the only Son
of the Baptism[55] and Transfiguration, then he understands this
son as a royal figure. In the parable, the only son is the same
son proclaimed at the Baptism and Transfiguration; he is the
Father's royal Son. And just as the nations conspired against
God's anointed in Ps. 2, so the tenants kill the son in order to
take his inheritance (*klēronomia*, 12:7). This inheritance may
well be a reference to Ps. 2:8.[56]

aitēsai par'emou kai dōsō soi ethenē ten klēronomian sou

In that case we would have still another indication that Mark
intended us to understand the son as a royal figure.

If we read the parable in the context of chapters 11-12,
then we see that Jesus is answering the religious authorities.
At the royal entry, he comes as the Messiah King to take possession of his temple (11:11). As Messiah King he teaches that
the temple will be called a house of prayer for all nations
(11:17). However, the religious leaders plot to destroy Jesus
because of his teaching (11:18), in order to keep the temple for
themselves. Finally Jesus responds that the authority for his
activity is his status as God's royal Son, the Son revealed at
the Baptism and Transfiguration.

There is still another indication that Mark intended his
readers to interpret the only Son of the parable as a royal
figure. At the end of this parable Mark concludes with an explicit quotation from Ps. 118:22 (LXX 117). In this quotation
he identifies the only son as a rejected stone which has become
the cornerstone. Why has the evangelist made this connection
and what relationship is there between the only Son and the
rejected stone? To answer these questions it is necessary to
undertake a brief study of Ps. 118.

The Rejected Stone in Psalm 118

Ps. 118 played a major role in the apologetic of the New
Testament (Mt. 21:42; Mk. 12:10-11; Lk. 20:17; Acts 4:11; I
Pt. 2:7)[57] and it was on the basis of this psalm that Rendal
Harris constructed much of his theory about a Book of Testimonies in early Christianity.[58] Lindars notes that the psalm
probably had such apologetic appeal since the notion of the
rejected stone has an aura of literal fulfillment.[59]

Peddinghaus suspects that the psalm had a special importance for the Markan community[60] because it is the only scriptural text quoted verbatim in the gospel. The placement of the
psalm at the beginning of the Jerusalem ministry (11:9b-10), the
allusions in 8:31,9:12, and its setting here (12:10-11) support
his suggestion.

The question which concerns us is the nature of Ps. 118
and the background against which we should interpret it. Is it
a psalm which celebrates the triumph and victory of an individual, or can we understand it against a royal background so that
the rejected stone is the rejected king?

For some years there has been a lively debate among Old
Testament scholars about the number of and the nature of the
psalms composed for the use of the Davidic king.[61] Gunkel
counted nine: 21 and 72 (coronation or birthday); 132 (anniver-
sary of the royal sanctuary or palace); 45 (royal wedding); 20
and 18 (before and after war); 2,101 and 110 (the king's enthronement). He looked upon the many psalms of the individual
as the utterances of a private person. He believed that those
which expressed the thanksgiving of the individual belonged to
the cult whereas the laments of the individual did not. Thus

he argued that the sufferer ". . . pours out his griefs in the
privacy of his room, while his thanksgiving must be public testimony."[62]

H. Schmidt and L. Delekat were not convinced by Gunkel's non-
cultic understanding of the laments and proposed " . . . a setting
in the juridical process of the sanctuary" and " . . . the asylum
of the Jerusalem Temple."[63] It was not until Mowinckel, however,
that the royal interpretation of the psalms began in earnest.
From Gunkel's laments of the individual he saw 28,61, and 63 as
royal. And from the laments of the people he counted 44,60,80,
and 83 as royal. Finally, as royal he added 66,68,84,118 and
I Sam. 2:1-10.

In Britain, A. R. Johnson[64] read a royal ritual in Pss. 18,
20,89, and 118. Meanwhile, Birkland saw the enemies of the individual in the psalms as foreign peoples and he convinced
Mowinckel that the " . . . 'I' is not just an 'Everyman' but
the king of the people, and the enemies are accordingly of a
national, political kind."[65]

Other studies came from Bentzen, Engnell and Ringgren, all
of which tended to increase the number of royal psalms.[66] They
formed a definite school of Scandinavian scholarship that found
a kinship with the Myth and Ritual School of English scholars.
Many of these studies, however, came under heavy criticism because they presupposed or read into the psalms a royal autumnal
festival which could not be documented. And yet the royal interpretation tended to explain such elements in the psalter which
otherwise could not be answered satisfactorily as the psalmist's
enemies, the magnitude of his deliverance.

Most recently the royal interpretation of the psalms has
been advocated by John Eaton, *Kingship and the Psalms*, and John
Gray, *The Biblical Doctrine of the Reign of God*.[67] Besides the
nine psalms that Gunkel counted as royal, Eaton would add the
following as clearly royal in content: 3,4,7,9-10,17,22,23,27,
28,35,40,41,57,59,61,62,63,66,69,70,71,75,89,91,92,94,108,118,
138,140,143. To this list he adds as less clear, but probably
royal, the following: 5,11,16,31,36,42-3,51,52,54,55,56,73,77,
86,102,109,116,120,121,139,141,142.[68]

It is usually objected that although these psalms may have
enjoyed a royal setting once, by the time of the New Testament

they were democratized so that they could be used by the ordinary people.[69] However, Eaton cautions that " . . . such 'democratization' should not be taken for granted in the Psalter, it is reasonable to regard royal items as evidence of royal psalms unless in a particular case there is adequate reason to the contrary."[70]

What we do know is that during the New Testament era Davidic authorship was attributed to a number of psalms. As Sanders writes, "whether David composed a single psalm is beside the point: the belief that the collection of psalms were of Davidic origin was unquestionably a stabilizing force in the diverse collections and compilations abroad in the Jewish world."[71] The importance of David as both a poet and prophet can be determined from the list of his compositions that comes from the Psalm Scroll of Qumran.

> And the Lord gave him a discerning and enlightened
> spirit. And he wrote 3,600 psalms; and songs to
> sing before the altar over the whole-burnt perpetual
> offering of the Sabbath, 52 songs; and for the
> offering of the New Moons and for all the Solemn
> Assemblies and for the Day of Atonement, 30 songs.
> And all the songs that he spoke were 446, and songs
> for making music over the stricken, 4. And the total
> was 4,050. All these he composed through prophecy
> which was given him from before the Most High.
> David's Compositions[72]
> Column 27

This picture of David as the author of the psalms who spoke prophetically is attested by the New Testament: Ps. 2/Acts 4:25-26; Ps. 16/Acts 2:25-28,31; Ps. 32/Rom. 4:6-8; Ps. 69/Acts 1:16-20; Rom. 11:9-10; Ps. 109/Acts 1:16-20; Ps. 110/Acts 2:34. Moreover, Mark explicitly named David as the author of Ps. 110 and showed that he spoke as a prophet by introducing the quotation in 12:35, *Dauid eipen en tǭ pneumati tǭ agiǭ*.

Although contemporary scholarship calls many psalms laments of the individual, we suggest that in terms of New Testament interpretation such a category can be restrictive and misleading. If the New Testament era looked upon David as the "author" of these psalms, an author who spoke through prophecy, then it clearly saw in them more than the lament of an individual. The royal imagery already present in many of these psalms, e.g.,

Ps. 118, and the prophetic voice of David, combine to give them
a royal and eschatological tone. Indeed it is precisely this
royal imagery and the prophetic voice of David which lends itself so well to a messianic interpretation. Psalms "composed"
by King David become prophecies for his royal descendant.

Psalm 118 is composed of 1) a brief thanksgiving song (1-
4), 2) the thanksgiving of an individual saved from danger
(5-21), and 3) a conclusion which appears to have been sung an-
tiphonally (22-29).[73] The question which concerns us is the
identity of this person who has experienced the Lord's deliverance. According to vv.10-13 all the nations surrounded him, a
fact which seems to imply that he is some sort of national
figure.[74] In v.15 there are " . . . songs of victory in the
tents of the righteous," an image which appears to refer to a
military campaign. Finally, the scope of this individual's victory is so great that it seems to occasion a major festival (22-
29). On the basis of these considerations, we suggest that the
only person in Israelite society who could command such attention so as to demand a national festal gathering for his deliverance is the king.

The king, then, is the rejected stone of v.22. For a moment he was rejected but now " . . . is glorified as the main
stone in the structure of God's society."[75] Thus the concluding
hymn, which is sung by the choir, is a royal welcome as the king
enters the sanctuary gates.

If we are correct, and the individual of vv.5-21 is the
king, then we probably have a word play in v.22.[76] That is, the
rejected stone, ᵓeben, is the rejected son, bēn, namely the
Israelite king who was seen as God's son. Thus the rejected
stone (ᵓeben) is the rejected son (ben), the Israelite King.

The Targum to Ps. 118:22 has employed this word play.[77] It
interprets the rejected stone (ᵓeben) as "the youth among the
sons of Jesse" (bennai benayya de Yishai) who was rejected when
Samuel came to anoint him (David) as king. Indeed, in this
section the Targum attributes different phrases of the psalm
to the builders, the sons of Jesse, Jesse and his wife, David,
the clans of the tribe of Judah and Samuel. Thus there is the
following dialogue.[78]

Builders:	This is the Lord's doing
Sons of Jesse:	It is marvelous in our sight
Builders:	This is the day which the Lord has made
Sons of Jesse:	Let us rejoice and be glad in it
Builders:	Save us we beseech thee O Lord
Jesse and wife:	O Lord we beseech thee give us success
Builders:	Blessed is he who enters in the name of of the Lord
David:	We bless you from the house of the Lord
Clans:	The Lord is God and he has given us light
Samuel:	Bind the festal procession with branches up to the horns of the altar
David:	Thou are my God, and I will give thanks to thee
Samuel:	O give thanks to the Lord, for he is good, for his steadfast love endures forever.

Moreover, in the Midrash on the Psalms "This is the Lord's
doing" refers to David as well as the freeing of the Israelites
from Egypt.

> *This is the Lord's doing* alludes to king David,
> king of Israel, who at one moment was keeping
> his father's sheep, and in the very next moment
> was made king, so that everyone exclaimed: One
> moment David keeps sheep, and the next he is
> king.
>
> *Midrash on Psalms*[79]

Thus it would seem that a strong royal Davidic tradition stood
behind this psalm.

Finally, Derrett has pointed to still another word play in
Ps. 118:22.[80] In this case he claims there is a pun latent in
habônîm, the builders. The builders can mean either the actual
builders or the metaphorical builders, i.e., the builders in
the Torah, the scholars. And, indeed, Acts 4:11 appears to employ the pun when it says, "This is the stone which was rejected
by you the builders . . . ," i.e., the rulers, elders and scribes
of Acts 4:5. If such a pun was current, then it also fits our
parable where the religious authorities, the "builders of the
Torah," reject the only son.

We summarize by saying that there is important evidence
that Ps. 118 is royal in content and that the rejected stone
refers to the rejected son/king.[81] Because of this royal content, and David's prophetic authorship, we believe that the New
Testament read the psalm in a royal and eschatological fashion,
and hence found it useful as an apologetic for the rejected

Messiah King. The only son of the parable is the royal Son of
the Baptism and Transfiguration. The quotation from Ps. 118:22
shows that this only son is also the rejected stone, that is,
the rejected stone/king. Thus in two ways, Ps. 2:7 and Ps.
118:22, we arrive at the same conclusion. That is, in the parable of the vineyard Mark continued to develop the royal theme.

In the second mockery the religious authorities questioned
Jesus' messianic credentials on the grounds that as King of
Israel he could not save himself. Now, however, that mockery
is directed at the Christian community which professes a crucified Messiah King for its savior. Mark's answer on behalf of
the community was that Jesus is indeed what they profess and
was sent as such by the Father (12:6). To those who challenge
the claim, he responded by asking whether or not they have ever
read the text of Ps. 118:22.[82] Understood as prophecy, the
passage foretold that the Messiah King must be rejected before
he can be exalted. Therefore, if Jesus had tried to save himself from the cross, he would have contradicted both his own
teaching (8:35) as well as the scripture (Ps. 118:22) his passion was intended to fulfill (8:31; 9:12).

The community realizes that even before the cross the
Father had already designated Jesus as Messiah King at the Baptism and Transfiguration. But just as in the case of the triumphal entry, so here, that kingship could not be publicly proclaimed lest it be misunderstood. But when Jesus is rejected
(Ps. 118:22) in the passion, then he will be proclaimed King
since there will be no possibility of misunderstanding the true
nature of his kingship. He is the royal Son revealed by the
Father (1:11; 9:7) and the rejected Messiah King that Ps. 118:22
prophesied.

IV. DAVID'S SON

The question about David's son (12:35-37) forms a bracket
with the triumphal entry (11:1-11) and challenges the reader to
interpret the events which occur between the two incidents in
its light. The pericope has not lacked attention.[83] Authors
have studied it from a variety of approaches (the historical
Jesus, *Sitz im Leben* of the church, Markan redaction) as well

as diverse understandings of the title "Son of David" (the
Messiah of Ps. Sol. 17, Exorcist in the tradition of Solomon).
As regards Mark, scholars have settled into one of two camps.
First, the evangelist did not deny Davidic descent but believed
that the Messiah would be more.[84] Second, the evangelist did
not consider Davidic descent essential for messiahship and
probably denied it.[85]

The question of David's son is one of four which occur after the parable of the vineyard (12:1-12). However, unlike the
first three questions (12:13-17; 18-27; 28-34a) nobody explicitly
poses this question to Jesus. In Mt. 22:41 the Pharisees ask
the question and in Lk. 20:41 Jesus directs the question to the
scribes (cf. 20:39). However, in Mark it is not clear whether
the scribes are present, although it does concern their doctrine.

For Matthew, the question about David's son is the *pièce de
résistance* which silences Jesus' opponents (22:46). It is not
so for Mark, who sees all debate ending after the scribe's question about the great commandment (12:34b). Moreover, although
Mark has already mentioned that Jesus is in the temple (11:27),
he now repeats that geographical notice in 12:35 and adds that
Jesus was teaching there (*didaskōn en tō heirō*). Therefore, no
matter how much the Son-of-David question is part of a fourfold
scheme, this pericope stands apart from the first three disputes
with the religious authorities.[86] It is a portion of Jesus' final teaching in the temple, a teaching of the Messiah about the
Messiah,[87] and it forces the reader to reassess his understanding
of what has happened since the triumphal entry.

Finally, although the question is not explicitly directed
at the scribes, it does concern their doctrine of the Messiah.
In Mark the scribes form the one group which opposes Jesus from
beginning to end (1:22; 2:6,16; 3:22; 7:1,5; 8:31; 9:11,14;
10:33; 11:18,27; 12:28,32,35,38; 14:1,43,53; 15:1,31). The
priests do not appear until 8:31 and the Pharisees disappear after 12:13. But the scribes are associated with the Pharisees as
early as 2:16, and with the priests and elders, with whom they
oppose Jesus, until the end of the gospel (8:31; 10:33; 11:18,
27; 14:1,43,53; 15:1,31). Moreover, in one instance (9:11) Mark
attributed a messianic doctrine to them; namely, Elijah must come

first. Jesus does not contradict that teaching but in 9:12 he
does supplement it with a new dimension: the Son of Man must
suffer many things and be rejected.

It is not surprising, then, that Jesus questions the messianic teaching of the scribes at this moment. They have opposed
his authority from the start; they hold messianic doctrines
known to the disciples; and, at the cross, they join the priests
in mocking Jesus as the Messiah King. It may even be that it
was a group of scribes which mocked the Markan community for
their messianic conviction about Jesus. In that case, this
pericope, like the second mockery, reflects the ongoing polemic
of the church.

Jesus' argument is well known. In Ps. 110 David spoke as
a prophet[88] (cf. Acts 1:16; 4:25) concerning the Messiah. Mark
emphasizes the prophetic nature of David's speech through the
phrase *en tō pneumati tō hagiō* (Ez. 11:24; 37:1; Rev. 1:10; 4:2;
17:3; 21:10).[89] In the Spirit, David heard what the Lord God
spoke to his Lord, the Messiah. Inasmuch as David himself calls
the Messiah his Lord, the father and son relationship between
the two comes into question. If David calls the Messiah "Lord,"
then how can the Messiah be his son since no father calls his
son his master?

One of the difficulties in interpreting this text is the
placement of emphasis. Has Mark employed it to combat Davidic
messiahship by denying Jesus' Davidic descent, or has he engaged
the text in order to raise the question of Jesus' true sonship
without prejudice to his physical origin? Those who espouse the
first position point to the plain and obvious meaning of the
text[90] in which the final question implies that he is not the
Son of David. On the other hand those opposed point to the
change of interrogatives from *pōs* to *pothen* and argue that the
switch is purposeful and that the latter should be read as "in
what sense?"[91] Or, they argue with Daube that this is a haggadha
question " . . . about apparent contradictions between passages
from Scripture . . . the answer implied is not that one notion
is right and the other wrong, but that both are right in different contexts."[92]

At this point we propose two avenues of approach. First,
we shall examine how this pericope functions within the

Jerusalem ministry of chapters 11-12. Second, we shall investigate the relationship between Ps. 110 as it occurs in this pericope and in the trial before the Sanhedrin (14:62).

If we examine the Son-of-David pericope as an isolated unit, the response it implies is in some sense negative. And at an earlier stage of the tradition particular groups may have enlisted the pericope to show that Davidic descent was not necessary for messiahship. However, we suggest that when the same pericope enters a wider narrative, that context alters the meaning. Thus, in the present setting, Mark raised this question almost immediately after the parable of the vineyard. Earlier we argued that in that parable, the redactor presented Jesus as the royal Son of the Baptism and Transfiguration. As the royal Son he inherits the Davidic promises (1:11; 9:7; 12:6). Moreover, in the Baptism, the Transfiguration, and the parable, Mark was at pains to emphasize that this royal Son is the only Son of the Father. Therefore, when Jesus asks how the Messiah is David's son, the reader already knows the answer. He is David's son inasmuch as he inherits the divine promises (1:11; 9:7; 12:6), but the origin of his sonship necessarily goes beyond physical descent because Jesus, the Messiah, is the Father's only Son. In other words, Jesus' sonship is a unique sonship which the scribal messianic doctrine cannot comprehend.

Here we find a similarity with 9:11-13. In this dialogue, which follows the Transfiguration, the three disciples question Jesus about another messianic doctrine of the scribes; namely, Elijah must come first (9:11). Jesus acknowledges that this scribal doctrine is essentially true but then he expands upon it in two ways. First, he points to the scripture that the Son of Man must suffer and be rejected (9:12). Second, again pointing to the scripture, he discloses that Elijah has already come (9:13). Thus the messianic doctrine of the scribes is true, but not sufficient. The Messiah does inherit the Davidic promises (1:11; 9:7; 12:6) but his sonship cannot be adequately explained in terms of physical descent. The Messiah, as Mark understood him, is the only Son of the Baptism, Transfiguration and parable. The scribes, like the Sadducees (12:24), have not understood the scriptures (9:12,13; 12:36). But why does David call the Messiah his Lord and what is the meaning of this title?

There is only one other instance when Mark employs Ps. 110.
In the trial before the Sanhedrin (14:62), he inserts a portion
of the psalm (*ek dexiōn kathēmenon*) within a free quotation from
Dan. 7:13.   In that scene the high priest asks Jesus if he is
the Christ, the Son of the Blessed, and Jesus responds with an
affirmative answer (*egō eimi*), and the mixed quotation we have
just noted.[93]   It is reasonable to assume, if Mark employed Ps.
110 in the messianic context of the trial and in the Son-of-
David question, that he saw some relationship between the two.[94]

By the quotation at the trial, Mark states that in his
eschatological capacity as the Son of Man the Messiah, the Son
of the Blessed, will be seated at the right hand of God.   This
Son of Man is a royal figure as the imagery from Daniel and Ps.
110 testifies.[95]   With this in mind, it becomes apparent why
David calls the Messiah his Lord.   He does so because in the
eschatological age the Messiah, the only Son (1:11; 9:7; 12:6),
the Son of the Blessed (14:62), will reign as the transcendent
Son of Man.   Thus even the great King David must address this
Messiah as his Lord.

Earlier in the triumphal entry, we suggested that Mark
employed *Kyrios* as a surrogate for king.   We suspect that the
royal messianic interpretation of *Kyrios* is precisely what Mark
intended in the Son-of-David question.[96]

Lucien Cerfaux has presented the case for the royal interpretation of *Kyrios* at some length.   The Old Testament refers
to the king as Lord in a number of instances:[97] 1) My Lord, Your
Lord (I Sam. 24:11; 25:28,41; II Kg. 9:7; 18:23); 2) My Lord the
King, Your Lord the King (I Sam. 26:17,19; 29:8; I Kg. 1:20,27,
36); 3) My Lord, Your Lord, King David (I Kg. 1:31,37); 4) Our
Lord David (I Kg. 1:11); 5) Your Lord Saul (II Sam. 2:7).   Moreover, the Psalms of Solomon make an identification between the
Christ and Lord.[98]   Thus in Ps. Sol. 17:36 we read:

> And there shall be no iniquity in his days in their
> midst for all shall be holy and that king is the
> Lord Messiah. (*Christos kyrios*)[99]

Likewise, Ps. Sol. 18:8 probably uses Lord in a royal context.
It reads:

> Under the rod of the chastening of Lord Messiah
> [*Christou Kyriou*] in the fear of his God: in the spirit
> of wisdom and of righteousness and of might.[100]

Thus, by addressing the Messiah as his Lord, David also salutes
him as his king. David does this because in his eschatological
capacity the Messiah, the Son of the Blessed, will reign as the
Son of Man.

In summary, our discussion shows that the Son-of-David question brings the royal theme in these chapters to a climax. The
Kyrios who enters the city (11:3) amid messianic allusions is
the *Kyrios* that David will salute as king (12:37). This *Kyrios*
is the only Son of the parable (12:6) whom the Father proclaimed
as his royal Son at the Baptism and Transfiguration. He is the
Kyrios whom Isaiah prophesied (1:3) and whom Mark identified as
Messiah (1:1,3).

V. IN RETROSPECT

If we read chapters 11-12 in light of the Son-of-David
question, it is evident that Mark has been redefining the concept
of Davidic messiahship all along.[101] Thus Jesus enters the
temple as a royal figure but is not publicly proclaimed because
the passion has not yet begun. He cleanses the temple but not
in the traditional manner.[102] Indeed, when we compare Jesus'
action to that which the zealots planned for the cleansing of
the temple (cessation of daily sacrifice for the emperor, ex-
clusion of Gentiles and the impure, enforcement of Pharisaic
halachah, installation of a new high priest), the very term
"cleansing" is misleading for Jesus' action in 11:15-17.[103]
Rather, Jesus presents himself as a teaching messianic King (11:
17). Such a Messiah no more corresponds to the traditional picture of the Davidic Messiah King than did the implication in
10:47 that a Nazarene could be the Son of David.[104]

The teaching of this Messiah King concerns the nations who
have been excluded from the temple (11:17)[105] and intimates that
there will be a new temple built on faith (11:21-25).[106] However, it is precisely this teaching (11:17) that results in the
plan to destroy Jesus (11:18).[107]

The priests, scribes and elders question the authority of
Jesus (11:27-33) but do not receive an answer because they have
refused to acknowledge John's baptism. And by refusing to
acknowledge that baptism, they have rejected what John taught

during the days of his ministry: Jesus is the more powerful one
who comes after John (1:7). As a result, 11:27-33 does not so
much concern John's baptism as it refers the reader to the opening of the gospel when John witnessed to Jesus as the coming
Messiah. Then, dressed as Elijah (Mk. 1:6/II Kg. 1:8), the
Baptist fulfilled even scribal expectations (9:11) and announced
the Coming One (1:7). The religious leaders must ask by what
authority Jesus performs these actions because they have rejected
the witness of John. Because they rejected the witness of the
Baptist, they do not understand that the Messiah King teaches in
their temple.

The parable of the vineyard shows that the only son (12:6)
is the royal Son announced at the Baptism and Transfiguration.
Moreover, this son is the rejected son/king foretold in Ps.
118:22.

Finally, the questions of the Pharisees, Sadducees and the
scribe take on added meaning in light of the Son-of-David question. The kingdom of the Messiah King will not compete with
that of Caesar's (12:13-17). Each king has his proper inscription (*epigraphē*).[108] For Caesar, the inscription occurs on a
coin (12:16): for the Messiah King, it will come on the cross
(15:26).

The debate about resurrection points to the Messiah King's
own resurrection. Here there is a basic misunderstanding about
the scripture and the power of God (12:24), the same misunderstanding that occurs in the second mockery. It is because of
their understanding of scripture and the power of God that the
Christian community can accept a crucified Messiah King. It is
because of their belief in the resurrection that they know he
will reign as the eschatological King.

Lastly, the debate about the greatest commandment reminds
the reader of the new community and cult that the Messiah King
is establishing. In that community, the proper relationship between members will be more important than cultic sacrifice.
The Messiah King has not cleansed the temple in order to reestab-
lish it " . . . as it was in the days of old" (Ps. Sol.
17:33),[109] but to transform it into a temple not made by hands
(14:58).

We urge that in chapters 11-12 Mark has been developing a
royal theme which prepares the reader for the royal theology of
chapter 15. Mark has not explicitly employed the title "King"
because he carefully reserves it for the moment when there can
be no misunderstanding the nature of Jesus' kingship. That
moment, of course, is the passion when the accusations of the
priests, the inscription and the mockeries will proclaim Jesus
a suffering, rejected king according to the pattern of Ps. 118.
However, in chapters 11-12 Mark has used *Kyrios* and *ho erchomenos*
as surrogates for the kingly title, and he has made clear that
the ground for Jesus' kingship is his divine sonship proclaimed
by the Father at the Baptism and Transfiguration. In what sense
is he a king? He is king after the pattern of Pss. 2, 110, 118,
namely, God's royal Son, the rejected stone which will become
the cornerstone.

CHAPTER VI

THE PASSION OF THE ONLY SON
AND THE REJECTION OF THE SON OF MAN

In the previous chapter we investigated Jesus' kingship in
light of chapters 11-12. We pointed to the presence of a royal
theme in this section and suggested that Mark's purpose was to
redefine royal messianism in order to prepare for the royal
theme of chapter 15. Although royal imagery abounded in chapters 11-12, Mark did not employ the title "King" lest the reader
misunderstand. Rather, he intentionally reserved the title for
the passion when there could be no misunderstanding the nature
of Jesus' kingship. The Christ, the King of Israel, is a suffering, rejected king. Thus the appearance of the royal titles
in chapter 15 is not so abrupt as it first appears. The attentive reader knows that the evangelist has carefully prepared
for this moment.

In this section we turn to the scenes before Pilate (15:1-
15; 42-47) and the mockery by the soldiers (15:16-20a) in order
to view another aspect of Jesus' kingship. Our objective is to
show that Mark has edited these scenes so that they refer the
reader to earlier material about the suffering, soon-to-be-
exalted, Son of Man. By this technique the redactor reminds us
that the only Son, the King of Israel, must suffer in his capacity as the Son of Man. Thus Mark's community reads the passion
as more than historical report or shameful failure. Because of
the Son-of-Man material, the believer realizes that everything
happens so that the scriptures might be fulfilled (14:49). The
believer is privy to the secret teaching granted the disciples
(8:31; 9:12,31; 10:33-34; 14:18) so that he understands that the
rejection of the only Son has been divinely ordained. On the
other hand, the historical actors and the detractors of Mark's
community were and are not privy to this mystery. Consequently,
they ridicule the authentic King of the Jews as a messianic
pretender.

In this chapter our procedure is threefold. First, we
shall examine the relationship between chapter 15 and the Son-
of-Man material in order to show how Mark has intertwined the
two. Thus, while the earliest community may have understood
Jesus to be the Suffering Just One, Mark has gone beyond this
and interpreted the Suffering Just One as the only Son who suffers in his capacity as the Son of Man but will soon be exalted.[1]

Second, we shall review the Son-of-Man material in the
gospel and argue that the concept which unifies it is the authority which the Son of Man possesses as the only Son. Moreover,
Mark understood this Son of Man as a royal figure and intended
his community to see the suffering Son of Man as one who would
come with regal power and glory.

Finally, we shall explain the scriptural necessity that the
only Son should suffer as the Son of Man. Once more we shall
point to Ps. 118:22 as a key text. By this scripture the evangelist constructed a bridge between the suffering Son of Man
(8:31; 9:12) and the rejected, only Son (12:6,10-11). In brief,
we shall endeavor to show that in Mark the Son-of-Man material
supports the royal theme. That is, the only Son suffers in his
capacity as the Son of Man, a soon-to-be-exalted, royal figure.

I. CHAPTER 15 AND THE SON OF MAN

Prediction and Passion

The simple fact that Mark has cast 8:31; 9:31 and 10:33-34
as predictions means that there will be some correspondence between them and the passion narrative. However, even the most
casual reader realizes that the third passion prediction is
more detailed than the first two so that for some it even appears to serve as an outline for the passion.[2] The linguistic
contacts between this prediction and the passion are so striking
that most commentators recognize some kind of interdependence.[3]

In recent years the passion predictions have attracted
scholarly attention[4] and there has been a tendency to understand
Mark as responsible in some way for their formation. Thus
Strecker argues that the evangelist produced the second and
third predictions on the basis of the first.[5] Minette de
Tillesse postulates an original logion on which Mark built up

all three sayings.[6] Perrin is convinced that " . . . the predictions are Markan literary productions, the individual parts
being mined from early Christian traditions."[7] Schenke claims
that except for 10:45 Mark composed all of the suffering Son-
of-Man predictions.[8] Finally, Hahn writes, " . . . the third
prophecy will have to be regarded as a sheer redactional development."[9] Below we have listed the linguistic contacts between
the third passion prediction and the passion.

Third Prediction	*Passion Narrative*
paradothēsetai tois archiereusin kai tois grammateusin	14:10,11,18,21,41,42-44
kai katakrinousin auton thanatō	14:64
kai paradōsousin auton tois ethnesin	15:1
kai empaixousin autō	15:20,31
kai emptysousin autō	14:65; 15:19
kai mastigōsousin auton	15:15 (*phragellōsas*)
kai apoktenousin	15:24,25 (*staurousin, estaurōsan*)
kai meta treis hēmeras	14:58 (*dia triōn hēmerōn*) 15:29 (*en trisin hēmerais*)
anastēsetai	14:28 (*egerthēnai*) 16:6 (*ēgerthē*)

On the basis of this chart we should like to make two observations. First, it is clear that although there are many
linguistic contacts between the prediction and the passion,
there remain a number of significant discrepancies. First, all
of the predictions (8:31; 9:31; 10:33-34) proclaim that the
Son of Man will be killed, but the passion consistently refers
to Jesus' crucifixion (15:13,14,15,20,21,24,25,27).[10] Second,
all of the predictions emphasize that the Son of Man will rise
(*anistēmi*), but the passion says that Jesus will be raised up
(*egeirō*).[11] Third, the predictions look for the resurrection
"after" (*meta*) three days while the passion prefers the expression "within" (*dia* or *en*) three days.[12] Fourth, the third prediction says that the Son of Man will be scourged (*mastigoō*),
a term usually applied to flogging as a punishment decreed by

the synagogue (Dt. 25:2f., Mt. 10:17),[13] but the passion employs
the Latin loan word *phragelloō* which refers to "a punishment
inflicted on slaves and provincials after a sentence of death
had been pronounced."[14] Finally, the general order of events
differs slightly between the prediction and the passion.[15]

Prediction	*Passion*
ridicule him	scourge him
spit on him	spit on him
scourge him	ridicule him

These discrepancies lead to a second observation; namely,
in forming the passion prediction and in arranging the passion
narrative Mark was dealing with different traditions.[16] Indeed,
if we observe the passion prediction closely, we notice that it
places a strong emphasis (10:34) upon the indignities which the
Gentiles will heap upon the Son of Man (mock, spit, scourge).[17]
However, when we arrive at the passion narrative, the role of
the Gentiles has been considerably diminished. In fact, in our
compositional analysis we pointed to the strong, anti-priestly
bias which characterizes the hearing before Pilate. Although
15:26 presupposes a political charge, at no point does the
governor officially pronounce Jesus guilty.[18] Rather, the emphasis falls upon the jealousy of the priests (15:10). It is
only in the first mockery (15:16-20a) that the Romans play an
evil role, and here nearly everything the soldiers do the
priests also do!

Spit	14:65 - members of Sanhedrin
	15:19 - Gentiles
Ridicule	15:20 - Gentiles
	15:31 - priests and scribes

What Mark has done is to take a prediction in which the Gentiles
are the primary evildoers and attribute some of their guilt to
the priests and other religious authorities. On the basis of
these observations, we suggest that Mark was working with essentially different traditions in the prediction and passion.

Nonetheless, the redactor has managed to coordinate and
intertwine these two diverse traditions. He accomplished this

in a number of ways. First, he pointed out, both in the predictions (8:31; 10:33) and passion, that the religious leaders
would share in the responsibility for the death of the Son of
Man. Second, he announced the death sentence in the prediction
(10:33) and the passion (14:64) in almost identical words.[19]
Third, the *paradidōmi* formula occurs in all three predictions
and at numerous points within the passion narrative. More
specifically, our compositional analysis showed that in the
hearing before Pilate, Mark employed *paradidōmi* as a means of
beginning and ending the hearing (*kai paredōken Pilatō* v.1, *kai
paredōken ton Iēsoun* v.15). And again in 15:10, a highly redactional verse, he referred to the priests as handing over
Jesus out of jealousy. Fourth, Mark appears to have purposely
coordinated the vocabulary of prediction and passion at two
specific instances: *emtyō* (10:34; 14:65; 15:19) and *empaizō*
(10:34; 15:20,31). Moreover, in two cases (14:65; 15:31) his
purpose seems to have been to show that what the Gentiles did
the religious leaders also did, namely, spit at and mock the
Son of Man.

What was the redactor's reason for intertwining these diverse traditions? An examination of Mk. 15:1-20 discloses that
there is a noticeable absence of Old Testament allusions in
this section.[20] Inasmuch as the passion occurs for Mark according to the scripture, this is a strange set of circumstances.
It is for this reason that the intertwining of prediction and
passion becomes important. By arranging the passion, and specifically this section, with the prediction in mind Mark grounded
it in the scripture. We now know that the King of the Jews,
God's only Son, suffers "as it is written of him" (9:12; 14:21).
By intertwining prediction and passion Mark has reminded the
reader that this humiliation and rejection does not occur by
chance. The only Son, the King of the Jews, suffers in his divinely appointed capacity as the Son of Man according to the
scriptures.

*The Passion of Jesus and the
Passion of the Baptist*

There is yet another section in which Mark notifies his
readers that the only Son, the King of the Jews, endures the

passion in his capacity as the Son of Man. This occurs in the
final scene before Pilate (15:42-47).

Earlier we noted that Mark created a relationship between
this scene and the hearing before Pilate by mentioning Pilate's
amazement for the second time (15:44). The notice of this
amazement comes in a section which Matthew and Luke have omitted
from their accounts (15:44-45). For the sake of convenience we
reproduce the stylized arrangement of these verses which we have
already attributed to the redactor.

ētēsato to sōma tou Iēsou (43c)
   ho de Pilatos ethaumasen ei ēdē tethnēken (44a)
      kai proskalesamenos ton kentyriōna (44b)
   epērōtēsen auton ei palai apethanen (44c)
kai gnous apo tou kentyriōnos edōrēsato to ptōma tǫ
                                              Iōsēph (45)

In these verses Mark has done three things. First, the presence
of the centurion reminds the reader of the confession made in
15:39. Second, the amazement of Pilate recalls the same reaction of the Roman procurator at the conclusion of the Roman
hearing (15:5). Third, the use of corpse (*ptōma*) calls to mind
the death of the Baptist in 6:29 when his disciples came for
his corpse (*ptōma*) and placed it in a tomb (*ethēkan auto en
mnēmeiǫ*, cf. 15:46). Since these are the only two places (6:29;
15:46) where Mark has employed this rather harsh term, which
some witnesses (A C W Ψ 0112, f[1,13], lat sy) replace with the
milder *sōma*, it appears that the redactor was drawing a deliberate parallel between the two events.

Throughout his narrative, Mark has paralleled the careers
of Jesus and John.[21] Thus, just as John was "handed over"
(1:14), so Jesus would be "handed over" (9:31; 10:33; 14:18,21,
42; 15:1,10,15). And just as the Baptist went the way recorded
of him by the scripture (9:13), so the Son of Man would suffer
as it was written of him (9:12). The identification between
John and Jesus is so great that Herod (6:14,16) and the people
(8:28) identify Jesus as the resurrected Baptist.

However, in Mark the parallel between Jesus and John comes
to a climax in the passion which each endures. Both John and
Jesus are arrested (6:17; 14:46) and bound (6:17; 15:1). In

each case the official in charge (Herod, Pilate) operates under
the instigation of a jealous party (Herodias, 6:19; priests,
15:10). Neither Herod nor Pilate is convinced of his prisoner's
guilt. The "trials" of John and Jesus take place on a festival
day (Herod's birthday, the coming Passover) when both Herod and
Pilate endeavor to act generously. Dialogues ensue between
Herod and the girl, and Pilate and the crowd, in which there is
a repeated vocabulary of "asking" and "wishing" (6:22,23,24,25,
26; 15:6,8,9,12). In both cases an intermediary (Herodias,
6:24; the priests, 15:11) counsels the one who is making the
request (the girl, the crowd) what to ask for. In order not to
break an oath before nobility (6:26), and in order to please
the crowd (15:15), Herod and Pilate reluctantly hand over their
prisoners to the executioners. Finally, both scenes conclude
with disciples (6:29) or a friend (15:43-46) taking the corpse
and placing it in a tomb. These striking similarities between
the two passions are strengthened by the following linguistic
contacts.

	John		Jesus
6:17	*ekratēsen*	14:46	*ekratēsan*
6:17	*edēsen*	15:1	*dēsantes*
6:19	*apokteinai*	14:1	*apokteinōsin*
6:20	*ephobeito*	11:18	*ephobounto*
6:29	*ptōma*	15:45	*ptōma*
6:29	*en mnēmeiō̦*	15:46	*en mnēmeiō̦*
6:22,23, 24,25	*aiteō*	15:6,8	*aiteō*
6:22, 25,26	*thelō*	15:9,12	*thelō*

What Mark has done here is similar to what we noticed in
our study of prediction and passion. There, by intertwining
prediction and passion, he made clear that the only Son, the
King of the Jews, was suffering in his capacity as the Son of
Man. Here, by drawing a similar comparison between John and
Jesus, he has made the same point in another fashion. That is,
the suffering of the King of the Jews, the only Son, is related
to the passion of the Baptist.

In the discussion after the Transfiguration (9:11-13) Mark
disclosed that John was indeed Elijah. Therefore, Jesus was

not the resurrected Baptist as Herod (6:14,16) and some of the
people mistakenly believed (8:28), but the Messiah (8:29) who
must suffer in his capacity as the Son of Man (8:31; 9:12). By
drawing a parallel between the passion of Jesus and the passion
of John, Mark has made plain to his readers that the King of
the Jews, whose silence (15:5) and rapid death (15:44) amazes
Pilate, is in fact the Messiah who comes after John to suffer
in his capacity as the Son of Man.

Most commentators agree that the death of the Baptist (6:
17-29) is a traditional story which Mark has received.[22] It
seems clear then that he has shaped his passion narrative, especially the two scenes which involve Pilate, so that they refer
the reader to the Baptist's own passion. In this manner Mark
assured his community that the only Son, the King of the Jews,
suffered as John did, i.e., according to the scriptures (9:12).

Therefore, we arrive at the same conclusion by separate
paths. Mark has constructed his narrative of the passion so as
to recall earlier instances in the gospel which point to the
suffering Son of Man; namely, the predictions and the death of
John. Thus the only Son, the King of the Jews, suffers in his
capacity as the Son of Man.

II. THE SON OF MAN AS A ROYAL FIGURE

The Son-of-Man Sayings

The literature on the Son of Man is immense.[23] However, in
most cases scholars have concerned themselves with historical
questions such as, which sayings are authentic, and to what extent did Jesus apply the title to himself? The necessity of
this research is self-evident but it will not be the focus of
our investigation. Rather, we seek to determine how Mark interpreted the title on a redactional level.[24] Therefore, we
shall endeavor to grasp the Markan Son-of-Man sayings as a
whole, and search for a concept by which we can unify them.

It is customary to divide these sayings into three categories:[25] 1) sayings which refer to the earthly activity of the
Son of Man; 2) sayings which refer to the suffering of the Son
of Man; 3) sayings which refer to the future coming of the Son
of Man. According to this classification the Markan material
can be divided as follows:

1)   2:10,28

2)   8:31; 9:9,12; 9:31; 10:33-34; 10:45; 14:21,41

3)   8:38; 13:26; 14:62

Most scholars have employed this classification in their quest
for the tradition-history of the material and in order to judge
the genuineness of the sayings in regard to the historical
Jesus.[26] If used judiciously, the classification is helpful
in reminding us that the present sayings are the product of different and complex tradition-histories.

However, as traditional as this classification may be, we
must avoid separating these sayings into airtight compartments.
Once the material enters the gospel, it enjoys a redactional
unity. Consequently, although the earthly Jesus may have looked
upon the future Son of Man as distinct from himself,[27] it is
apparent that the gospel does not.[28] Or whereas the sayings of
group one refer to the earthly work of Jesus, it is quite possible that the evangelist employed the title in an exalted
sense.[29]

Finally, any attempt to understand the Son-of-Man sayings
must necessarily deal with all of them. We make this remark because there is a temptation to emphasize one group at the expense
of the others, or to begin the investigation only after the confession at Caesarea Philippi.[30] Consequently, we intend to look
at each of the three categories in order to determine what common theme unites them.

The earthly activity of the Son of Man. There are only two
passages which describe the earthly activity of the Son of Man
(2:1-12, 23-28). However, each occurs within the same series
of controversy stories, 2:1 - 3:6. In both the common theme
appears to be the present authority of the Son of Man.[31] Thus
in the healing of the paralytic (2:1-12), Jesus appeals to his
authority (*exousia*) as the Son of Man to forgive sins. In the
controversy about the Sabbath (2:23-28), he asserts that the Son
of Man is Lord (*Kyrios*) even of the Sabbath. Although Mark applied the title to the earthly activity of Jesus, it is apparent
that he intended his readers to understand that Jesus acts with
the authority of the exalted Son of Man.[32] Otherwise both pericopes lose their meaning if all Mark asserted is that man has

the authority to forgive sins. Rather, looking back, Mark's
readers know that even then Jesus possessed the authority of the
exalted Son of Man.[33] Mark concluded these controversies with
the notice of the plot by the Herodians and Pharisees to destroy
Jesus (3:6). The importance of this verse as a major division
of Mark's gospel has long been noticed.[34] Here it discloses
that what the religious leaders oppose is the claim to authority
which Jesus makes as the Son of Man. Thus 2:10 and 2:28 reveal
that Jesus claimed authority as the Son of Man to forgive sins
and to be Lord of the Sabbath, an authority which the religious
leaders rejected.

The Suffering Son of Man. By far these are the most prominent of the Son-of-Man sayings in Mark.[35] Among them 8:31;
9:31 and 10:33-34 enjoy a certain primacy as passion predictions
because they are also determinative for the structure of the
narrative from 8:27-10:45.[36] Within this section there are two
other sayings, 9:12 which closely parallels 8:31, and 10:45
which serves as a climax and summary to the entire section.
Finally, two sayings, 14:21,41, concern the betrayer and are the
only ones to occur in the passion narrative.

Perhaps the most distinctive characteristic of these
sayings as a group is that Jesus directs them to his disciples
as part of their private instruction.[37] Nobody but the disciples, or the three, is privy to the knowledge that the Son of
Man must suffer. However, the teaching is continually misunderstood and leads to controversy within the inner circle. Peter
(8:32), the twelve (9:33-34), James and John (10:35-40), and the
ten (10:41) do not comprehend Jesus' instruction. What they do
not grasp, however, becomes clear in 10:45 where Jesus explains
the nature of his authority.[38]

In the verses which immediately precede 10:45, Jesus draws
a comparison between how the rulers of the world exercise authority and how the members of his community should exercise authority. Worldly rulers lord it over (*katakyrieuousin*) their sub-
jects and exercise authority (*katexousiazousin*) over them (10:
42). But members of Jesus' community must strive for service
after the pattern of the Son of Man who came not to be served
but to serve (10:45). In 10:42-45 it becomes clear that what

the disciples have misunderstood about the Son of Man is the
nature of his authority; it is not self-serving authority, but
self-effacing authority. Just as the religious leaders rejected
Jesus' claim to exercise authority as the Son of Man, so his
disciples have misunderstood how he exercises this authority
which he possesses as the Son of Man.

The function of 10:45 is two-fold. On the one hand it summarizes the great section in which Jesus teaches his disciples
about the nature of the Son of Man's authority. On the other
hand it points forward to the passion, and more specifically to
the Last Supper (14:22-25). There, after a passion saying (14:
21), Jesus once more shows that his life will be given for many
(*hyper pollōn*, 14:24; *anti pollōn*, 10:45). It is this new concept of authority, founded on service, which unites the suffering Son-of-Man sayings. It is this new authority which the
disciples cannot understand.

The Coming Son of Man. Minette de Tillesse has noted that
the three future sayings about the Son of Man form a counterpart
to the three major passion predictions.[39] Three times Jesus
solemnly announces his passion and three times he solemnly promises his coming glory. Donahue has examined these sayings and
shown that as a group they manifest a number of common characteristics, e.g., coming, power, glory, clouds of heaven, seeing.[40]

coming	8:38	13:26	14:62
glory	8:38	13:26	
angels	8:38	(13:27)	
seeing	(9:1)	13:26	14:62
power	(9:1)	13:26	14:62
clouds		13:26	14:62
seated			14:62

(Verses within parentheses are not a part of the Son
of Man saying proper but are closely united to it.)

Moreover, when we compare these sayings with the future sayings
in the Q material we immediately notice that the latter group
lacks the imagery of the Markan sayings.[41]

Many authors argue that the primary function of the future
Son-of-Man sayings in Mark is judgment.[42] We suggest, however,

that in addition to judgment Mark also emphasized the aspect of
vindication. Thus, in 8:38 the Son of Man comes in his Father's
glory with the angels and stands before those, who like Peter
(8:32),[43] were ashamed of him. Here the logion portrays the
Son of Man not only as judge but also as a type of witness before God.[44] He has been vindicated by the Father to the shame
of those who were ashamed of him.

In 13:26 the Son of Man comes " . . . in clouds with great
power and glory," to gather his elect. What will happen to
those left behind Mark does not say. Will the Son of Man judge
them? Will the Father judge them? But it is evident that the
appearance of the Son of Man will be a moment of vindication.
The one rejected as unable to save himself (15:31) will return
with the power and glory to gather his elect.

Finally, in 14:62 Jesus stands before his judges and points
to the future coming of the Son of Man. Then the Son of Man's
enthronement at the right hand will be his vindication that he
is who he claims to be. One naturally assumes that some sort
of judgment will follow, but Mark does not describe it.

But why must the Son of Man be vindicated? Once more it is
a question of the authority of the Son of Man. The religious
leaders rejected the claim of that authority. The disciples
were ashamed of the manner in which the Son of Man exercised
that authority. Therefore, in the future coming, that authority
will be vindicated both to the world and to the disciples of the
Son of Man. We can summarize by saying that in the second gospel the Son of Man material finds its unity in the claim of
Jesus' *exousia* which has been rejected by the religious leaders,
misunderstood by the disciples, but will be vindicated at the
future coming.

If we return to chapter 15, it is clear that in the first
mockery and the Roman trial it is Jesus' royal authority which
the soldiers ridicule (15:18) and which the crowd, inspired by
the priests, rejects (15:13-14). Therefore, it is important
for Mark's readers to know that this King of the Jews, the only
Son, suffers in his capacity as the Son of Man. Only at his
coming can the glorious and powerful aspect of his authority
be revealed. Then that authority will be vindicated. But in

the passion, the soon-to-be-exalted Son of Man must suffer as
a mocked and rejected king.

The Source of the Son of Man's Authority[45]

A study of how Mark employed *exousia* in his gospel suggests
that it is closely aligned with the notion of sonship. It leads
us to believe that the source of the Son of Man's authority is
this divine sonship.

In his gospel Mark announces Jesus' authority almost immediately. The first mighty work which Jesus performs is related
to his authority as a teacher (1:21-27). As commentators have
noted, the emphasis of this pericope falls upon the authority
of Jesus as a teacher rather than on his power as an exorcist.[46]
In the rather extended introduction, and in the conclusion, the
evangelist refers twice to Jesus' authority as a teacher (1:22,
27). However, what the crowd does not know, and what the reader
does, is the revelation of the Baptism (1:10-11). As Best has
remarked, Mark's gospel " . . . is not a mystery story in which
the identity of the main character has to be guessed; from the
outset it is made clear who this is - the Son of God."[47] Consequently, the reader can appreciate that Jesus teaches with
authority because he knows that he is the Father's only Son.
Moreover, as we noted earlier, since the background of Mk. 1:11
is primarily Ps. 2:7, the authority of this only Son is a royal
authority.

In the next two instances Jesus grants authority to the
twelve to cast out demons (3:14-15; 6:7). Moreover, in each
case there is a prior reference or allusion to Jesus' sonship.
Thus the demon identifies Jesus as the Son of God (3:11), and
then Jesus chooses the twelve (3:13-19). In chapter six, Jesus'
fellow citizens claim to know him because his mother is Mary,
and his brothers are James, Joseph, Jude and Simon. Therefore,
they are scandalized by him. In the next incident, Jesus sends
the twelve on mission (6:7-13) and grants them authority. However, the reader knows that physical descent cannot explain
Jesus' true origin. Thus the reference to his mother and
brothers reminds the reader that Jesus' real origin is found in
his sonship to the Father (1:11). This parallel structure of

sonship and authority intimates that Jesus bestows authority
upon the twelve as the only Son of the Father.

Between the Baptism and the two instances that we have just
considered fall the controversy stories of 2:1-3:6 in which the
Son of Man exercises his authority to forgive sins (2:10) and
rule over the Sabbath (2:28). From what we have said thus far,
it becomes apparent that the source of the Son of Man's authority
is rooted in the same sonship that was revealed at the Baptism.

The great debate about Jesus' authority, however, occurs
in chapter 11 when the priests, scribes and elders question him
(11:27-33). The fact that Mark has named all three groups which
compose the Sanhedrin adds to the solemnity of the occasion and
gives it the overtones of a preliminary trial (cf. 14:53).[48]
Jesus' response is to question the authorities about the baptism
of John. If they will identify the origin of that baptism,
then Jesus will disclose the source of his authority. As we
observed in our last chapter, the scene refers the reader to
the opening of the gospel. It demonstrates that because the
authorities have rejected John's witness, they cannot recognize
the identity of the one in their midst. Thus Mark has further
identified the fate of John and Jesus. Moreover, John's baptism
recalls the baptism of Jesus when the Father revealed him as
the only Son. *This* is the source of Jesus' authority, a royal
authority, which the leaders cannot grasp because they have refused to acknowledge the source of John's baptism.

However, according to Mark, Jesus' explicit answer to the
religious leaders is the parable of the vineyard (12:1-12).
Jesus is the only Son (12:6) who comes to claim the inheritance
(12:7), and by rejecting him they have rejected his authority.
Through the parable Jesus finally answers their question. He
can do what he does because the Father has sent him (12:6), the
same Father who revealed him as the only Son at the Baptism
(1:11).

Mark's final reference to authority comes in a parable contained in the eschatological discourse (13:34-37). Here the
householder is the Son of 13:32. He has entrusted authority to
his disciples until he, the Lord of the household (13:35), returns. However, only he who possesses authority can dispense

it. In this case it is clear that it is as Son that the householder, Jesus, possesses his authority.

A summary of our survey discloses that in Mark the source
of Jesus' authority is his divine sonship revealed at the Baptism. Because of that sonship he teaches with authority (1:22,
27), forgives sins with authority (2:10), and grants authority
to his disciples (3:15; 6:7; 13:34). In his dispute with the
religious leaders (11:27-33) he refers them to John's baptism
and so to his own baptism where the Father revealed him as his
only Son.

Finally, we note two places where Mark has brought this
sonship into relationship with the Son of Man and shows that by
rejecting the Son of Man, one rejects the only Son empowered by
the Father. In the first, Mark has bracketed the Transfiguration
account between two major teachings about the Son of Man (8:31-
9:1; 9:9-12). The Transfiguration, of course, is the second
proclamation of Jesus' sonship (9:7). The fact that Mark has
situated the Transfiguration within these two teachings about
the Son of Man is not accidental. It means that in rejecting
the Son of Man (8:31; 9:12), one also rejects the Son empowered
by the Father. As the only Son, Jesus must suffer in his capacity as the Son of Man; as the Son of Man, he possesses the
authority of the only Son of the Father.

Second, Mark has brought together the only Son and the Son
of Man in the Gethsemane account. The cry *Abba ho patēr* (14:36)
makes it clear that he is the Son in an exclusive sense. As
Son he asks that the cup be taken away from him (14:36). The
cup, of course, is the same cup which he told James and John
(10:38) he must drink in his capacity as the suffering Son of
Man (10:33-34). It is the same cup which will be poured out
for many (14:23-24) because the Son of Man came to give his life
as a ransom for many (10:45). However, in this very hour the
Son of Man is handed over into the hands of sinners (14:41).

Here is the deepest irony. The reader knows that the Son
of Man has been empowered with an authority that belongs to the
one who can call God his Father (14:36), i.e., the only Son.
However, the one filled with all authority now submits to the
hands of sinners.

The Son of Man sayings find their unity in the concept of
authority, and that authority is rooted in the divine sonship
disclosed at the Baptism and Transfiguration. As the suffering
Son of Man, the hidden Son of God exercises his authority in
humble service. As the coming Son of Man, the revealed Son of
God (14:62) will have that authority vindicated in power and
glory.

The Eschatological Kingship of the Son of Man

Thus far we have argued that Mark intended his readers to
interpret the sufferings of the only Son, the King of the Jews,
in light of the sufferings of the Son of Man. This Son of Man
exercises an authority which is rooted in divine sonship. In
the present age, this authority is rejected and misunderstood,
but in the future age it will be revealed and vindicated. It
is now incumbent upon us to make more explicit in what sense
this Son of Man is a royal figure.

The Son of Man in Daniel. Of the three sayings which describe the future glory of the Son of Man, two, 13:26 and 14:62,
contain references to Dan. 7:13. Therefore, we suggest that the
starting point for interpreting the Markan Son of Man is the
Book of Daniel.

Daniel 7 has been a storm center of controversy for Old
Testament as well as New Testament scholars. Students of Daniel
continue to debate the identity of the "saints of the Most High"
(7:18,22,25,27).[49] How they resolve this question, of course,
colors their interpretation of the "one like a son of man,"
i.e., he is either a representative of the angelic hosts or of
the historical Israel. However, inasmuch as Mark has already
individualized the Son of Man by identifying him with Jesus, it
will not be our task to resolve that exegetical problem. Rather,
we shall point to the imagery of this scene as one of the keys
for understanding the Markan Son of Man.

In Daniel 7, the one like a son of man is compared to four
beasts. The first was like a lion (7:4), the second like a
bear (7:5), and the third like a leopard (7:6). Only the fourth
beast (7:7), presumably because of its fearsomeness, is not

compared to any animal. The one like a son of man (7:13), then,
is merely compared to a man rather than identified with a particular earthly or heavenly individual. His humanlike quality
is a way of demonstrating his superiority to the four beasts.

What interests us is the function of this one like a son
of man. Unlike the son of man in Ethiopian Enoch (62:3) Daniel's
son of man is not a judge. The judgment has already been accomplished by the Ancient One before the son of man arrives.
Rather, in Daniel, the one like a son of man is the recipient of
" . . . dominion--glory and kingship" (7:14).[50] Just as the
four beasts before him represented four kings (7:17),[51] so the
son of man is a kingly figure who represents the kingdom of the
"saints of the Most High."

In 7:18,22,27 the saints of the Most High inherit the kingdom (malkûtā'). Although the imagery shifts from son of man to
the saints of the Most High, it is clear that Daniel intends the
reader to make the association between the son of man and the
saints. The former is the representative of the latter and
serves as a type of corporate personality.[52] Thus, whether we
look at the son of man or at the saints of the Most High, the
basic image of kingdom and kingship remains. The saints of the
Most High, represented by the one like a son of man, will inherit a royal power.

The Markan Son of Man differs from the son of man in Daniel
in a number of ways. As Hartmann says, there appears to be an
original interpretation here.[53] In the gospel, the Son of Man
is no longer a corporate personality but is identified with
Jesus. Likewise, there is no revelation of God or his judgment;
rather, the Son of Man assumes a more active role by coming to
gather his elect with the assistance of the angels.

But despite this reinterpretation, the Markan Son of Man
is more firmly rooted in the imagery of Daniel than in any other
source we know. Just as Daniel's son of man comes with the
clouds of heaven, so in Mark he comes in/with the clouds of
heaven.[54] This relationship between Mark and Daniel suggests
that we should interpret the coming of the Son of Man in power
and glory in terms of the same royal imagery we find in the book
of Daniel. Of course the main difference is that in Daniel the

son of man receives dominion, honor and kingship (7:14), whereas
in Mark he appears as a figure in possession of power and glory
(13:26) and is already enthroned (14:62). However, his presence
in/with the clouds of heaven assures us that he is of the same
royal lineage as Daniel's "one like a son of man."

The use of Psalm 110. In 14:62, Mark strengthens the royal
imagery that we have observed by the insertion of a reference
to Ps. 110, *ek dexiōn kathēmenon.*[55] This verse has been the fo-
cal point of an exaltation/parousia debate as scholars have attempted to determine the precise nuance which Mark intended, i.e.,
the return of the Son of Man or his exaltation.[56] However,
as many have pointed out, if the Son of Man is to be exalted,
it is strange that his enthronement is mentioned before his arrival with the clouds of heaven.[57] Rather, in 14:62 it appears
that the Son of Man is already enthroned at the moment of his
parousia; he does not come to be enthroned as in Daniel but returns as the enthroned one.[58] The verb *opsesthe* promises that
Jesus' judges will see both his enthronement and his coming
simultaneously with no time lapse between the two events.[59]
Therefore, the Son of Man returns as the enthroned one.

Ps. 110 is closely akin to Ps. 2 and was probably uttered
by court prophets on the occasion of the King's enthronement.[60]
The fact that these words were addressed to the Davidic King
" . . . laid open the possibility that they might later be applied to the king to come, the Messiah."[61] The messianic interpretation of Ps. 110, however, is not firmly attested to, except
in Christian sources, before the second half of the third century.[62] In rabbinic sources, the psalm is linked with Abraham
as well as with David, and Justin Martyr says that in his day
it was connected with Hezekiah.[63] Nonetheless, Billerbeck, followed more cautiously by Hay and Loader, judges that the psalm
could have been used with reference to the Messiah in the New
Testament era.[64]

Hay has made an extensive study of the imagery involved in
sitting or being at the right hand and summarizes his results
as follows:

> In ancient paganism and Judaism generally the right
> side symbolized potency and honor. Long before the

Christian era pagans spoke of kings and gods exalted
to thrones at the right hand of other gods, and they
sometime described bliss after death in terms of
right-hand location. The Hebrew scriptures and later
Jewish writings spoke of men and supernatural beings
gaining right-hand or heavenly thrones, often without implying any particular function was linked with
such elevation.

Glory at the Right Hand, p. 58

The use of right hand imagery in 14:62 suggests that Mark intended his readers to interpret the Son of Man as possessing a
royal dignity.

Royal Figure or Judge? In our discussion of the royal na-
nature of the Son of Man thus far we have limited ourselves to
the texts of 13:26 and 14:62 because they contain clear imagery
from the book of Daniel. However, the combination of *en tē
doxē* and *en dynamei* in 8:38-9:1, which recalls the *meta dynameōs
pollēs kai doxēs* of 13:26, suggests that the first saying of the
coming Son of Man should also be drawn into the same orbit.
Therefore, we would judge all three sayings of the coming Son
of Man as possessing a royal dimension.[65]

However, the royal aspect of these sayings has often been
overlooked by commentators who have chosen to emphasize the
Son of Man as an apocalyptic judge. Pesch presents the case for
such a view in his discussion of 13:26[66] where he also draws
14:62 and 8:38 into the debate. Because he has made such a
strong case for the Son of Man as judge, we wish to engage him
in discussion.

In *Naherwartungen* Pesch argues that the appearance of the
Son of Man in 13:26 is contemporaneous with, and not subsequent
to, the signs of vv. 24-25 which point to the day of judgment.
He does this on the basis of the *kai tote* in vv. 21 and 26, noting
that it has the force of correlating the events rather than setting out a chronological order (first the judgment, then the
Son of Man). Therefore, the Son of Man comes with the signs of
the last time in order to judge.

Second, Pesch argues that the unexpressed subject of *opsontai* (13:26) must be all those who will be judged rather than the
elect or the three disciples to whom Jesus is speaking. Just
as Jesus' judges will see him (14:62), so will all the world

see him (13:26) and be judged. The verb cannot be impersonal
since Mark does not use the impersonal with verbs of seeing.

Third, he maintains that the coming of the Son of Man in
8:38; 13:26 and 14:62 corresponds to the eschatological judgment
of Yahweh rather than to the imagery of Dan. 7. Whereas the
clouds may remind us of Dan. 7:13, their real significance is
to point to the presence of God and to participation in his
power and majesty. Finally, Pesch suggests that the picture of
the Son of Man's power and glory (13:26) does not come exclusively from Dan. 7:14 but derives from Enoch 62:5,7.

We do not deny that there are elements of judgment in the
sayings about the coming Son of Man, but we do believe that
Pesch has overstated his case to the detriment of the royal imagery which is present. Moreover, we wonder if Pesch presumes
what he must prove, i.e., the Son of Man in Mark is a judge.

The *kai tote* of 13:26 does show that the Son of Man comes
in the circumstances just mentioned in 13:24-25.[67] However, we
urge that the signs of these verses function as unmistakable
signs of the Son of Man's coming so that " . . . the end will
come in a form no one will be able to miss."[68] In other words,
there is a contrast here between the signs which are preliminary
and which can lead one astray (13:5b-23), and the great signs
which nobody can mistake (13:24-27). To claim that these signs
point to the function of the Son of Man as judge, or to argue
that the subject of *opsontai* is those who are to be judged, seems
to presume what must be proven. The subject may well be all men
but it does not necessarily mean that they will all be judged
by the Son of Man. The problem which Pesch encounters, and which
every commentator must face, is that there is no explicit scene
of judgment in Mk. 13.

Moreover, 14:62 does not speak of an explicit judgment.
Therefore, it is not permissible to interpret 13:26, as Pesch
does,[69] in the light of 14:62. Once more he appears to presume
what he must prove. In this case he must first establish that
14:62 is a judgment scene before he can interpret 13:26 as a
judgment scene in its light.

Finally, it seems imprudent to argue away the clear Daniel
imagery of 13:26 and then appeal to Enoch. This is especially

hazardous if, as some believe, the Similitudes of Enoch are to
be dated in the first century A.D.[70] One has the feeling that
the picture of the Son of Man as judge that we find in Enoch has
had an undue influence upon the interpretation of Mark's Son of
Man. Once more we are not denying the allusions to judgment in
8:38; 13:26 and 14:62, but we caution that they should not be
emphasized to the detriment of the royal imagery.[71]

In light of Dan. 7 and Ps. 110 we propose that the future
sayings present the Son of Man as both judge and royal figure
(cf. Mt. 25:31-34 where the Son of Man is a royal judge). A
part of the judgment will consist in his vindication before those
who have rejected his authority (13:26; 14:62) or misunderstood
it (8:38). In the coming age they will see the only Son enthroned as the Son of Man. They will understand that the one
whom they rejected, or of whom they were ashamed, was indeed a
royal figure. Herein lies the true judgment, the vindication of
the suffering Son of Man as the enthroned Son of Man.

Excursus - The Testament of Job. An intriguing use of Ps.
110 occurs in the *Testament of Job* which probably predates the
Christian era.[72] In the *Testament,* Job suffers because he has
razed to the ground the temple of Satan (5:2,3). Previously,
God granted Job the authority (*exousia*) to purge the temple
(*naon,* 3:5-7) with the understanding that suffering would ensue
(4:4-5). However, if Job endures this suffering, the Lord promises that Job's name will be renowned, his possessions restored,
and he will be raised in the resurrection (4:6-9). Therefore
Satan, disguised as the King of the Persians, accuses Job before
the city of having torn down the temple of God and of destroying
the place of libation. Thus begin Job's trials.

After twenty years, the kings hear of the things which have
happened to Job (28:1). Eliphaz, the King of the Temanites,
asks, "Are you Job, our fellow-king?" (29:3b) Job answers, *egō
eimi* (29:4). However, the kings do not believe that such a suffering one can be a king and so they collapse on the ground for
three days as if dead (30:1b). After seven days they approach
Job again. Then, after three days of fumigating the area because of the stench, they approach and ask once more,

> Are you Job, our fellow king?
> Are you the one who formerly had vast splendor?
> Are you the one who was like the sun which shines
> by day in all the earth?
> Are you the one who was like the moon and the stars
> that appear at midnight? (31:4-6)

A litany follows in which the kings ask eleven times "Where
now is the splendor of your throne?" (32:1-12). It is at this
point that Job finally responds.

> Be silent! And now I will show you my throne
> and the splendor of its majesty which is among
> the holy ones.
> My throne is the supra-terrestrial realm,
> and its splendor and majesty are from *the right hand*
> [emphasis mine] of (the Father) in the heavens.[73]
> My throne is eternal --
> the whole world shall pass away and its splendor
> shall (fade)
> and those who cling to it shall be (caught) in its
> demise.
> But my throne is in the holy land
> and its splendor is in the unchanging world.
> The rivers will dry up
> and their heights of exaltation descend
> to the depths of the abyss.
> But the rivers of my (land), in which is my throne,
> are not drying up, nor will they disappear,
> (but they shall remain) in perpetuity.
> These kings will pass away and these rulers are
> passing away,
> and their splendor and boast will be as in a mirror,
> But my kingdom is forever and ever,
> and its splendor and majesty are in the chariots of
> the Father.
>
>   (33:2-9)

We quote this episode for two reasons. First, it provides a
clear example of how the right-hand imagery of Ps. 110 could be
employed to denote a supraterrestrial kingship. Here it is
plain that Job will rule as a king from a throne in heaven.
Second, there is an analogy between the situation of Jesus and
Job. Both were unjustly persecuted; the accusation concerned
a temple; and the true glory of both could not be recognized because of the present suffering. The litany against Job is not
a mockery, as occurs in the gospel, but it does reveal the un-
belief of Job's fellow kings. We are not suggesting that there
is a dependence of the gospel upon the *Testament of Job*, but we
are indicating that similar ideas are operative in both works,

namely, a suffering just one whose kingship is vindicated in
another realm.

 Excursus - Psalm 80. Some years ago C. H. Dodd pointed to
Ps. 80:18 ("But let thy hand be upon the man of thy right hand,
the son of man whom thou has made strong for thyself") as pro-
viding " . . . direct scriptural justification for the fusion
of the two figures in Mk. XIV. 62"[74] However, for the most part
Dodd's suggestion was not accepted, since Ps. 80 is not otherwise attested in the New Testament.[75] Nonetheless the psalm
continues to attract attention,[76] especially since the Targum
to v.16 reads:

> And the stock which Thy right hand has planted
> and upon the King Messiah whom Thou has made
> strong for Thyself.[77]

Thus the question arises as to the identity of the son of man
in this psalm. Does the son of man refer to the people of Israel[78] or to the King of Israel? What relationship is there
between this son of man and the Messiah King?

 Recently Gelston has tried to demonstrate that the son of
man in Ps. 80:18 originally referred to the king, later understood as the Messiah, and that this " . . . paved the way for
the later interpretation of Dan. 7:13 in messianic terms alike
by Jesus and the Jews."[79] David Hill's interpretation is
slightly different. He sees a relationship between Ps. 80 and
Ps. 89 on the basis of the verb *ʾms* which occurs in the piel in
Ps. 80:18b and Ps. 89:22 (the only other occurrence of the piel
is in Isa. 41:10). In Ps. 89:22 it refers to Yahweh strength-
ening the king, that is, " . . . the securing of David's authority as King (2 Sam. vii 13; Ps. lxxxix 20, 36f.) and the estab-
lishment of the father-son relationship (2 Sam. vii 14; Ps.
lxxxix 26f.)."[80] On the basis of this usage, and the similarity
of the two psalms (glorious past, calamitous present), Hill aims
to demonstrate that the son of man in Ps. 80:18 refers to the
king and " . . . that the *bēn ʾādām* whom Yahweh has 'strengthened' was open to interpretations in terms of the promise of
David, in an expansion of *the* messianic oracle that 'Yahweh will
strengthen him.'"[81]

On the basis of Gelston's and Hill's work we suggest that
Ps. 80 offers some evidence that son of man could be applied to
the king. Moreover, it is possible that the author of Daniel
had this text in mind when he composed the vision of chapter
seven.[82] Perhaps a prudent conclusion is that son of man enjoyed
a limited royal background through Ps. 80 and may have influenced the background of Dan. 7:13. In that case the biblical
tradition knows of a royal side to the expression son of man,[83]
precisely the point we have been urging for the coming Son-of-
Man sayings in Mark. In these sayings, the Son of Man does not
refer exclusively to a coming judge, although this element is
present. There is also a royal element which identifies the
coming Son of Man as an eschatological king.

IV. THE FULFILLMENT OF THE SCRIPTURES

Thus far we have shown that by allusions to the Son of Man
in chapter 15, Mark understood that the only Son, the King of
the Jews, suffers in his divinely appointed capacity as the Son
of Man. Furthermore, we have argued that the concept of the
Son of Man was especially suited to Mark's needs since it could
be understood both in terms of suffering and future glory, i.e.,
kingship. Therefore, those who know the secret of the Son of
Man realize that the mocked King of the Jews is in fact what his
persecutors ridicule him of being, a royal figure. But why does
this king submit to such humiliation? For Mark, the mystery was
hidden in the divine imperative contained in the scriptures that
the Son of Man must suffer. Three times (8:31; 9:12; 14:21)
Mark makes it clear that the suffering of the Son of Man was
grounded in the scriptures. Therefore, when Jesus finally approaches his passion, it is evident to the reader that the King
of the Jews, the only Son, suffers in his capacity as the Son of
Man according to the scriptures.

There is an ambivalence regarding which scriptures govern
the sufferings of the Son of Man in Mark. On the one hand, the
statement in 14:49 " . . . but that the scriptures may be fulfilled," does not appear to refer to any specific text.[84]
Rather, just as the time was "fulfilled" and the Kingdom drew
near (1:15), so here the time has arrived "to fulfill" the

scriptures about the Son of Man. Likewise, 14:21 does not refer
to a specific text but to the death of the Son of Man in a general fashion.[85] Although there is a scriptural allusion to Ps.
41:10 in the immediate vicinity (14:18),[86] it does not appear to
be the scripture to which 14:21 alludes. In 14:18 the emphasis
is on the betrayer, whereas in 14:21a the *kathōs gegraptai* refers
to the Son of Man's death. Therefore, just as in 14:49, so in
14:21, the evangelist did not have a specific scripture in mind.

On the other hand, we have already mentioned, and Tödt has
effectively argued, that *apodokimasthēnai* and *exoudenēthē* in
8:31 and 9:12, respectively, are allusions to Ps. 118:22.[87]
Evidently, Mark has inherited two versions of the saying and
has decided to keep both. Each contained a different introductory formula (*dei*, 8:31; *pōs gegraptai*, 9:12)[88] and synonym
(*apodokimasthēnai*, 8:31; *exoudenēthē*, 9:12) for *māᵓas* which is
found in the Massoretic text of 118:22.

Recently, W. J. Bennett has argued aginst Tödt's position
on the basis of *dei*.[89] In a thorough analysis he shows that in
apocalyptic texts *dei* is synonymous with "God wills it" rather
than "as it is written." In other words, he reverses Tödt's
argument and interprets *gegraptai* by *dei* rather than vice ver-
sa.[90] However, we find Bennett's otherwise excellent study
wanting since it does not interpret 8:31 and 9:12 in terms of
Mark. We grant that at an earlier stage the sayings may have
had a general apocalyptic necessity rather than Ps. 118:22 in
mind. However, once the sayings have been drawn into the gospel,
the quotation of Ps. 118:22, found in Mk. 12:10-11, reinterprets
them. Thus it is difficult to believe that Mark did not have
12:10 in mind when he introduced 8:31 since these are the only
two places where he employs *apodokimazō* in the gospel.[91]

The case of 9:12 is more difficult inasmuch as one might
refer *exoudenēthē* to LXX Ps. 21:7,25; LXX Ps. 68:34; LXX Ps.
88:39, as well as LXX Ps. 117:22.[92] However, the parallel structure of "suffer" and "be rejected" that we find in both 8:31
and 9:12 makes it more probable that Mark also saw this text in
light of LXX Ps. 117:22. Therefore, despite Bennett's important
observations about the apocalyptic use of *dei*, we contend that
Tödt's arguments stand and that in 8:31 and 9:12 we have explicit
references to Ps. 118:22.

There is still one text that we have not considered because
it does not refer directly to the Son of Man; namely, 14:27. It
is, moreover, the only text of the passion that is introduced by
an introductory formula.[93] Recently, Schenke has argued that
the primary focus of this citation is not Jesus but the disciples.[94] He points out that the primary reason for the Zechariah
text is the consequence which Jesus' death holds for his disciples rather than the death itself. Because of the death, the
disciples will be scattered. This shift in emphasis from the
death of Jesus to the dispersion of the disciples may explain
why the Son of Man is not connected with this particular text.

What interests us, however, is the change that Zechariah
13:7 has undergone in Mark.[95] *Pataxate* has been altered to
pataxō so that God becomes the subject.[96] What 9:31 contains
cryptically in the passive form of *paradidotai*[97] this verse
says openly; namely, it is God who delivers Jesus into the hands
of sinners. Mark has made the same point in 14:36 where Jesus
asks the Father to remove the cup of suffering. Likewise, in
14:41, when he says that the hour has come, it is clear that
for Mark the hour is the time determined by the Father alone
(13:32). In other words, whereas one can "hand over" Jesus from
person to person (Judas to the Jews, the Jews to Pilate, Pilate
to the soldiers), it is ultimately the Father who "hands over"
Jesus to men.

We can summarize by saying that for Mark the passion of
the Son of Man was rooted in the divine necessity of scripture.
In part, the evangelist was content to leave the references
general (14:21,49). But he was also specific (8:31; 9:12) and
explained that the rejection of the only Son was foreseen in
Ps. 118. Moreover, and perhaps more surprisingly, it is ultimately the Father who hands over Jesus to sinful men (9:31;
14:27). Consequently, as Mark's community hears the passion of
the only Son, the King of the Jews, they know that nothing has
happened by chance. The rejection and mockery were foreseen by
the scripture itself, especially Ps. 118. Moreover, even though
Judas, the religious leaders and Pilate "hand over" Jesus to
each other, the Christian community realizes that ultimately
these men have no authority since it is the Father who has

handed over the Son of Man to them. The mystery of the passion
is more than the evil of men; it is grounded in God's plan of
salvation.

Finally, we need to say a word about the relationship of
this chapter to the previous chapter of our study. There we
dealt with Mark's reinterpretation of royal messiahship as seen
in chapters 11-12. Here we have considered the concept of the
Son of Man as seen in chapters 2,8-10,13-14. At first there
seems to be no relationship between these two sections inasmuch
as the Son-of-Man title disappears during chapters 11-12. However, Mark has given us a bridge by which to cross from one side
to the other in the allusions to Ps. 118:22 that we find in
8:31; 9:12, and the explicit quotation of Ps. 118:22 in 12:10-11.
By crossing the bridge, we discover that the suffering Son of
Man is the rejected, only Son of 12:6-8. That son is the royal
Son of 1:11; 9:7. By throwing a bridge between the suffering
Son of Man and the only Son of the parable, Mark has disclosed
that the one who suffers as the Son of Man is the only Son, a
royal figure. For the evangelist, the Son of Man and the only
Son are one and the same person as the reference in 8:38 to the
Son of Man and his Father shows (*en tē doxē tou patros autou*).

Therefore, when Mark's readers arrive at chapter 15, they
fully understand who the King of the Jews is. The frequent allusions to the Son of Man in this chapter notify them that the
sufferings of the King of the Jews constitute the passion of the
Son of Man. This Son of Man is the only Son, the royal Son of
the Father. In the present moment the kingship of this Son can
only be proclaimed in ridicule and mockery because the Son of
Man "must" suffer. However, in the coming age, that kingship
will be revealed when the coming Son of Man sits enthroned at
the right hand of the Power. In the present age, kingship is
hidden and can only be understood by those who know the secret
of the Son of Man. In the coming age, kingship will be revealed
to all, and the royal authority that the only Son possesses will
be revealed in the parousia of the exalted Son of man. For
Mark the glory and the power of kingship are reserved for the
coming age. In the present age, Jesus exercises kingship in
suffering and by enduring mockery.

CHAPTER VII

THE ROYAL SON OF GOD

In previous chapters we have examined Mark's view of kingship in light of the first and second mockeries. Our results suggested that the royal theme is not limited to the fifteenth chapter. Rather, in chapters 11-12 and in the Baptism and Transfiguration accounts, Mark has prepared for the royal theme of chapter 15. Moreover, by interpreting the passion of the only Son in light of the suffering, but soon-to-be-exalted, Son of Man, the evangelist has readied the reader for the transcendent nature of this kingship. The gospel makes its first public proclamation of Jesus' kingship only when the passion has begun and there can be no mistaking the nature of that kingship. The King of Israel is a suffering and rejected Messiah with no claim to political power.

In this chapter we propose to examine the great cry, the Elijah incident, the tearing of the temple curtain and the centurion's confession in order to ascertain what clarification they bring to the royal theme. Our procedure is threefold. First, we shall investigate the nature of the Elijah incident. Have the bystanders misunderstood Jesus? Or, are they mocking the Messiah King?

Second, because the immediate occasion for the Elijah incident is the great cry, the opening verse of Ps. 22, we shall investigate this psalm and its role in the passion narrative. Did the redactor intend the reader to hear only the opening verse or the whole psalm? Is the cry one of despair or of victory? What role does the psalm play in the rest of the New Testament?

Finally, we shall compare the two reactions in face of the great cry; namely, that of the bystanders and that of the centurion. What allows the latter to confess what the former mocks or misunderstands? What is the meaning of the temple curtain? How should we interpret the title "Son of God?" What relationship does it have to the royal theme?

Through an examination of these incidents, we seek to demonstrate that Mark utilized them in order to support and develop
the royal motif. Moreover, we shall show that "Son of God" is
one with the royal titles of vv.2,9,12,18,26,32, and that it is
best understood in terms of royal messianism.

I. THE NATURE OF THE ELIJAH INCIDENT

The presence of a third mockery in chapter 15 has not been
obvious to all commentators. For example, Schreiber maintains
that the bystanders have misunderstood $El\bar{o}i$ for the prophet's
name. Thus, while Jesus cries to God in his deepest need, his
opponents misunderstand the cry as the occasion for a miracle,
i.e., they hope to see Elijah's return.[1] Linnemann and Gese
take the same line.[2] They interpret the attempt to give Jesus
a drink as a cruel but sincere desire to prolong his life in the
hope that Elijah will come. We urge that there is not a misunderstanding here and that the bystanders do not expect a miracle to occur. Rather, this is the third in a series of mockeries which Mark employed to exploit the royal theme.

Authors who interpret the text as a misunderstanding rather
than as a mockery argue from one of two positions. On the one
hand, commentators have endeavored to explain the misinterpreta-
tion of Jesus' cry ($El\bar{o}i$) for the prophet's name ($'\bar{E}l\hat{i}y\bar{a}h$) in
terms of the historical event. Consequently, some scholars
claim that the text of Mt. 27:46, which uses the Hebrew form of
the divine name, preserves the original words of Jesus.[3] In that
case, the confusion between the divine name ($\bar{E}l\hat{i}$) and the prophet's name ($\bar{E}l\hat{i}y\bar{a}h$) seems plausible. In the same vein, others
have tried to show that Dead Sea scroll evidence proves that
Jesus' cry, "My God," could have been $'\bar{E}l\hat{i}ya$ since the Hebrew of
the second century B.C. still employed iya as a first person suf-
fix.[4] Or they have argued that $'\bar{E}l\hat{i}$ was a short form of
$'\bar{E}l\hat{i}yahu$.[5] Still others assert that Jesus cried out in Hebrew
$'\bar{E}l\hat{i}'att\bar{a}h$ (You are my God, cf. Pss. 22:11; 63:2; 118:28; 140:7)
but that the bystanders misunderstood it as the Aramaic $'\bar{E}l\hat{i}a$,
tha (Elijah, Come!).[6]

The difficulty with such explanations is that they presuppose an original historical event in which Jesus uttered a great

cry that was misunderstood. However, in our compositional analysis we showed that 15:35-36 resulted from a combination of traditions in which Mark was responsible for inserting *dramōn de
tis [kai] gemisas spoggon oxous peritheis kalamọ epotizen auton
legōn* between *ide Ēlian phōnei* and *aphete idōmen ei erchetai
Ēlias kathelein auton*. The fact that this scene is a literary
construction composed of diverse traditions warns us that the
solution to the problem may not lie on the level of historical
conjecture.[7]

Others, such as Linnemann, approach the problem from a
literary stance. She argues that Mark employed the misunderstanding as a literary device to express the bystanders' expectation that perhaps Elijah will save Jesus from the cross in
a miraculous manner.[8] In this way Mark heightened Jesus' abandonment as well as the blindness of his enemies.[9] According to
Linnemann, the difficulty of confusing *Ēloi* with *'Ēlîyāh* would
not have presented a problem to Mark's Greek readers for whom
Ēlōi was a foreign word. Such readers would simply have accepted that somehow the word *Ēlōi*, foreign to them, could be
confused with the prophet's name.[10]

Linnemann's approach on the literary level is a step in
the right direction. However, her explanation fails to appreciate the extent to which the Elijah incident continues the
ridicule of the second mockery.[11] In 15:31 the priests and
scribes mock Jesus because he cannot save himself. In 15:36 the
bystanders, whose anonymity seems to relate them to the anonymous passersby of 15:29, mock Jesus because even Elijah will
not save him. In other words, there is a progression in the
second and third mockeries. First, Jesus cannot save himself
(15:31); second, even Elijah will not come to his aid (15:35).

Moreover, the attitude of the bystanders, who seek to see
(*idōmen*) whether or not Elijah will take Jesus down from the
cross (*kathelein*), establishes a parallel with the mocking attitude of the priests and scribes, who challenge Jesus to descend from the cross (*katabatō*) in order that they can see
(*idōmen*) and believe. The structure implies that the Elijah
incident is also a mockery.

Finally, the language of 15:36 should not be overlooked.
The RSV translates 15:36b, "wait, let us see whether Elijah will

come to take him down," implying by the prohibition that the
bystanders seek a miracle and maintain a faint hope that perhaps
Elijah will rescue Jesus. However, the correct translation of
aphete idōmen is, as Taylor notes,[12] closer to "do let us see,"
since the imperative *aphete* is on its way to becoming a mere
auxiliary. Accordingly there is no attempt to prohibit anyone
from anything, there is merely the mocking taunt "do let us see
if Elijah will come to take him down" [trans. mine].

We suggest that the Elijah incident is not a misunderstanding on either the historical or literary level. Rather, Mark
intended his reader to hear a third and final mockery. Thus it
is significant that the Elijah material, *ide Ēlian phōnei . . .
aphete idōmen ei erchetai Ēlias kathelein auton*, brackets an
allusion to LXX Ps. 68:22.[13]

> *kai edōkan eis to brōma mou cholēn
> kai eis tēn dipsan mou epotisan me oxos.*

In the psalm the gesture is clearly one of mockery (cf. vv.20-
21) which leads us to suspect the same for the action of the bystanders in 15:35-36.

As a mockery the Elijah incident continues the royal theme.
The cry of Jesus from the cross is more than the call of a suffering, just man.[14] Throughout the chapter, and especially in
the second mockery, the evangelist has emphasized that Jesus suffers as the Messiah King. Consequently, the bystanders of 15:35-
36 hear his call as a cry of a false Messiah King. It may even
be, as Martinez argues, that they deliberately misquote Jesus'
speech.[15] In that case, the bystanders hear the cry of Ps. 22,
but they mockingly twist Jesus' words into a last, desperate
cry to Elijah for help. In their eyes there is no possibility
that Elijah will come because Jesus is a false Messiah King.[16]
They do not expect a miracle; rather, like the soldiers, the
passersby, the priests, the scribes, and the thieves, they mock
Jesus as a pretender.

Finally, Mark has contrasted the bystanders (*parestēkotōn*)
who hear (*akousantes*) with the centurion standing opposite
(*parestēkōs*) Jesus who sees (*idōn*). In this manner, he has established two reactions in face of the great cry, a response of
mockery and a response of confession. Below we shall argue that

Mark intended a single cry (15:37 being a reprise of 15:34) so
that we arrive at the following structure:

> Cry of Ps. 22 (v.34)
> Response to cry (vv.35-36)
> Death and torn curtain (vv.37-38)
> Response to cry (v.39)

In the following sections we shall explore the significance of
this arrangement for the royal theme.

II. PSALM 22 AND THE GREAT CRY

The proximate occasion for the third mockery is the great
cry of Jesus. Jesus cries out the first verse of Ps. 22 and
immediately the Elijah mockery follows. In this section we
shall examine that great cry of Ps. 22 in order to determine why
Mark has juxtaposed it with the Elijah incident and the centurion's confession.

Scholars have often concerned themselves with the question
of historicity. Was there a great cry? Did Jesus utter a
second, wordless cry or was there only the lament of Ps. 22?
The opinions form a spectrum that varies between Bultmann's
judgment that " . . . v. 34 is a secondary interpretation of the
cry in v. 37"[17] to the confident assurance of Cranfield that
with the quotation from Ps. 22 " . . . we are on the firmest
historical ground."[18] Our own approach will not be to enter into
this debate. Rather, we shall remain on the redactional level.
Did the final redactor intend us to hear one cry or two? After
we have wrestled with this problem, we shall be in a better
position to determine the nature of the cry and its relationship
to the events which follow.

A Single Cry

In an earlier chapter we maintained that while it is possible to interpret the text as containing two cries, an examination of Markan style can also argue for a single cry.[19] Our
contention is that Mark's purpose in mentioning the *phōnēn
megalēn* in v.37 was to form a bracket with *phōnę̄ megalę̄* in v.34
around the third mockery. Moreover, as is often the case when
Mark repeats earlier material, the seemingly redundant second

member adds a further clarification.[20] In this case while repeating the cry, Mark added that Jesus died (*exepneusen*). Thus
both the bystanders and the centurion react to the same cry but
there is a significant difference. *According to Mark's arrangement of the material*, the reaction of the centurion occurs after
Jesus' death and after the temple curtain has been torn from
top to bottom.

We suggest that this arrangement of the material is deliberate. It was Mark's way of saying that although the bystanders
and centurion react to the same cry, they do it at different
points in time. The centurion's reaction is subsequent to and
the result of Jesus' death and the tearing of the temple curtain.
The bystanders' reaction, according to the arrangement of the
material, is prior to both.[21]

In Matthew's account it is clear that the evangelist envi-
sions a second cry because he has added *palin* to his Markan
source. However, the insertion of this word, which Matthew
otherwise omits,[22] serves as a negative indicator that Mark intended only one cry. If, like Matthew, the second evangelist
understood a second, wordless cry, there would have been nothing
more natural than for him to add one of his favorite words;
namely, *palin*.

However, it is important to note that even though Matthew
clarifies or understands Mark in terms of two cries he has
" . . . put the two cries of 27:46 and 27:50 on a parallel
plane"[23] by using the verb *krazō* which is found three times in
Ps. 22 (vv.3,6,25). In other words, although Matthew speaks of
two cries, he maintains the general Markan perspective, showing
that his second, wordless cry is somehow related to the first
cry by means of a reference (*krazō*) to Ps. 22. So Senior can
write: "It is possible, then, that Matthew has identified the
wordless cry of 27:50 as another confident prayer to his Father
for deliverance."[24]

Furthermore, since the great cry does not lead to confession, as it does in Mark, Matthew may not have been so concerned
as Mark to maintain a single cry whose content is Ps. 22. In
the first gospel, the centurion and those with him confess Jesus
as the Son of God on the basis of the earthquake and the

accompanying events (27:54). In Mark, however, the confession
is intimately bound with the great cry. The centurion confesses
Jesus because he sees the manner in which Jesus died (*hoti
houtōs exepneusen*), i.e., with a great cry. We suggest that the
great cry was of more significance to Mark than it was to
Matthew. Mark was intent upon showing that the bystanders and
the centurion react to the same cry with different results.

If, as we have argued, the bystanders and the centurion
react to the same cry, what is the sense of that cry? Is it a
cry of dereliction or of victory? Did Mark and his community
understand the psalm as simply descriptive of abandonment or do
they contemplate the entire psalm? Before we answer these questions we must undertake a brief study of Ps. 22. Only then shall
we have an adequate background against which to answer the
questions we have posed.

Psalm Twenty-two

Contemporary scholarship classifies Ps. 22 as the lament
of an individual.[25] The structure of the psalm is clear. The
first half (2-22) is composed of three laments (2-3,7-9,13-19),
each of which is followed by an expression of trust (4-6,10-12,
20-22). Each of these sections begins in a similar fashion by
addressing God in the second person: "Yet thou are holy" (4),
"Yet thou art he who took me from the womb" (10), "But thou, O
Lord, be not far off!" (20).

The second part of the psalm concludes with a hymn of
thanksgiving (23-32) which includes a hymn of eschatological
praise (28-32).

Today most commentators view the psalm as a unity although
there is some discussion about the final eschatological hymn
(28-32).[26] The occasion for the psalm and the nature of the individual's affliction remain in dispute. Schmid claims that
the petitioner is afflicted by sickness (vv.15f,18).[27] Gese
disagrees and states that v.19 points in the direction of someone about to be executed.[28] Eaton refers the entire psalm to
the sacral king and claims that the enemies possess an archetypal
character.[29]

For our purposes it is important to note that the psalm not
only alternates between lament and hope, but that there is also

a development which culminates in an eschatological kingdom.
The psalmist moves from remembrance of the past (4-6), to his
own birth (11-12), to a call for immediate help (20-22). His
thanksgiving spreads from the congregation of his brethren (23)
to the ends of the earth (28). Gese draws attention to the relationship between the Holy One enthroned in v.4 and God's kingship in v.29 ("For dominion belongs to the Lord, and he rules
over the nations") which finds a climax in the eschatological
hymn of vv.28-32.[30] For Gese this eschatological hymn brings
an apocalyptic theology to expression in which the redemption of
the petitioner from death foreshadows the inbreaking of God's
kingdom.

Within the Markan passion there are explicit references to
Ps. 22 in at least two other places besides the great cry: the
dividing of Jesus' garments (15:24) which corresponds to 22:19,
and the mockery of the passersby (15:29) which finds its reference in 22:8.

However, a number of authors maintain that Ps. 22 is at
the origin of a pre-Markan passion narrative and that more references, albeit not explicit, can be found.[31] Peddinghaus, for
example, sees the original passion narrative as composed of Mk.
14:44-47,50-53a; 15:1,15b,20b-22,24,27,29f,32c,34a,35-36a,37,
39.[32] He argues that within this narrative Ps. 22 is the basis
of the story which comprises 15:24,27,29f,32c,34-36a,37,39.
Therefore, he draws attention to the following parallels:

Mark	*Ps. 22*
15:24	22:19
15:27	22:13ff., 17a
15:34	22:2f.,12,20-22
15:36	22:16
15:39	22:28

The result is that Peddinghaus sees the following verses from
Ps. 22 as significant for the pre-Markan narrative which he believes he has isolated: vv.2f,7-9,12,16f,19,20-22,28. So he
concludes that the entire psalm was employed in the construction
of a pre-Markan narrative.[33]

In a somewhat similar vein, Julius Oswald argues for a pre-
Markan narrative built upon Ps. 22. He begins by indicating
the parallels found in Mk 15:24,29,34a. To these he adds the
following:[34]

Mark	*Ps. 22*
15:27	22:17
15:31b	22:9
15:32	22:7
15:39	22:28f

His argument for Mk. 15:31b is the presence of *sōzein* in both
the narrative and the psalm. However, it should be noted that
in the narrative the mockers challenge Jesus to save himself
whereas in the psalm the mockers challenge God to save the suffering just one. Between Mk. 15:27 and Ps. 22:17 there are no
word parallels but, like Peddinghaus, Oswald sees a similarity
in the situation of Jesus and the suffering just one. In the
case of Mk. 15:32 and Ps. 22:7, Oswald points to *ōneidizon* and
oneidos as the connecting links. Finally, just as did Peddinghaus, Oswald sees the confession of the centurion as the fulfillment of the eschatological hymn found in 22:28ff.[35]

If we take the explicit quotations of Ps. 22 and combine
them with the suggestions of Peddinghaus and Oswald, we arrive
at the following list:

Mk. 15		*Ps. 22*	
*24	(garments)	19	(garments)
27	(thieves)	13ff.,17a	(bulls, dogs)
*29	(mockery)	8	(mockery)
31b	(save)	9	(save)
32	(deride)	7	(scorn)
*34	(cry)	2f,12,20-22	(cry)
36	(thirst)	16	(tongue cleaves)
39	(universal salvation)	28f.	(ends of earth)

* explicit reference

The studies of Oswald and Peddinghaus are suggestive but
remain at the level of hypothesis. There simply are not enough
linguistic contacts in the parallels which they have brought
forth to secure their position. Nonetheless, their work suggests that the whole of Ps. 22 gave shape to early traditions
concerning the passion. The early community was intensely conscious of the entire psalm and its parallels with the passion
of Jesus.

Outside of the gospels Ps. 22 plays an important role.[36]
The enemies listed in the psalm (roaring lion 14b, dogs 17a, the
lion's mouth 22) now become the enemies of Christians, sometimes
in a spiritual sense (I Pet. 5:8) and other times in a human

sense (Phil. 3:2; II Tim. 4:17). In Heb. 2:12, the psalm verse
(22:23) is placed in the mouth of the Risen Christ and is associated with Isa. 8:17-18 (cf. Heb. 2:13). In the Isaiah text,
the prophet binds up his testimony and waits for the Lord who
is hiding his face from the house of Jacob. The connection between the Isaiah text and Ps. 22 seems to be that just as God
hid his face from the house of Jacob, so he hid it from the
righteous sufferer, Jesus, who is the representative of the
whole house of Israel.[37] However, just as the prophet committed
his case to Yahweh in hope of vindication, so Jesus committed
his case to the Father, and found vindication.

Finally, there are two allusions to Ps. 22 in the Book of
Revelation. In Rev. 11:15, the seventh angel blows his trumpet
and loud voices in heaven proclaim that "the Kingdom of the world
has become the Kingdom of our Lord and his Christ, and he shall
reign forever and ever." Here the allusion is to Ps. 22:29,
part of the eschatological hymn. In Rev. 19:5, after the twenty-
four elders and the four living creatures worship God, a voice
cries from the throne, "praise God, all you his servants, you
who fear him, small and great." Here the allusion is to Ps.
22:24, the beginning of the hymn of thanksgiving. In both instances the author of Revelation employs the latter half of the
psalm in order to express some aspect of God's eschatological
victory. This use of Ps. 22 outside of the passion narrative,
especially in Heb. 2:13 and Rev. 11:15; 19:5, intimates that
the New Testament was reading Ps. 22 in a messianic manner; that
is, the psalm was an apt vehicle for describing God's eschatological victory[38] as well as the sufferings of Jesus.

Among the Church Fathers, it was taken for granted that
the entire psalm applied to Christ and that King David spoke it
in prophecy.[39] Clement, in his letter to the Corinthians (95
A.D.), quotes vv.7-9 in conjunction with Isa. 53:1-12. Then, in
his introduction to the psalm quotation, he makes it clear
that Christ himself spoke the psalm.

> And again He says Himself: "But I am a worm and no
> man, the reproach of men, and the outcast of the
> people."
>   I Cor. 16:15-16

In his First Apology (138-156 A.D.) Justin Martyr points
to David as a prophet (also cf. chapter 38).

> Again [the Prophetic Spirit] says, in other words,
> through another Prophet: "They have pierced My hands
> and My feet, and have cast lots for My clothing."
> David, however, the King and prophet who spoke
> these words, endured none of these sufferings, but
> Jesus Christ stretched out his hands when He was
> crucified by the Jews who contradicted Him and
> denied that He was the Messiah.
>
> I *Apology* 35

It is interesting that Justin points to David as king as
well as prophet. Later, in his *Dialogue with Trypho* (155-161
A.D.), he offers one of the most detailed commentaries of the
psalm which we possess from this period. It extends from chapter 97-106. As the Apologist begins his commentary he writes:

> You are indeed blind when you deny that the above-
> quoted Psalm was spoken of Christ, for you fail to see
> that no one among your people *who was ever called King
> had his hands pierced while alive* [emphasis mine] and
> died by this mystery (that is, of the cross) except
> this Jesus only.
>
> *Dialogue with Trypho* 97

The implication here is that Justin understands the psalm as
in some sense referring to a royal figure. On the basis of the
previous quotation, he may be thinking of David. But in any
case he knows that the psalm was uttered in prophecy by David
and must apply to a royal figure.

Although the patristic evidence is later than the composition of the gospels, it indicates the trajectory which evolved,
and perhaps it gives us a hint as to how the psalm was understood even in the biblical period. First, the New Testament
understood the psalm in terms of God's eschatological victory
as well as Jesus' sufferings. Second, because the psalm was
ascribed to David, the prophet and king, it was read as a prophetic word, the prophecy of a king. On this last point we refer
the reader to our discussion in chapter five on Ps. 118 and the
importance of Davidic authorship. For the New Testament, the
one heard in Ps. 22 was more than an anonymous individual; it
was King David speaking prophetically. The step from a suffering
David to a suffering Messiah King was the next move as the
patristic period shows.

The Meaning of the Great Cry

We are not in a position to return to our original question; namely, the meaning of the great cry and the role of Ps.
22. First, there can be no doubt that the great cry expresses
the depth of abandonment which the crucified one experiences.[40]
In the gospel, all of Jesus' supporters gradually abandon him
with the result that on the cross he must endure even the absence of his Father.[41] However, there is no question of despair
here in the manner that contemporary philosophies, such as exis-
tentialism, propose. The anguish of the just one is anchored
in the theology of the psalms of lament. Here, as Lothar Ruppert
has shown, the passion of the Suffering Just One has become by
the intertestamental period a "dogma."[42] The just one must
suffer.

Moreover, the structure of Ps. 22 from which the great cry
arises supports this thesis. The psalm alternates between complaint and trust and concludes with thanksgiving. The lament
which the suffering just one utters in v.2 describes the distance he experiences between himself and his God.[43] The psalm
is especially appropriate, then, to express that in his passion
Jesus is alone.[44] But the development of this theme does not
exclude either hope or victory.

Finally, the placement of the cry, after the three hours
of darkness, and not within the three hours, argues that the
evangelist did not interpret it as a sign of despair or defeat.[45]

The three hours of darkness finds its immediate Old Testament reference in Amos 8:9.[46]

> And on that day, says the Lord God "I will make the
> sun go down at noon, and darken the earth in broad
> daylight. I will turn your feasts into mourning, and
> your songs into lamentations; I will bring sackcloth
> upon all loins and baldness on every head. I will
> make it like the mourning for an only son, and the
> end of it is like a bitter day."

The quotation interprets the darkness in terms of judgment. However, we suggest that Mk. 13:24 may be just as important for
understanding the darkness as is Amos 8:9 since it is the only
other place where the evangelist speaks of darkness.[47] Once
more there is a reference to the Old Testament, Isa. 13:10.

However, here Mark seems to have employed the darkness as one
of the final signs which announces the coming of the Son of Man.
As we noted earlier, this series of signs (13:24-25) is distin-
guished from the preliminary signs of 13:5b-23, and serves to
announce the end in a fashion that no one will miss. On the
basis of 13:24 and Amos 8:9, we suggest that the three hours of
darkness in 15:33 contains a note of judgment and acts as an
eschatological sign preparing the reader for the cry of Jesus
and his death. Just as darkness announces the coming of the
Son of Man (13:24), so darkness announces the great cry of Jesus
and the events which result from it.

We now wish to argue that for Mark's community the psalm
verse is more than a descriptive phrase of Jesus' abandonment.
The great cry of the Crucified One brings to mind the entire
psalm.[48] *To that extent Mark's community understands the cry
of 15:34 as the cry of the Messiah King*, a cry first uttered by
David himself. Thus, by juxtaposing the great cry of Ps. 22
and the Elijah mockery, the evangelist shows in still another
way that the bystanders mock Jesus as Messiah King, i.e., the
Messiah King who cries out the opening verse of David's lament.

Not all commentators agree, however, that Mark intended
his community to go beyond the opening verse.[49] X. Léon-Dufour
presents four arguments to the contrary.[50]

1) The evangelist did not explicitly say that he was
   citing the psalm.
2) The context militates against the presence of a
   long prayer and invites us to emphasize the abandonment of Jesus.
3) If the quotation was originally expressed in Aramaic
   this does not favor a liturgical recitation of the
   text.
4) The Greek translation, provided by the evangelist,
   has the purpose of giving Jesus' words a sense of
   authenticity as in Mk. 5:41 where he translates
   talitha koum.

Although Mark did not introduce the psalm in an explicit manner,
this is no argument that he and his community did not understand
the entire psalm when they heard the first verse. As we have
already shown, the crucifixion and death narrative contains
many references and allusions to Ps. 22.[51] The surrounding of
the great cry with so many allusions to the same psalm is unlike

any other scriptural quotation in Mark and leads us to suspect
that his community was intimately familiar with the entire psalm.

Although the context may not be conducive to a long prayer
by Jesus, this is not our contention. Mark did more than describe historical events, and his purpose was not to tell us
what Jesus may or may not have said. Rather, he has juxtaposed
traditions (great cry and mockery) and made his point by suggestion and allusion. In this case, the psalm verse brings to mind
the entire psalm of the Suffering Just One.

Finally, it is true that the Aramaic quotation gives Mark's
narrative a sense of realism for his Greek readers. However,
this does not eliminate the possibility that the evangelist intended his audience to go beyond the opening verse. There is
a significant difference between a comment such as *talitha koum*
(5:41), where there is no possibility of further allusion, and
a psalm verse where there is.

We are arguing, then, that when the Markan community received the text of the great cry, they understood it in terms
of the entire psalm. In favor of this, we note the following.
First, the passion narrative alludes and quotes from more than
Ps. 22:2. This concentration of quotation and allusion indicates that the tradition, the evangelist, and his community were
keenly aware of the entire psalm. Second, the New Testament
writings outside of the gospels continued to refer to the psalm.
Many of them saw the psalm from the viewpoint of the Risen Christ
(Heb. 2:12) and God's eschatological victory (Rev. 11:15; 19:5).
Third, by the end of the first century, Clement understands
Christ as the speaker of the entire psalm. In the middle of
the second century, Justin has already written an entire commentary on the psalm in terms of Christ. He knows that David has
spoken in prophecy and that the psalm was written for a royal
figure. This movement among the Fathers seems to be related to
an understanding of the psalms as compositions of David the
prophet-king. It is not surprising, then, that Mark and his
community would also understand such psalms as 118 and 22 as
prophetically spoken by David.

For Mark's community, the messianic content of the cry derives from the nature of the entire psalm and its Davidic

authorship. The hymn of vv.28-32 becomes a proclamation of
eschatological victory which the centurion announces by confessing Jesus as God's Son.[52] John Eaton writes that "such is the
scope of the concluding hymn (vv.23-32) that it can hardly be
interpreted of the salvation of anyone but the sacral king,
God's 'son,' focus of the cause of God's kingdom and the health
of all the world."[53] Although we do not agree with all of
Eaton's arguments for sacral kingship, we believe that his point
is well taken. In the psalm, the scope of thanksgiving is such
that it easily lends itself to a messianic and eschatological
interpretation. We suspect that it is precisely for this reason that the Christian community chose this psalm. Not only
does it describe the suffering of the just one, it also portrays
his victory in language that is susceptible to messianic and
eschatological interpretation.

Finally, we should not underestimate the power of Davidic
authorship. We have already seen that in the case of Ps. 110
Mark understood David as a prophet. Therefore, it is not unrea-
sonable to conclude that he also interpreted Ps. 22 as a prophetic composition of King David.[54] In that case David speaks
prophetically of the Messiah King. The great cry becomes a
messianic cry which Mark has juxtaposed with the Elijah mockery,
and the Markan community comprehends the eschatological dimen-
sions of this cry.[55]

III. THE CENTURION'S CONFESSION

If, as we have argued, Mark understood the cry of 15:37 as
a reprise of 15:34 then the confession of the centurion is a
response to the same cry which the bystanders have mocked. Thus
the evangelist has drawn a deliberate contrast between the response of the bystanders (*parestēkotōn*) and of the centurion who
stands (*parestēkōs*) opposite Jesus. The bystanders seek to see
(*idōmen*) if Elijah will come; the centurion sees (*idōn*) how
Jesus dies.

This contrast extends to the second mockery by the use of
the catchword "see." There (15:32) Mark described the priests
and scribes as challenging Jesus to descend from the cross so
that they can see (*idōmen*) and believe. Here the centurion

sees not the descent of Jesus from the cross but the manner of
his death, and so confesses his belief.[56]

Finally, there is a contrast between the centurion's confession and the first mockery (15:16-20a). There the Roman
soldiers mock Jesus; here a Roman soldier confesses him.[57] There
the mockers fulfill the passion prediction (10:33-34) that the
Gentiles will ridicule the Son of Man; here the Gentiles find
access to the kingdom. There the soldiers worship (*prosekynoun*)
Jesus in mock homage; here the centurion fulfills the prophecy
found in the eschatological hymn of Ps. 22:28.[58]

kai proskynēsousin enōpion sou pasai hai patriai
tōn ethnōn

Moreover, if we observe the structure of chapter 15 it now becomes clear that Mark intended three mockeries to follow three
events with the confession of the centurion standing in juxta-
position to all three.[59]

I.   A. Jesus is tried as King of the Jews (1-15)
     A. Jesus is mocked as King of the Jews (16-20a)
     B. Jesus is crucified as King of the Jews (20b-26)
     B. Jesus is mocked as Messiah, King of Israel (27-32)
     C. Jesus cries out at Messiah King (33-34)
     C. Jesus is mocked as Messiah King (35-36)

II. D. Jesus dies (37)
         Curtain is torn (38)

III. E. Centurion confesses Jesus as Son of God (39)

IV. F. The Son of God is buried (40-47)

It is clear from Mark's arrangement of the material that
the death of Jesus and the tearing of the temple curtain form a
watershed in the second gospel. Mark offered no reason in the
course of his narrative why the centurion, who has heard the
same cry as the bystanders, should be able to confess what they
deny. For him and his community the answer is found on the
level of theology. By the arrangement of his material, he states
that the centurion, like his community, stands on the other side
of two great events, the death of Jesus and the tearing of the
temple curtain. Before these events there can be no possibility
of confessing Jesus as Son of God. Indeed, as the three mockeries demonstrate, before the death of Jesus and the tearing of

the temple curtain, the reaction to Jesus is ridicule. Therefore, the centurion does not make his confession on the basis of special knowledge or moral growth but because he has been fortunate enough to stand on the other side of Jesus' death and the tearing of the temple curtain. The centurion is the representative of the Markan community. That community can only confess Jesus as the Son of God when they, like the centurion, stand on the other side of Jesus' death. Then they know that the only Son suffers in his capacity as the suffering Son of Man, and that he will reign in his capacity as the exalted Son of Man.

According to Mark, the centurion confesses Jesus as the Son of God because he saw that he died thus (*houtōs exepneusen*).[60] Here the *houtōs* refers to the last mention of the great cry found in v.37 which we have judged is a reprise of v.34. Thus the centurion's confession is, like the mockery, related to the cry of Ps. 22. Above we noted that for Mark the cry was more than one of abandonment. It brought to mind the entire psalm so that it becomes Jesus' messianic cry. If this interpretation is correct, then the *houtōs* takes on new meaning. The centurion does not make his confession because he saw a man die in utter abandonment, but because the crucified one dies with a messianic cry.[61] The centurion, who functions as a representative of the Markan community, has properly understood the messianic nature of the great cry.

What allows the centurion to recognize what the bystanders cannot? We have mentioned already that according to the arrangement of the material, the centurion stands on the other side of Jesus' death. However, in Mark's perspective, there was also another interpretive fact; namely, the tearing of the temple curtain.

The Temple Curtain

The tearing of the temple curtain remains one of the classic problems of Markan scholarship.[62] Most commentators recognize the evangelist's hand here since there is such a clear reference to the temple theme. Usually the question has been posed in terms of whether Mark intended the inner or the outer curtain. If he meant the outer curtain, then he probably understood the tearing of that curtain to symbolize the destruction

of the temple. On the other hand, if he interpreted it as the
inner curtain, the event takes on a more positive function;
namely, the revelation of God's holiness to all mankind.[63]

In the temple there were two curtains, an outer curtain
(*māsāk*) between the temple and the forecourt, and an inner curtain (*pārōket*) between the holy place and the holy of holies.
In the Septuagint, *katapetasma* could denote either curtain,
whereas *kalumma* (used in the New Testament for Moses' veil, II
Cor. 3:13,14,15,16) is employed only for the outer veil. Josephus uses *katapetasma* for both curtains.[64]

In the New Testament the only other occurrence of *katapetasma* outside of the gospels comes in Hebrews. Twice it refers
to the inner veil (6:19,9:3) and once it signifies the flesh of
Jesus (10:20), but in such a manner that Jesus is the new veil
before the holy of holies.[65] Therefore, on the level of word
usage there are some arguments for considering the veil in 15:38
as referring to the inner veil.

On the other hand, there are objections to this position.
First, as Donahue points out,[66] neither the Septuagint nor the
Letter to the Hebrews calls the holy of holies the *naos*. Therefore, he doubts that Mark intended the holy of holies by the
tearing of the curtain of the *naos*. Second, we must reckon with
the anti-temple theme that begins with Mk. 11.[67] The cleansing
of the temple sandwiched between the two notices of the cursing
of the fig tree (11:12-14,21-24); Jesus' prophecy that the temple
will be destroyed (13:2); the temple charge against Jesus (14:
57-59); and the mockery at the cross (15:29) all favor an interpretation in terms of the outer veil with its symbolism that the
temple will be destroyed.[68]

Nonetheless, we note that in chapters 11-13 Mark consistently used the term *hieron* for temple, whereas beginning with
the trial, the vocabulary changes to *naos*. This seems to indicate, as Juel notes, that " . . . the use of *naos* in the temple
charge at Jesus' trial rules out any clear identity between the
prediction in 13:2 (which refers to the buildings) and the charge
at the trial."[69] It would appear that by the tearing of the
curtain of the *naos* Mark had more in mind than the destruction
of the *hieron*.

We suggest that to attempt to determine which veil Mark
understood is to ask more than the author intended. The tearing
of the temple curtain is a rich image with both positive and
negative poles. As Lamarche writes, " . . . un voile qui déchire
de haut en bas, c'est en même temps une destruction irrémédiable
et une ouverture décisive."[70] Thus, on the basis of the temple
theme it is manifest that in some sense the temple and its cult
have come to a conclusion with the death of Jesus. But at the
same time the destruction of the temple, symbolized in the
tearing of the curtain, means that God has revealed his hidden
glory to all.[71]

The word which Mark employed to describe the tearing of
the curtain is *schizō* and it occurs only one other time in the
gospel, the Baptism of Jesus (1:10). In that incident the heavens are torn apart (Matthew and Luke use *anoigō* instead of
schizō), the spirit descends and there is a voice (*phōnē*) from
heaven proclaiming Jesus is the only Son. In 10:38-39 Mark has
already notified the reader that Jesus' death will be his baptism.[72] The usage of *schizō* in these two incidents is hardly
accidental. Rather, we urge that the redactor has established
a relationship between the Baptism and the tearing of the
temple curtain.[73]

Baptism	*Curtain*
schizomenous tous ouranous	*to katepetasma tou naou eschisthē*
ho huios mou ho agapētos	*huios theou* .

The centurion can proclaim Jesus as Son of God because the veil
which forbade such a public proclamation before the death of
Jesus has been torn in two. Just as the tearing of the heavens
provided an opening for the Father's proclamation, so the tearing
of the temple veil grants the centurion access to the divine
glory and allows him to make the first public proclamation of
the gospel, by a human being, that Jesus is the Son of God.

Returning to our original question, we can now respond that
it is the tearing of the temple curtain which allows the centurion (and Mark's community) to confess what the bystanders can
only mock. The centurion recognizes the great cry of Ps. 22 as
a messianic cry because by Jesus' death the curtain which

veiled his divine sonship has been torn in two. Before this
moment there could be no possibility of confessing Jesus as
Son of God. But after Jesus' death has torn the curtain from
top to bottom, this possibility is open to all. It is this
reality which Mark's community now enjoys. As they read the
gospel, they know that the centurion stands in their place.

The Son of God

     In Mark's passion, the death of Jesus and the tearing of
the temple curtain allow the centurion to confess Jesus as
God's Son.[74] Inasmuch as this confession is the final identification of Jesus' person, its importance cannot be overestimated
for the passion narrative or for the gospel. Mark refers to
Jesus as Son in only eight instances (1:1,11; 3:11; 5:7; 9:7;
13:32; 14:62; 15:39), but the placement of 1:11; 9:7; 15:39
suggests the significance of this title for him.[75] Twice the
Father identifies Jesus as the only Son (1:11; 9:7), and at the
conclusion of the gospel a human being confesses him as God's
Son for the first and only time. Moreover, if the reading of
א B D L W for Mk. 1:1 is accepted, then Mark announces that the
content of his gospel is Jesus Christ, God's Son.[76]

     In Markan studies scholars have disputed the meaning of
this title. Basically they question whether Son of God should
be read from a Palestinian or a Hellenistic[77] background. Moreover, if they opt for the former they dispute whether Mark intended the imagery of the Servant,[78] the Suffering Just One,[79]
or the royal Messiah.[80] On the basis of our analysis thus far,
we propose that royal messianism is the most fruitful manner in
which to interpret the confession.

     Our investigation has revealed that Mark composed this
chapter in terms of the kingship of Jesus. If, as we have maintained, Mark saw an ironic truth in the royal titles,[81] then he
proclaimed Jesus as Messiah King. Moreover, it follows that
somehow the centurion's confession relates to Jesus' kingship
which is the primary charge in the hearing before Pilate (15:2)
and the content of the inscription on the cross (15:26).

     The Old Testament ascribes sonship to angelic beings, to
Israel and to the king. The angelic beings (Gen. 6:2,4; Jb. 1:6;
2:1; 38:7; Dan. 3:25; Ps. 29:1; 82:6; 89:7) belong to the

heavenly court and form God's assembly, congregation or inner
circle around his throne.[82] On a number of occasions Israel is
called God's son, the Lord's first born (Ex. 4:22; Jer. 31:9),
a dear child (Jer. 31:20) summoned out of Egypt (Hos. 11:1).
God is Israel's Father (Dt. 32:6,18; Jer. 3:4) and the people
his sons and daughters (Dt. 14:1; 32:5,19; Isa. 43:6; 45:11;
Hos. 2:1) so that Israel can speak of God as "our Father" (Isa.
63:16; 64:7; Mal. 2:10).[83] However, in the person of the king,
sonship was concentrated in a unique manner so that he became a
visible sign not only of his own election but of Israel's.[84]
The classic texts are the prophecy of Nathan, II Sam. 7:14 (taken
up again by I Chron. 17:13; 22:10; 28:6; Ps. 89:27-28), and
Ps. 2:7. In the first, Yahweh promises that David's descendant
will be his son: "I will be his father, and he shall be my
son." I Chron. 17:13 repeats the promise but does not include
the warning of II Sam. 7:14b: "When he commits iniquity I will
chasten him with the rod of men, with the stripes of the sons
of men." This seems to indicate that the prophecy was moving
towards a messianic interpretation.[85] In Ps. 89:27-28 the
promise to David is again taken up. However, this time the
Anointed cries out, "Thou art my Father!" and Yahweh names him
the "first-born." Finally, in Ps. 2:7 we probably possess part
of a coronation ritual. The king announces Yahweh's decree:
"He said to me, 'You are my son, today I have begotten you.'"
Here there has been an advancement over the oracle in II Sam.
7:14 inasmuch as the royal decree speaks of God as "begetting"[86]
the king as his son on the day of enthronement (cf. Ps. 110:3).

Despite the references to the heavenly beings, Israel, and
the king as God's son, it is important to note that the Old
Testament does not speak of the "Son of Yahweh."[87] This omission is an eloquent testimony on behalf of the metaphorical nature of sonship in the Old Testament, especially as regards the
people and the king. The Israelites and the king are God's
son(s) but not in a physical or mythical sense.[88]

During the intertestamental period, references to sonship
dealt primarily with the people and with the just man. Once
more Israel is called God's first-born son (Sir. 36:12; II Esd.
6:58). However, in the absence of the Davidic dynasty, the

promise of II Sam. 7:14 and Ps. 2:7, which was originally made
on behalf of the king, has now been transferred to the people
as a whole.

> And after this they will turn to Me in all upright-
> ness and with all (their) heart . . . , and I will
> create in them a holy spirit, and I will cleanse
> them so that they shall not turn away from Me from
> that day unto eternity. And their souls will cleave
> to Me and to all My commandments, . . . and I will
> be their Father and they shall be my children.
> Book of Jubilees 1:23-24[89]

During this period the sacred writings also pointed to individ-
uals as sons of God (Sir. 4:10; 51:10; Ps. Sol. 13:8). By far
the most important witness here is the Book of Wisdom where
the righteous man claims to be God's son (2:16, 18)[90] and is
vindicated and numbered among the sons of God (5:5).

However, despite the absence of a king, the Psalms of
Solomon and the writings of Qumran demonstrate that the hope of
royal messianism was not forgotten. Moreover, Ps. Sol. 17:26
contains a reference to Ps. 2:9 which suggests that Ps. 2 was
being read in terms of royal messianism.[91]

> He shall thrust out sinners from the inheritance,
> utterly destroy the proud spirit of the sinners,
> *and* as potter's vessels [*hōs skeuē kerameōs*] with
> a rod of iron shall he break in pieces all their
> substance.

At Qumran the messianic florilegium of cave four " . . .
shows that the tradition of the *king* as a 'son of God' was not
completely lost."[92] The commentary on II Sam. 7:14a is:

> This is the Branch of David who will arise with
> the Seeker of the Law and who (12) will sit on the
> throne of Zion at the end of days; as it is written,
> *I will raise up the tabernacle of David which is fallen.*
> This *tabernacle* (13) *of David which is fallen* (is) he who
> will arise to save Israel.
> 4Q Flor. 1:11-13

The context is manifestly messianic (the Branch of David) and
indicates that the royal messianic hopes associated with II
Sam. 7:14 were not lost.

In 1QS[a] 2:11f. there appears to be a reference to Ps. 2:7
in another messianic context.

(11) [Concerning the mee]ting of the men of renown
[called] to assembly for the Council of the Community when [Adonai] will have begotten (12) the
Messiah among them.

If, indeed, there is a reference to Ps. 2:7 here, we have another
indication that the psalm was still being read in terms of royal
messianism, and perhaps even that the Messiah was thought of
in terms of God's Son.[93]

Finally, we must mention the mysterious Aramaic fragment
from Cave four.[94] Fitzmyer judges that the text does not supply
sufficient evidence for " . . . the alleged *messianic* use of
the title 'son of God' in pre-Christian Palestinian Judaism."[95]
However, it does, as Hengel points out, make clear " . . . that
the title 'Son of God' was not completely alien to Palestinian
Judaism."[96]

The purpose of this survey has been to show that the concept
"Son of God" was interpreted in a variety of ways within the
Old Testament. Moreover, it suggests that the royal messianic
aspect of the title was not lost so that we are permitted to
employ that interpretation for Mk. 15:39. Indeed, in light of
the six-fold use of "king," we suggest that the royal messianic
meaning of Son of God is more satisfying than any of the other
usages mentioned above. What the mockeries deny by ridicule
(Jesus is king), the centurion affirms in confession (Jesus is
God's Son/King). Jesus is the King of the Jews, the Messiah,
the King of Israel, the Messiah who utters David's lament, because he is God's royal Son. The confession of the centurion
is the belief of Mark's community that in the crucified King
of the Jews, God has fulfilled his messianic promises.[97]

If we return to the Baptism and Transfiguration accounts,
we find a corroboration of our thesis that Mark intended Son
of God to be understood in terms of royal messianism. As we
have already noted, in 1:11 and 9:7 the primary scriptural allusion is to Ps. 2:7, a psalm which the tradition appears to
have associated with the promises of II Sam. 7:14. In Heb. 1:
5-6, we find Ps. 2:7 associated with references to precisely
this text (cf. Heb. 1:5) as well as Ps. 89:28 (cf. Heb. 1:6).
Earlier we noted that both of these texts were applied to the
king as God's son. The association of these same texts in

Heb. 1:5-6 with Ps. 2 seems to indicate that the psalm was understood in terms of royal messianism and the Davidic promises.[98]
However, as Acts 2:35-36 reveals, the promises now find their
fulfillment in a new manner; namely, the resurrection where Jesus
is appointed Messiah. The presence of Ps. 2 in the Baptism and
Transfiguration suggests that Mark understood Son of God in this
royal tradition. However, now the psalm does not point to an
earthly king but to the eschatological ruler.[99] Therefore, at
the crucifixion the centurion confesses, after the death of
Jesus and the tearing of the curtain, what no human has been
able to confess but what the Father has already announced;
namely, Jesus is God's Son, the messianic King.

We find a further tradition of Jesus' eschatological kingship in I Cor. 15:24-28 and Col. 1:13. The last reference is
especially interesting since in the context of Jesus' kingship
it employs language similar to the Baptism and Transfiguration.

> He has delivered us from the dominion of darkness
> and transferred us to the kingdom of his beloved
> son [*tou huiou tēs agapēs autou*].

Finally, we point out that in 14:61 Mark drew a parallel
between *Christos* and *ho huios tou eulogētou*.[100] It is true that
the high priest understood this messiahship in a manner different from Jesus as the reference to the Son of Man in 14:62
shows. But for Mark, *Christos* and *ho huios tou eulogētou* were
synonymous and completely acceptable when understood in terms
of suffering. The use of Son of the Blessed (14:61), a surrogate for Son of God, in connection with *Christos* indicates that
Mark intended Son of God in 15:39 to be interpreted in light of
royal messianism.

We can summarize the results of this chapter by stating
that the Elijah episode is a genuine mockery which continues the
royal theme of the first two mockeries. Mark has juxtaposed the
great cry with a mockery and the centurion's confession, just
as earlier he juxtaposed the trial with the first mockery, and
the crucifixion with the second mockery. In the hearing, Pilate's question (15:2) announced Jesus' kingship. In the crucifixion the inscription (15:26) proclaimed it. In the great
cry Jesus cries out as Messiah King. Only the centurion,

however, understands the mystery of this cry. He functions as
a representative of all who confess Jesus now that he has died
and the temple curtain has been torn. His confession stands in
sharp contrast to the three mockeries, so that King of the Jews,
Messiah, King of Israel[101] are interpreted in light of Son of
God. In turn, the clue to the correct understanding of Son of
God is found in the titles which have been mockingly applied to
Jesus. Son of God finds its roots in royal messianism because
Jesus is the expected Messiah in a most unexpected manner.

CONCLUSION

In chapter four we summarized the results of our compositional analysis. Consequently, it is not necessary for us to review that material again. It is sufficient to say that the final conclusion of our study is that the present shape and form of chapter 15 reveal a surprising degree of Markan redactional activity. In light of this evidence, we propose that Mark assembled the chapter from earlier traditions in much the same way as he constructed the rest of his gospel. Moreover, we suspect that he composed it in such a manner so as to highlight a royal theme. The burden of chapters five, six and seven has been to demonstrate that the redactor has carefully prepared for this theme in other sections of the gospel. Therefore, although the royal title only surfaces in chapter 15, we suggest that its absence is purposeful, and that intimations of the royal theme can be found elsewhere. In this concluding section we shall synthesize the results of chapters five, six and seven, and then formulate some implications which arise from this study.

We maintained that in chapters 11-12 Mark sustained a royal theme alongside the temple theme. There, Jesus entered the temple as king but was not publicly proclaimed. He cleansed the temple, but not in the traditional manner expected of kings. Rather, Mark presented Jesus as a teaching Messiah who came for the Gentiles who had been excluded from the temple. In the parable of the vineyard, the evangelist portrayed Jesus as the rejected son, the only Son of the Baptism and Transfiguration. As such Jesus is the royal Messiah of Ps. 2:7 as well as the rejected king of Ps. 118:22. The dispute over taxes revealed that both Caesar and Jesus possess royal inscriptions; Caesar's is on a coin, Jesus' is upon a cross. Finally, the Son-of-David question proclaimed that even David will call the Messiah (Jesus) his king when he calls him "my Lord." Thus the royal theme ran through chapters 11-12, but Mark refused to employ the title "King" until chapter 15 when the passion had begun. In this manner he demonstrated that Jesus' kingship cannot be

understood apart from rejection and suffering. Thus it is no
accident that Mark announced Jesus as the King of Israel for the
first time in the midst of mockery.

The evangelist continued the royal theme by the manner in
which he drew a relationship between the passion narrative and
the Son-of-Man material. So we flagged the linguistic and literary contacts between 1) the hearing before Pilate, the first
mockery and the third passion prediction, and between 2) the
passion of Jesus and the passion of John the Baptist. Mark
deliberately intertwined the passion material with the Son-of-
Man material in order to alert the reader that the only Son,
the King of the Jews, suffered in his divinely appointed capacity
as the Son of Man.

We urged that Mark portrayed this Son of Man as a royal
figure rooted in the imagery of Dan. 7 and strengthened by the
royal overtones of Ps. 110. Thus the Son-of-Man material supported the royal theme and the evangelist foresaw a glorious
aspect to Jesus' kingship. However, even here that kingship
could not be recognized until the only Son had suffered in his
capacity as the Son of Man.

Mark built a bridge between the Son-of-Man material and the
only Son by means of Ps. 118. In the predictions of 8:31 and
9:12, we learned that the Son of Man would be rejected according
to the pattern of Ps. 118:22; and in the parable of the vineyard,
we discovered that the rejected stone of Ps. 118:22 is the only
Son of the Baptism and Transfiguration. Consequently, when the
evangelist made his allusions to the Son of Man in chapter 15,
we realized that the only Son, the King of the Jews, suffered
in his capacity as the rejected but soon to be exalted Son of
Man, a royal figure. Now the rejected Son suffers in his capacity as the suffering Son of Man. Soon the revealed Son will
rule in his capacity as the exalted Son of Man.

The royal theme attained its climax in the centurion's
confession. There the evangelist juxtaposed the great cry, the
Elijah incident and the centurion's confession in order to make
his final statement about kingship. Thus, whereas the cry described the depth of Jesus' abandonment, it also functioned as
the messianic cry of the great king.

As the symbolic representation of the Markan community,
the centurion confessed what the bystanders mocked because, like
Mark's community, he stood on the other side of Jesus' death.
Once more the redactor referred his reader to the baptismal
scene. The centurion could confess Jesus' sonship because the
torn temple curtain revealed the Father's glory, just as the
torn heavens revealed the Spirit and the Father's voice.

In light of the six-fold use of the title "King" and the
three mockeries, we urge that Mark intended his readers to interpret "Son of God" in terms of royal messianism. Just as the
king was God's son, so Jesus is the Son of God. However, the
baptismal proclamation emphasizes the uniqueness of this sonship,
and Jesus' capacity as the coming Son of Man discloses the transcendent nature of that sonship.

On the basis of our study, we submit that for Mark kingship
comprised the following components:

1. Kingship is inseparable from rejection and
   suffering. Mark consistently refuses to make
   a public proclamation of Jesus as King of
   Israel until the passion has begun.

2. Kingship possesses a glorious aspect which
   will be revealed when the only Son returns
   in his capacity as the Son of Man. But
   this kingship cannot be disclosed until
   Jesus has completed his suffering and death.

3. Kingship finds its supreme title in "Son of
   God" but no one can make this proclamation
   until the temple curtain has been torn.
   This event, the result of Jesus' death,
   allows the Markan community and all believers
   to confess Jesus as God's Son.

We therefore urge that the second part of this study confirms
the first, and that the first prepares for the second. That is,
Mark is responsible for the composition of chapter 15 and he
has arranged the chapter in order to highlight a royal theme.
Moreover, he has carefully prepared for the royal motif throughout his gospel.

A first implication flowing from this study regards the
passion narrative in general. If, as we have argued, Mark has
fashioned a coherent narrative, then it is questionable to what
extent we can speak of a pre-Markan passion narrative. The
royal theme of chapter 15 complements earlier motifs in the gospel supporting our contention that Mark has not simply appropriated an older passion story. Rather, we believe that he has
carefully redacted the gospel from start to finish.

Second, we propose that there is a need to examine Mark's
Christology in light of the royal theme. Our investigation suggests that royal messianism may be the linchpin of Markan
Christology. Thus, in chapters 11-12 we noted that Mark appears
to have employed *Kyrios* (11:3; 12:37) and *ho erchomenos* (11:9)
as surrogates for King. We pointed out that there is a royal
element in the Son-of-Man material which the apocalyptic judge
motif must not submerge. Christ and Son of David, of course,
are more clearly associated with the royal theme. In the case
of the former, Mark coupled it with Son of God (1:1; 14:61) and
King of Israel (15:32). Son of David occurs just before Jesus'
royal approach (10:47-48), while during the entry he arrives as
the bringer of David's kingdom (11:10). The royal Christology
comes to a climax in chapter 15, and we have seen that the six-
fold use of the title "King" in this chapter has been carefully
planned. These titles, however, find their center of gravity
in the centurion's confession that Jesus is the Son of God. With
that confession it becomes clear that what the soldiers, the
religious leaders and the bystanders have spoken in mockery is
eminently true. Jesus is the King of the Jews and the King of
Israel because, as the centurion correctly confessed, he is the
royal Son of the Baptism, the Transfiguration and the parable
of the vineyard. Thus the royal theme may be the thread which
runs through the titles of Mark's gospel.

Finally, there is a need to investigate further the question of royal messianism. Authors have tended to downplay this
theme in the second gospel.[1] Of the synoptics, this gospel appears the least interested in the great themes of Old Testament
messianism and the most open to apocalyptic expectation. However, our study suggests that Mark and his community may have

been besieged by opponents who argued that Jesus did not fulfill
the messianic expectations of the Old Testament. Kingship seems
to have been intensely important to Mark, and one of his problems
was to explain how the King of Israel could be a crucified Messiah. For Mark the answer was contained in the scriptures, especially Pss. 22 and 118. In these psalms David himself foretold
that the Messiah King would suffer before he inaugurated his
kingdom, and that the rejected king would become the cornerstone.
But most importantly, the evangelist discovered that the kingship of this Messiah could only be understood on the other side
of the torn curtain.

[1]The following authors provide surveys of the research: John R. Donahue, "Introduction: From Passion Traditions to Passion Narrative," in *The Passion in Mark: Studies on Mark 14-16*, ed. Werner H. Kelber (Philadelphia: Fortress Press, 1976), pp. 1-20; Detlev Dormeyer, *Die Passion Jesu als Verhaltensmodell: Literarische und theologische Analyse der Traditions- und Redaktionsgeschichte der Markuspassion*, NTAbh, Bd. 11 (Münster: Verlag Aschendorff, 1974), pp. 1-23; Gerhard Schneider, "Das Problem einer vorkanonischen Passionerzählung," *BZ* (1972/2): 222-44.

[2]Rudolf Bultmann, *The History of the Synoptic Tradition*, trans. John Marsh, rev. ed. (New York: Harper & Row Publishers, 1963), pp. 262-284; Martin Dibelius, *From Tradition to Gospel*, trans. Bertram Lee Woolf (New York: Charles Scribner's Sons, n.d.), pp. 178-217; Karl Ludwig Schmidt, *Der Rahmen der Geschichte Jesu: Literarkritische Untersuchungen zur ältesten Jesusüberlieferung* (Berlin: Trowitzsch & Sohn, 1919), pp. 303-09.

[3]Dibelius, *From Tradition to Gospel*, p. 180.

[4]Schmidt, *Der Rahmen der Geschichte Jesu*, p. 303.

[5]George Bertram, *Die Leidensgeschichte Jesu und der Christuskult: Eine formgeschichtliche Untersuchung* (Göttingen: Vandenhoeck & Ruprecht, 1922); Gottfried Schille, "Das Leiden des Herren: Die evangelische Passionstradition und ihr 'Sitz im Leben,'" *ZTK* 52 (1955/2): 161-205.

[6]Bultmann, *The History of the Synoptic Tradition*, p. 279; Dibelius, *From Tradition to Gospel*, p. 185.

[7]Willi Marxsen, *Mark the Evangelist*, trans. James Boyce (Nashville: Abingdon Press, 1969) is regarded as the first such study in Mark.

[8]Johannes Schreiber, *Theologie des Vertrauens: Eine redaktionsgeschichtliche Untersuchung des Markusevangeliums* (Hamburg: Furche-Verlag, 1967).

[9]Ibid., pp. 32-40. The historical tradition comprised 15:20b-22,24,27. The apocalyptic tradition comprised 15:25, 26,29a,32c,33,34a,37,38.

[10]Eta Linnemann, *Studien zur Passionsgeschichte* (Göttingen: Vandenhoeck & Ruprecht, 1970), pp. 139-146.

[11]Carl Daniel Peddinghaus, "Die Entstehung der Leidensgeschichte: Eine traditionsgeschichtliche und historische Untersuchung des Werdens und Wachsens der erzählenden

Passionstradition bis zum Entwurf des Markus" (Dissertation, Heidelberg, 1965).

[12]Linnemann, *Studien zur Passionsgeschichte*, p. 171.

[13]Ludger Schenke, *Studien zur Passionsgeschichte des Markus: Tradition und Redaktion in Markus 14, 1-42*, Forschung zur Bibel, Bd. 4 (Würzburg: Echter Verlag Katholisches Bibelwerk, 1971).

[14]Wolfgang Schenk, *Der Passionsbericht nach Markus: Untersuchungen zur Überlieferungsgeschichte der Passionstraditionen* (Leipzig: Gütersloher Verlagshaus, 1974).

[15]Dormeyer, *Die Passion Jesu als Verhaltensmodell*. He labels these: T, a catechetical document and the oldest tradition of Mark's passion; Rs, a secondary redaction of T which introduced christological elements; Rmk, the final redaction of Mark's passion which introduced the Son-of-Man title and the cosmic dimension.

[16]Rudolf Pesch, *Das Markusevangelium II. Teil: Kommentar zu Kap. 8,27-16,20*, Herders theologischer Kommentar zum Neuen Testament, Bd. 2, T. 2 (Herder: Freiburg, 1977), p. 10. After their initial citation all commentaries, regardless of title, will be cited as *Mark*.

[17]*The Passion in Mark: Studies on Mark 14-16*, ed. Werner Kelber (Philadelphia: Fortress Press, 1976).

[18]Pesch, *Mark*, p. 12.

[19]Dibelius, *From Tradition to Gospel*, p. 179.

[20]Bultmann, *The History of the Synoptic Tradition*, p. 275.

[21]Franz Neirynck, "L'Évangile de Marc (II): À propos de R. Pesch, *Das Markusevangelium*, 2 Teil," *ETL* 55 (1979): 1-42.

[22]Franz Neirynck, *Duality in Mark: Contributions to the Study of the Markan Redaction*, BETL, no. 31 (Louvain: Leuven University Press, 1972).

[23]Ibid., p. 72.

[24]Detlev Dormeyer, *Der Sinn des Leidens Jesu: Historisch-kritische und textpragmatische Analysen zur Markuspassion*, SB, Bd. 96 (Stuttgart: Verlag Katholisches Bibelwerk, 1979); Olivett Genest, *Le Christ de la passion perspective structurale: Analyse de Marc 14,52-15,47, des parallèles bibliques et extra-bibliques*, Recherches, no 21 théologie (Montréal: Bellarmin, 1978); Daniel Patte and Aline Patte, *Structural Exegesis: From Theory to Practice: Exegesis of Mark 15 and 16 Hermeneutical Implications* (Philadelphia: Fortress Press, 1978).

[25]Paul J. Achtemeier, *Mark*, Proclamation Commentaries: The New Testament Witnesses for Preaching (Philadelphia: Fortress Press), p. 83, writes: "Analysis of the Markan narrative,

and of the passion narratives in the other Gospels, leads to
the same kind of conclusions that earlier analysis of the pre-
ceding narrative in Mark had led, namely, Markan editorial work
is as surely evident in this part of his Gospel as in earlier
parts." Donahue, "Introduction: From Passion Traditions to
Passion Narrative," p. 14, concludes: "The very discovery of
a complex history behind the Mkan Passion Narrative casts some
doubt on the validity of postulating an independent and coherent
Passion Narrative prior to Mk." Michael J. Cook, *Mark's Treatment of the Jewish Leaders*, Supplements to Novum Testamentum,
vol. 51 (Leiden: E. J. Brill, 1978), 52-76, presents a view
opposing Achtemeier and Donahue. Werner Kelber, Anita Kolenkow,
and Robin Scroggs, "Reflections on the Question: Was there a
pre-Markan Passion Narrative?" A Report Prepared for the Markan
Task Force of the Society of Biblical Literature, *Seminar Papers*,
2:503-85, Scroggs thinks that there was a connected narrative
prior to Mark; Kolenkow feels that Mark followed a traditional
pattern; Kelber believes that Mark is the virtual creator of
the present narrative.

[26]Bultmann, *The History of the Synoptic Tradition*, pp.
275-77.

[27]Ludger Schenke, *Der gekreuzigte Christus: Versuch einer
literarkritischen und traditionsgeschichtlichen Bestimmung der
vormarkinischen Passionsgeschichte*, SB, Bd. 69 (Stuttgart:
Verlag Katholisches Bibelwerk, 1974), p. 135, sees part of a
pre-Markan passion narrative in 15:1, 3-5, 2,15b, 16-20, 22-
27, 29a, 31b, 32,34a,36a,37,39, 42-47.

[28]The reader will note that in the exegesis which follows
we have accepted the priority of Mark and the general reliability
of the Two-Source Theory. We are aware, however, that the
priority of Mark has been called into question and that there
is a renewed interest in the Griesbach Hypothesis. Some of the
pertinent literature is, M.-E. Boismard, "The Two-Source Theory
at an Impasse," 26 *NTS* (1980): 1-17; George Wesley Buchanan,
"Has the Griesbach Hypothesis Been Falsified?" 93 *JBL* (1974):
550-572; William Farmer, *The Synoptic Problem: A Critical
Analysis* (Western North Carolina Press: Dillsboro, North Carolina, 1976); Thomas R.W. Longstaff, *Evidence of Conflation in
Mark? A Study in the Synoptic Problem*, SBL Dissertation Series,
no. 28 (Missoula, Montana: SBL, 1977); Bernard Orchard and
Thomas R. W. Longstaff, ed., *J. J. Griesbach: Synoptic and
Text-Critical Studies 1776-1976*, SNTSMS, no. 34 (Cambridge:
Cambridge University Press, 1978); Hans-Herbert Stoldt, *History
and Criticism of the Marcan Hypothesis*, trans. and ed. by Donald
L. Niewyk, with an Introduction by William R. Farmer (Macon,
Georgia: Mercer University Press, 1980).

NOTES - CHAPTER I

[1]George Braumann, "Markus 15:2-5 and Markus 14:55-64," *ZNW* 52 (1961): 273-80; Gerhard Schneider, "Gab es eine vorsynoptische Szene "Jesus vor dem Synedrium'." *NovT* 12 (1970): 22-39.

[2]Linnemann, *Studien zur Passionsgeschichte,* p. 135, points out that Braumann does not take this into account in his comparison between the two accounts.

[3]Braumann, "Markus 15:2-5 und Markus 14:55-64," p. 278.

[4]Genest, *Le Christ de la passion perspective structurale,* pp. 89-92; Schneider, "Gab es eine vorsynoptische Szene 'Jesus vor dem Synedrium'?" p. 33.

[5]John R. Donahue, *Are You the Christ?,* SBL Dissertation Series, no. 10 (Missoula, Montana: SBL, 1973), pp. 53-102.

[6]Pierre Benoit, *The Passion and Resurrection of Jesus Christ,* trans. Benet Weatherhead (New York: Herder & Herder, 1969), p. 79; Bultmann, *The History of the Synoptic Tradition,* p. 272; Eugene Ruckstuhl, *Chronology of the Last Days of Jesus: A Critical Study,* trans. Victor J. Drapela (New York: Desclée Co., 1965), p. 42.

[7]C. E. B. Cranfield, *The Gospel According to Saint Mark: An Introduction and Commentary,* Cambridge Greek Testament Commentary (Cambridge: Cambridge University Press, 1959), p. 448; Joachim Gnilka, *Das Evangelium nach Markus: 2 Teilband Mk 8, 27-16,20,* Evangelisch-Katholischer Kommentar zum Neuen Testament, Bd. 2, T. 2 (Zurich: Benziger Verlag, 1979), pp. 198-99; Ernst Lohmeyer, *Das Evangelium des Markus,* Kritisch-exegetischer Kommentar über das Neue Testament, Bd. 2, 12 aufl. (Göttingen: Vandenhoeck & Ruprecht, 1952), p. 334; Erich Klostermann, *Das Markusevangelium,* Handbuch zum Neuen Testament, Bd. 3, 5 aufl. (Tübingen: J. C. B. Mohr [Paul Siebeck], 1971), p. 194.

[8]*A Greek-English Lexicon of the New Testament and Other Early Christian Literature,* 2d ed. rev. and augmented by F. Wilbur Gingrich and Frederick W. Danker from Walter Bauer's 5th ed., 1958 (Chicago: The University of Chicago Press, 1979), s.v. *symboulion.*

[9]Josef Blinzler, *Der Prozess Jesu: Das jüdische und das römische Gerichtsverfahren gegen Jesus Christus auf Grund der ältesten Zeugnisse dargestellt und beurteilt,* 3 erweiterte aufl. (Regensburg: Verlag Friedrich Pustet, 1960), p. 149, n. 75.

[10]Unless otherwise specified all biblical quotations are taken from *The Holy Bible: Revised Standard Version Containing the Old and New Testaments with the Apocrypha/Deuterocanonical Books: An Ecumenical Edition* (New York: Collins, 1973).

[11]Donald P. Senior, *The Passion Narrative According to Matthew: A Redactional Study*, BETL, no. 39 (Louvain: Leuven University Press, 1975), p. 215.

[12]Neirynck, "L'Évangile de Marc (II)," p. 33.

[13]Gnilka, *Mark*, p. 297. Schneider, "Gab es eine vorsynoptische Szene 'Jesus vor dem Synedrium'?" p. 29.

[14]Neirynck, *Duality in Mark*, pp. 96-97, refers to this as "Double Statement: General and Specific."

[15]Schneider, "Gab es eine vorsynoptische Szene 'Jesus vor dem Synedrium'?" pp. 28-9.

[16]Eduard Schweizer, *The Good News According to Mark*, trans. Donald H. Madvig (Richmond: John Knox Press, 1970), p. 74; Vincent Taylor, *The Gospel According to St. Mark: The Greek Text with Introduction, Notes, and Indexes*, 2d ed. (New York: St. Martin's Press, 1966), p. 220.

[17]Neirynck, *Duality in Mark*, p. 132. By bracketing we mean that Mark tends to enclose material between similar words and phrases. This is akin to, but different from, intercalation. In the latter case the author tends to break the flow of the narrative in order to interpolate new material. See Howard Clark Kee, *Community of the New Age: Studies in Mark's Gospel* (Philadelphia: The Westminster Press, 1977), pp. 54-56; Donahue, *Are You the Christ?*, pp. 58-63. We suspect that Mark's penchant for bracketing is a part of his wider style of duality, i.e., the tendency to repeat words, phrases, etc.

[18]Senior, *The Passion Narrative According to Matthew*, p. 216; C. H. Turner, "Marcan Usage: Notes, Critical and Exegetical on the Second Gospel," *JTS* 28 (1926): 15-19.

[19]Eduard Schweizer, "Anmerkungen zur Theologie des Markus," *Neotestamentica: Deutsche und Englische Aufsätze 1951-1963* (Zurich: Zwingli Verlag, 1963), p. 97.

[20]Franz Neirynck, "ANATEILANTOS TOU HĒLIOU (Mc, 16,2)," 54 *ETL* (1978): 70-108; Achtemeier, *Mark*, pp. 84-85.

[21]Loisy, Schreiber, Schenk, Dormeyer. See the chart provided by Neirynck in "ANATEILANTOS TOU HĒLIOU (Mc, 16,2)," p. 96.

[22]Hugh Anderson, *The Gospel of Mark*, The New Century Bible (Greenwood, S.C.: Attic Press, 1976), p. 304; Neirynck, "ANATEILANTOS TOU HĒLIOU (Mc, 16,2)," p. 98. Both authors understand *meta dyo hēmeras* (14:1) as the inclusive Jewish mode of reckoning so that the expression means the next day.

[23]Neirynck, "ANATEILANTOS TOU HĒLIOU (Mc, 16,2)," p. 28.

[24]Achtemeier, *Mark*, p. 86.

[25]According to the Jewish mode of reckoning pascha is 14 Nisan and the first day of unleavened bread is 15 Nisan.

However, according to the Roman mode of reckoning time both
feasts can begin on the same Roman day. 15 Nisan would begin
in the evening which, according to the Roman day, is the end of
the first day of pascha (14 Nisan). Thus, 14:12 seems to show
that Mark was working with a Roman time scheme. See Anderson,
Mark, p. 308, and Neirynck, "ANATEILANTOS TOU HELIOU (Mc, 16,2),"
pp. 98-99.

[26]Bultmann, *The History of the Synoptic Tradition*, p. 272;
Alfred Loisy, *L'Evangile selon Marc* (Paris: Émile Nourry,
1912), p. 444; Schweizer, *Mark*, p. 335.

[27]Senior, *The Passion Narrative According to Matthew*, pp.
224-25.

[28]Bultmann, *The History of the Synoptic Tradition*, p. 272.

[29]Schenke, *Der gekreuzigte Christus*, pp. 52-53.

[30]Gerhard Schneider, *Die Passion Jesu nach den drei älteren
Evangelien*, Biblische Handbibliothek, Bd. 11 (Munich: Kösel-
Verlag), p. 86.

[31]T. A. Burkill, "The Condemnation of Jesus: A Critique
of Sherwin-White's Thesis," 12 *NovT* (1970): 323.

[32]John C. Hawkins, *Horae Synopticae: Contributions to the
Study of the Synoptic Problem*, 2d ed., rev. and supp. (Oxford:
Clarendon Press, 1968), pp. 143-49; Max Zerwick, *Untersuchungen
zum Markus-Stil: Ein Beitrag zur stilistischen Durcharbeitung
des Neuen Testaments* (Rome: Pontificio Instituto Biblico,
1973), pp. 49-57, study this usage in Mk.

[33]Donahue, *Are You the Christ?*, p. 85; E. J. Pryke, *Redactional Style in the Marcan Gospel: A Study of Syntax and Vocabulary as Guides to Redaction in Mark*, SNTSMS, no. 33 (Cambridge: Cambridge University Press, 1978), p. 147.

[34]Schweizer, *Mark*, p. 335.

[35]Eduard Norden, *Agnostos Theos: Untersuchungen zur Formen-
geschichte religiöser Rede* (Leipzig, Berlin: Verlag B. G.
Teubner, 1913), pp. 183-88.

[36]Donahue, *Are You the Christ?*, p. 88.

[37]In Matthew 11:3; 14:28; 16:16; 26:63; 27:11 the formula
refers to Jesus, but in 16:18 to Peter. In John 1:49; 3:10;
4:19; 6:69; 10:24; 11:27; 18:33,37; 21:12 it refers to Jesus,
but in 1:21,25 to John, and in 1:42 to Peter.

[38]Norden, *Agnostos Theos*, pp. 196-97, no. 2, writes:
"Meine Annahme, dass dieser zweiter Teil des Pilatusverhörs eine
Dublette zum ersten des Synedrionverhörs ist, . . . ".

[39]Donahue, *Are You the Christ?*, pp. 241-43, lists 15:2-4
as characteristic of the Markan insertion technique; Neirynck,

Duality in Mark, p. 131, lists it under "Correspondence and Narrative."

[40]Mark uses *thaumazō* in 5:20; 6:6 15:5, 44 and *thaubeomai* in 1:27; 10:24; 10:32 as typical reactions to Jesus.

[41]For Mark's use of *polla* see Schenk, *Der Passionsbericht nach Markus*, p. 245; Taylor, *Mark*, p. 579. For *ide* see John Charles Doudna, *The Greek of the Gospel of Mark*, JBL Monograph Series, vol. 12 (Philadelphia: SBL, 1961), pp. 63-65. For *palin* see Hawkins, *Horae Synopticae*, p. 13. For the double negative see Neirynck, *Duality in Mark*, p. 88.

[42]Donahue, *Are You the Christ?*, p. 87, says that Lk. 23:9, 10 seems to preserve a remnant of this tradition.

[43]Braumann, "Markus 15:2-5 und Markus 14:55-64," pp. 276-77; M. J. Lagrange, *Evangile selon Saint Marc*, Études Bibliques, édition corrigée et augmentée (Paris: Librairie Lecoffre, 1947), pp. LXXVII-LXXIX.

[44]Pryke, *Redactional Style in the Marcan Gospel*, p. 79; Taylor, *Mark*, p. 61; C. H. Turner, "Marcan Usage: Notes, Critical and Exegetical, on the Second Gospel," *JTS* 28 (1927): 352-353.

[45]Mark uses *ochlos* twenty-four times with the artical and thirteen times without the article. In the thirteen cases he does not employ the article he uses an adjective with *ochlos* (often *polys*) nine times. Thus, in only four instances does he utilize *ochlos* without adjective or article; 14:43 is in this category. It would appear that Mark distinguishes this crowd from "the" crowd.

[46]C. H. Turner, "Marcan Usage: Notes, Critical and Exegetical, on the Second Gospel," *JTS* 26 (1925): 145-156. The use of *archiereis* back to back in vv.10-11 also leads us to suspect that Mark has added v.10.

[47]C. H. Bird, "Some *gar* clauses in St. Mark's Gospel of the New Testament," *JTS*, n.s. 4 (1953): 171-187; Turner, "Marcan Usage: Notes, Critical and Exegetical, on the Second Gospel," 26 *JTS* (1925): 145-56; Pryke, *Redactional Style in the Marcan Gospel*, pp. 126-35.

[48]Gnilka, *Mark*, p. 298.

[49]Senior, *The Passion Narrative According to Matthew*, p. 236.

NOTES - CHAPTER II

[1]Ernest Best, *The Temptation and the Passion: The Markan Soteriology*, SNTSMA, no. 2 (Cambridge: Cambridge University Press, 1965), p. 96; Schneider, *Die Passion Jesu nach den drei älteren Evangelien*, p. 105; Schweizer, *Mark*, p. 339; Taylor, *Mark*, p. 584.
Other authors are not convinced there has been an insertion: Cranfield, *Mark*, p. 452; Gnilka, *Mark*, p. 306; Lohmeyer, *Mark*, p. 340.
Bultmann, *History of the Synoptic Tradition*, p. 271, says the incident is an expansion of 15:15b; Pesch, *Mark*, p. 468, considers it a part of his pre-Markan passion narrative.

[2]Senior, *The Passion Narrative According to Matthew*, p. 263.

[3]Raymond E. Brown, *The Gospel According to John (xiii-xxi): Introduction, Translation, and Notes*, The Anchor Bible, vol. 29A (Garden City, New York: Doubleday & Co., 1970), p. 886, is not convinced of John's dependence on Mark at this point but he does note " . . . that of the seven episodes in the Pilate trial, this one lends itself best to such a theory of Johannine dependence."

[4]Vincent Taylor, *The Passion Narrative of St. Luke: A Critical and Historical Investigation*, ed. Owen E. Evans, SNTSMS, no. 18 (Cambridge: Cambridge University Press, 1972), p. 89, writes " . . . 5-16 was composed by Luke himself out of traditions contained in the non-Markan source."

[5]Neirynck, *Duality in Mark*, p. 106, terms this "Synonymous Expression."

[6]P. Willibrord Hillmann, *Aufbau und Deutung der synoptischen Leidensberichte: Beitrag zur Kompositionstechnik und Sinndeutung der drei älteren Evangelien*, (Freiburg im Breisgau: Herder & Co. G.m.b. H Verlagsbuchhandlung, 1941), p. 122.

[7]Anderson, *Mark*, p. 338; Dormeyer, *Die Passion Jesu als Verhaltensmodell*, p. 191; Gnilka, *Mark*, p. 306; Schweizer, *Mark*, p. 340; Taylor, *Mark*, p. 586.

[8]This chart is taken from Senior, *The Passion Narrative According to Matthew*, p. 267.

[9]Taylor, *The Passion Narrative of St. Luke*, p. 99, writes: " . . . we must conclude that in Lk xxiii 33-49 verses 34b,38, 44f., and 49 are Markan insertions or additions in a non-Markan source."

[10]In Mark the inscription (15:26) is tightly knit with the third hour (15:25). Just as the sixth hour (15:33) marks the beginning of the three hours of darkness, so the third hour (15:25) notes the hour of the crucifixion and of the inscription.

[11]See chapter 1, n. 25.

[12]Senior, *The Passion Narrative According to Matthew*, p.
279, n. 1, writes: "Mark's description of the Passion is encom-
passed in a strict 24 hour chronological framework beginning
with *opsia* (14:17) and moving through *alektorophōnia* (14:72),
prōi (15:1), the 'third hour' (15:25), 'sixth hour to ninth
hour' (15:33), and finally *opsia* (15:42)." We agree with the
parallelism between 14:17 and 15:42. It does not, however,
eliminate a crucifixion day which runs from 15:1-42. Mark is
more careful in marking time in chapter 15 than he is in chapter
14, as can be seen in his use of the hours.

[13]Ibid., p. 282, "In Mark the historical present *staurousin*
(in the active, cf. vs.24a) plus the phrase *syn autǭ* convey the
fact that the two thieves were crucified simultaneously with
Jesus. However, the Old Testament quotation in Mk. 15:24 and
the description of the title in 15:26 make their simultaneity
disjointed."

[14]Mark speaks of three entries into Jerusalem (11:1, 11,
27), three servants sent to the tenants of the vineyard (12:2,
4,5), three movements in the Garden of Gethsemane (14:37,40,41),
and three denials by Peter (14:68,70,71). Pesch, *Mark*, pp. 15-
20 sees the passion narrative constructed on the basis of thirteen groups, each group composed of three members. See
Neirynck's discussion of the schema in "L'Evangile de Marc (II),"
pp. 35-42.

[15]Taylor, *Mark*, p. 592.

[16]Bruce M. Metzger, *A Textual Commentary on the Greek New
Testament: A Companion Volume to the United Bible Societies'
Greek New Testament (Third Edition)* (United Bible Societies,
1971), p. 75, says that the reading in Mk. 1:34 is probably derived from the parallel in Lk. 4:41.

[17]Ibid., p. 73, *huiou theou* is absent from ℵ[*] θ 28[C] al.
However, according to Metzger, the combination of B W D al in
support of the reading is strong evidence.

[18]Brown, *The Gospel According to John* (xiii-xxi), pp. 913-
16, is not inclined to see a direct dependence of John upon
Mark at this point.

[19]Cranfield, *Mark*, p. 459, and Taylor, *Mark*, p. 595, are
typical of authors who conjecture about the historical event.

[20]Anderson, *Mark*, p. 346; Taylor, *Mark*, p. 595.

[21]Loisy, *Mark*, p. 469, notes further: "Il est évident que
les paroles sur Élie, et la présentation du vinaigre ont été
conçus indépendamment du miracle des ténèbres."

[22]Gnilka, *Mark*, p. 322.

[23]Metzger, *A Textual Commentary on the Greek New Testament*,
p. 119.

[24]Taylor, *The Passion Narrative of St. Luke*, p. 80,
" . . . Luke's account is not an edited version of Mk xiv 65,
but represents his own rewriting of material from his special
source."

[25]In Mark the common attachment formula is *kai elegen
autois*.

[1]D. E. Nineham, *The Gospel of St. Mark*, The Pelican Gospel Commentaries (Baltimore: Penguin Books, 1963), p. 421.

[2]Hans Ruedi Weber, *The Cross: Tradition and Interpretation*, trans. Elke Jessett (Grand Rapids, Michigan: William B. Eerdmans Publishing Co., 1975), p. 44, gives a chart which shows how seven scholars (Bultmann, Finegan, Grant, Taylor, Peddinghaus, Schweizer, Linnemann) perceive the primitive narrative within vv. 20b-41b. The seven agree only on the following verses, 22a and 24a.

[3]Bultmann, *The History of the Synoptic Tradition*, p. 273.

[4]Jack Finegan, *Die Überlieferung der Leidens-und Auferstehungsgeschichte Jesu*, Beihefte zur Zeitschrift für die neutestamentliche Wissenschaft, Beih. 15 (Giessen: Verlag von Alfred Töpelmann, 1934), p. 78.

[5]Taylor, *Mark*, p. 587.

[6]Ibid., p. 658.

[7]Cranfield, *Mark*, p. 453.

[8]Schweizer, *Mark*, p. 342.

[9]Schneider, *Die Passion Jesu nach den drei älteren Evangelien*, p. 109.

[10]Gnilka, *Mark*, p. 326.

[11]Also, Johannes Schreiber, *Die Markuspassion: Wege zur Erforschung der Leidensgeschichte Jesu* (Hamburg: Furche-Verlag, 1969).

[12]Schreiber, *Theologie des Vertrauens*, p. 32.

[13]Ibid., p. 33.

[14]Schenk, *Der Passionsbericht nach Markus*, p. 24.

[15]Dormeyer, *Die Passion Jesu als Verhaltensmodell*, p. 209.

[16]Ibid., pp. 288-89.

[17]Linnemann, *Studien zur Passionsgeschichte*, pp. 139-43.

[18]Ibid., p. 146.

[19]Ibid., p. 146.

[20]Ibid., pp. 168-69.

[21]Bultmann, *The History of the Synoptic Tradition*, p. 273.

[22]Nineham, *Mark*, p. 421.

[23]Schenk, *Der Passionsbericht nach Markus*, p. 16; Schreiber, *Theologie des Vertrauens*, pp. 24-26.

[24]Dormeyer, *Die Passion Jesu als Verhaltensmodell*, pp. 26-8.

[25]Besides Linnemann, Schenk and Schreiber, see Gnilka, *Mark*, pp. 310-14. He sees a "Grundbericht" composed of 20b-22a, 24,26f,29,31f,34,35f,36a,40 which has been interpreted through the help of apocalyptic material found in vv.25,29b,30,33,37,38.

[26]Bultmann, *History of the Synoptic Tradition*, p. 274, writes: "The time reference in vv.33,34 is the editorial work of Mark, as it is also in v.25."

[27]Taylor, *The Passion Narrative of St. Luke*, pp. 90,92.

[28]Schneider, *Die Passion Jesu nach den drei älteren Evangelien*, p. 115, disagrees with Taylor and writes: " . . . hat er dennoch keine Sondervorlage für den gesamten Bericht zur Verfügung gehabt."

[29]Hawkins, *Horae Synopticae*, p. 143.

[30]Ibid., p. 144.

[31]W. M. A. Hendriks, "Zur Kollektionsgeschichte des Markusevangeliums," in *L'Évangile selon Marc: Tradition et redaction*, ed. M. Sabbé, BETL, no 34 (Louvain: Leuven University Press, 1974), p. 47, writes: "Auch in Mk kann das praesens in einigen Gruppen eingeteilt werden, jedoch sind die Grenzen nicht so scharf unterschieden wie in Mt." Zerwick, *Untersuchungen zum Markus-Stil*, divides the gospel into seventy-eight pericopes and finds the historic present in all but nineteen. He draws general conclusions about the usage of this tense on pp. 55-7.

[32]Hendriks, "Zur Kollektionsgeschichte des Markusevangeliums," p. 52, points to 1:21a; 8:22a; 10:46a; 11:15a and 11:27a as essentially redactional and claims that these introduce " . . . einer oder mehrerer Perikopen" (p. 54).

[33]Zerwick, *Untersuchungen zum Markus-Stil*, p. 54.

[34]Ibid., p. 55.

[35]Nineham, *Mark*, p. 421.

[36]The use of the historic present as a criterion for determining sources has been criticized by Linnemann, *Studien zur Passionsgeschichte*, p. 140; and by Hendriks, "Zur Kollektionsgeschichte des Markusevangeliums," p. 49, who writes: "Dass in diesen Versen älteste Gemeindetradition zu sehen ist, wie es

Schreiber behauptet, ist nicht von vornherein vorauszusetzen.
Vielmehr handelt es sich auch hier um eine sekundare Uberarbei-
tung."

[37]Zerwick, *Untersuchungen zum Markus-Stil*, p. 55.

[38]The RSV translates the *kai* as "when." F. Blass & A.
Debrunner, *A Greek Grammar of the New Testament and Other Early
Christian Literature*, trans. & rev. by Robert W. Funk from 9th-
10th German ed. incorporating supplementary notes of A. Debrunner (Chicago: University of Chicago Press, 1961), p. 227
(442:2), sees the *kai* as co-ordination with a temporal designation.

[39]Neirynck, *Duality in Mark*, pp. 97-101, designates this
as "Double Statement: Repetition of the Motif." He gives six-
ty-two examples.

[40]Neirynck, *Duality in Mark*, pp. 76-77, gives a list of
verses with cognate accusatives or datives in Mark. LaGrange,
Mark, p. lxxiii refers to this as pleonasm.

[41]C. H. Turner, "Marcan Usage: Notes, Critical and Exegetical, on the Second Gospel," 26 *JTS* (1926): 12.

[42]Neirynck, *Duality in Mark*, pp. 106-7, gives a list of
these phrases.

[43]Taylor, *The Passion Narrative of St. Luke*, p. 96, writes:
"The entire narrative, 33-40, it may be suggested, is the Lukan
setting of an earlier source supplemented by Markan additions
in vv.34b,38,44f., and 49."

[44]Neirynck, *Duality in Mark*, p. 113, designates this as
"Correspondence in Narrative."

[45]Ibid., pp. 75-76, calls attention to the use of the preposition *apo* with an adverb ending in *then* as a sign of Markan
duality.

[46]Philipp Vielhauer, "Erwägungen zur Christologie des Mark-
usevangeliums," in *Zeit und Geschichte: Dankesgabe an Rudolf
Bultmann zum 80. Geburtstag*, ed. Erich Dinkler (Tübingen:
J. C. B. Mohr [Paul Siebeck], 1964), pp. 155-69.

[47]Among the important literature is the following: Josef
Blinzler, *Die Brüder und Schwestern Jesu*, SB, Bd. 21 (Stutt-
gart: Verlag Katholisches Bibelwerk, 1967), pp. 82ff.; *Der
Prozess Jesu*, pp. 299ff.; Ingo Broer, *Die Urgemeinde und das
Grab Jesu: Eine Analyse der Grablegungsgeschichte im Neuen
Testament*, SANT, Bd. 31 (Munich: Kösel-Verlag, 1972); Martin
Hengel, "Maria Magdalena und die Frauen als Zeugen," in *Abraham
Unser Vater: Juden und Christen im Gespräch über die Bibel.
Festschrift für Otto Michel zum 60. Geburtstag*, ed. Otto Betz,
Martin Hengel, and Peter Schmidt (Leiden: E. J. Brill, 1963),
pp. 243-256; Ludger Schenke, *Auferstehungsverkündigung und
leeres Grab: Eine traditionsgeschichtliche Untersuchung von*

Mk 16, 1-8, SB, Bd. 33 (Stuttgart: Verlag Katholisches Bibelwerk, 1968); Kennard J. Spencer Jr., "The Burial of Jesus,"
74 *JBL* (1955): 227-38.

[48]Senior, *The Passion Narrative According to Matthew*, pp.
328-29.

[49]Blinzler, *Die Brüder und Schwestern Jesu*, pp. 82ff.

[50]The best witnesses (B ℵ[corr]A K Δ33 al.) include *tou*.

[51]Lohmeyer, *Mark*, p. 348.

[52]Finegan, *Die Überlieferung der Leidens- und Auferstehungsgeschichte Jesu*, p. 76f.

[53]Pesch, *Mark*, pp. 504-07.

[54]Blinzler, *Die Brüder und Schwestern Jesu*, p. 84.

[55]Neirynck, *Duality in Mark*, pp. 108-12.

[56]Broer, *Die Urgemeinde und Das Grab Jesu*, pp. 97ff. says
that identifying a mother by her son is strange. Blass-De-
brunner, *A Greek Grammar of the New Testament and other Early
Christian Literature*, p. 89 (162:3) say that the genitive of
origin can also identify a mother by her son. However, they
make this deducation by using Mk. 15:47 as the example, and
then refer to 15:40 to clarify the relationship.

[57]Broer, *Die Urgemeinde und das Grab Jesu*, p. 132;
Schenke, *Auferstehungsverkündigung und leeres Grab*, pp. 26ff.

[58]Broer, *Die Urgemeinde und das Grab Jesu*, p. 135;
Schenke, *Auferstehungsverkündigung und leeres Grab*, p. 19.

[59]Schenke, *Auferstehungsverkündigung und leeres Grab*, p. 14.

[60]Schenke and Broer disagree here. The former sees v.47 as
a part of the original story (p. 18), while the latter does
not (p. 114).

[61]Dormeyer, *Die Passion Jesu als Verhaltensmodell*, p. 207;
Schneider, *Die Passion Jesu nach den drei älteren Evangelien*,
p. 138; Taylor, *Mark*, pp. 622-23.

[62]Senior, *The Passion Narrative According to Matthew*,
p. 322.

[63]Broer, *Die Urgemeinde und das Grab Jesu*, pp. 116-131,
makes a detailed analysis of the vocabulary and grammatical
style of 15:40f. He concludes: "Die Vokabelstatistik und die
Stilanalyse bestätigen insofern unser oben gewonnenes Ergebnis,
dass Mk 15:40f redaktionell verfasst hat." (p. 131)

[64]Taylor, *The Passion Narrative of St. Luke*, p. 99, writes:
"Luke's source is Mark, without any clear sign of a second

source except a knowledge of Johannine traditions." Brown, *The Gospel According to John (xiii-xxi)*, p. 958, concurs with Dodd and sees John as " . . . drawing upon an independent tradition similar to those behind the Synoptic Gospels rather than on the Synoptic Gospels or pre-Gospel traditions themselves."

[65]Broer, *Die Urgemeinde und das Grab Jesu*, p. 183, sees four general tendencies in the growth of the tradition: 1) the general motif of the Sabbath falls away; 2) the character of Joseph is heightened; 3) there is a greater interest in the grave; 4) the worth of the grave increases.

[66]Nineham, *Mark*, p. 435.

[67]Broer, *Die Urgemeinde und das Grab Jesu*, p. 167; Dormeyer, *Die Passion Jesu als Verhaltensmodell*, p. 217; Gnilka, *Mark*, p. 331; Schenk, *Der Passionsbericht nach Markus*, p. 256.

[68]Broer, *Die Urgemeinde und das Grab Jesu*, pp. 167-69.

[69]Blass-Debrunner, *A Greek Grammar of the New Testament and Other Early Christian Literature*, p. 237 (454:1).

[70]Neirynck, *Duality in Mark*, p. 122, terms this "Request and Realization."

[71]Finegan, *Die Überlieferungsgeschichte der Leidens- und Auferstehungsgeschichte Jesu*, p. 90; Lohmeyer, *Mark*, p. 350.

[72]Eduard Lohse, *History of the Suffering and Death of Jesus Christ*, trans. Martin O. Dietrich (Philadelphia: Fortress Press, 1967), p. 101; Taylor, *Mark*, p. 601.

[73]Walter Grundmann, *Das Evangelium nach Markus*, Theologischer Handkommentar zum Neuen Testament, bd. 2 (Berlin: Evangelische Verlagsanstalt, 1959), p. 318; Nineham, *Mark*, p. 433.

[74]Pesch, *Mark*, p. 510. Even he agrees this may be an insertion.

[75]Anderson, *Mark*, p. 350; Broer, *Die Urgemeinde und das Grab Jesu*, pp. 180ff; Gnilka, *Mark*, p. 332; Schenk, *Der Passionsbericht nach Markus*, p. 255; Schweizer, *Mark*, p. 362.

NOTES - CHAPTER IV

[1]Paul J. Achtemeier, "Mark as Interpreter of the Jesus Traditions," 32 *Int* (1978): 339-352.

[2]A number of authors have pointed to the royal theme, or the royal elements of this chapter. Hans Conzelmann, "History and Theology in the Passion Narratives of the Synoptic Gospels," trans. Charles B. Cousar, *Int* 24 (1970): 178-197; Donahue, "Temple, Trial, and Royal Christology (Mark 14:53-65), " in *The Passion in Mark*, pp. 72-8; Hillmann, *Aufbau und Deutung der synoptischen Leidensberichte*, p. 127, gives an outline of the chapter with a strong emphasis on kingship; Donald Juel, *Messiah and Temple: The Trial of Jesus in the Gospel of Mark*, SBL Dissertation Series, no. 31 (Missoula, Montana: Scholars Press, 1977), p. 49, writes that "the theme unifying the passion story is the royal theme." Grant R. Osborn, "Redactional Trajectories in the Crucifixion Narrative," *EvQ* 51 (1979), pp. 85-6 says " . . . Mark's theological emphasis is on the suffering of the Messianic King as an anticipation of His enthronement." Norman Perrin, "The High Priest's Question and Jesus' Answer," in *The Passion in Mark*, p. 94 writes that "for Mark the crucifixion narrative is the narrative of the enthronement of Christ as King." Vielhauer, "Erwägungen zur Christologie des Markusevangeliums," pp. 155-69, sees 15:39 as an act of enthronement.

[3]G. Minnette de Tillesse, *Le secret messianique dans L'Évangile de Marc*, Lectio Divina, no 37 (Paris: Les Éditions du Cerf, 1968), pp. 338-39, shows how the title grows in chapter 15 " . . . avec une insistance de plus en plus irrésistible."

[4]Bultmann, *The History of the Synoptic Tradition*, pp. 272-3, denies the historicity of the charge. It is defended by Nils Alstrup Dahl, "The Crucified Messiah," in *The Crucified Messiah and Other Essays* (Minneapolis, Minnesota: Augsburg Publishing House, 1974), pp. 10-36; and Wayne A. Meeks, *The Prophet-King: Moses Traditions and the Johannine Christology*, Supplements to Novum Testamentum, vol. 14 (Leiden, E. J. Brill, 1967), p. 79.

[5]Peddinghaus, "Die Entstehung der Leidensgeschichte," pp. 160-65.

[6]Ibid., p. 160.

[7]Schenke, *Der gekreuzigte Christus*, p. 85, attributes the titles to the tradition because v.32a corresponds with 14:61f.; 15:2,26 which he sees as traditional. We have argued, however, that 15:2,26 show redactional activity.

[8]In 10:37 James and John ask for seats at Jesus' right and left (*aristerōn*). In 10:40 Jesus says that the seats at his right and left (*euōnymōn*, the same word used in 15:27) have already been appointed for others. Mark may have brought the

two words for "left" into line in order to show the relationship between these two pericopes.

[9]*TDNT*, s.v. "*Ēl(e)ias*," by Joachim Jeremias, 2:935. "Elijah
as helper in time of need. This is recognized only as a popular
Jewish belief in the NT. . . . The Messianic claim of Jesus
was shattered in Jewish eyes when Elijah failed to help."

[10]Ernesto R. Martinez, *The Gospel Accounts of the Death of
Jesus: A Study of the Death Accounts Made in the Light of the
New Testament Traditions, The Redaction and the Theology of the
Four Evangelists* (Rome: Pontificia Universitas Gregoriana,
1970), p. 44, notes that " . . . the Elijah scene is simply a
part of the mocking of Jesus on the cross." To that extent
then, Jesus is mocked as a royal figure in 15:35-36.

[11]Martin Hengel, *The Son of God: The Origin of Christology
and the History of Jewish-Hellenistic Religion*, trans. John Bowden (Philadelphia: Fortress Press, 1975), p. 44, referring to
the fragment from Cave IV writes: " . . . the tradition of the
king as a 'son of God' was not completely lost." Juel, *Messiah
and Temple*, p. 82, " . . . we can only assume that 'Son of God'
is being used by Mark as a royal title."

[12]Minette de Tillesse, *Le secret messianique dans L'Évangile
de Marc*, p. 338.

[13]Donahue, *Are You the Christ?*, p. 199, "However, the relationship between 'king of Israel' and 'king of the Jews' still
remains unsolved. Caution must be exercised in simply equating
the titles as, for example, Cullmann does when he treats them
as synonyms. Juel, *Messiah and Temple*, p. 50, "'King of the
Jews' and 'the Christ the King of Israel' are both used to describe the same reality; but they describe that reality from
different perspectives. 'King of the Jews' is a Roman, i.e.,
a non-Jewish formulation."

[14]Juel, *Messiah and Temple*, p. 47; Robert C. Tannehill, "The
Gospel of Mark as Narrative Christology," *Semeia* 16 (1979): 80,
writes: "So the mocking scenes in Mark's passion story are
Christological. They covertly proclaim Jesus as prophet, king,
and powerful savior who does not use his power for himself."
However, Aloysius M. Ambrozic, *The Hidden Kingdom: A Redac-
tional-Critical Study of the References to the Kingdom of God
in Mark's Gospel*, the CBQ Monograph Series, no. 2 (Washington:
The Catholic Biblical Association of America, 1972), p. 38, says
that " . . . irony, with the possible exception of 7:2-3 and
10:42 is not one of his characteristics."

[15]Juel,*Messiah and Temple*, p. 71.

[16]Best, *The Temptation and the Passion*, p. 96.

[17]Klaus Berger, "Die königlichen Messiastradition des Neuen
Testaments," *NTS* 20 (1973): 1-44; and "Zum Problem der Messianität Jesu," *ZTK* 71 (1974): 1-30. Berger argues that the
content of "King of the Jews" must be drawn from chapter 15,

especially the second mockery. Jesus' opponents do not attack him because he failed to free them from the Romans but because he did not save himself and rebuild the temple. The one who does these things is the King of the Jews, the Messiah. Berger connects the title with the Son of David title in the sense of Solomon's son, the exorcist. Then, he ties the title to *Wisdom* 2-5 and argues that the King of the Jews, the Son of David, is the son of God in the sense of this book. That is, he is a charismatic person, with a special relationship to God, whose power has failed him. Later we shall look to royal messianism as a better way to understand "Son of God."

[18]Donahue, *Are You the Christ?*, p. 197.

[19]Berger, "Zum Problem der Messianität Jesu," p. 182, writes: "Die Christologie der Evangelien steht wesenlich im Horizont der Legitimationsfrage." Also Peddinghaus, "Die Entstehung der Leidensgeschichte," p. 182.

[20]Juel, *Messiah and Temple*, pp. 211-12, writes, "One of the purposes of Mark's story seems to be to prove to his readers that, contrary to all appearances and despite the obvious differences between Jesus and the image of the Messiah in popular expectation, the crucified Jesus is the Messiah, the Son of God."

[21]The temple theme has been investigated by Donahue and Juel as well as Lloyd Gaston, *No Stone on Another: Studies in the Significance of the Fall of Jerusalem in the Synoptic Gospels*, Supplements to Novum Testamentum, no. 23 (Leiden: E. J. Brill, 1970); and Werner Kelber, *The Kingdom in Mark: A New Place and a New Time* (Philadelphia: Fortress Press, 1974).

[22]Taylor, *Mark*, p. 436, outlines the similarities between prediction and passion.

[1]See our earlier discussion based on Neirynck and Achtemeier. However, Klemens Stock, "Gliederung und Zusammenhang in Mk 11-12," *Bib* 59 (1978): 481-515, has analyzed the section on the basis of a three day schema.

[2]Fritz Neugebauer, "Die Davidssohnfrage (Mark XII 35-37 Parr.) und der Menschensohn," *NTS* 21 (1974): 83-84.

[3]David Daube, *The New Testament and Rabbinic Judaism*, Jordan Lectures 1952 (London: Athbone Press, 1956), p. 167, disagrees.

[4]Gerhard Schneider, "Die Davidssohnfrage (Mk 12, 35-37)," *Bib* 53 (1973): 87-90.

[5]Paul J. Achtemeier, "'And He Followed Him' Miracles and Discipleship in Mark 10:46-52," *Semeia* 11 (1978): 127, sees a growing denial of Jesus as Son of David rather than a growing affirmation. See Christoph Burger, *Jesus als Davidssohn: Eine traditionsgeschichtliche Untersuchung*, FRLANT, Hft. 98 (Göttingen: Vandenhoeck & Ruprecht, 1970), pp. 42-71, for an opposing view.

[6]Peddinghaus, "Die Entstehung der Leidensgeschichte," p. 132.

[7]Gaston, *No Stone on Another*, pp. 216-17; Barnabas Lindars, *New Testament Apologetic: The Doctrinal Significance of the Old Testament Quotations* (Philadelphia: Westminster Press, 1961), pp. 170-171; *TDNT*, s.v. "paschō," by Michaelis.

[8]Lindars, *New Testament Apologetic*, p. 81, does not agree, and on the basis of the reading in Aquila, Symmachus and Theodotion he refers *exoudeneō* to Isa. 53:3. In the next chapter we present an argument for our position.

[9]Ambrozic, *The Hidden Kingdom*, p. 42; Minette de Tillesse, *Le secret messianique dans L'Evangile de Marc*, p. 284.

[10]Ambrozic, *The Hidden Kingdom*, pp. 40-42; Rudolf Pesch, *Naherwartungen: Tradition und Redaktion in Mk 13*, Kommentare und Beiträge zum Alten und Neuen Testament (Düsseldorf: Patmos-Verlag, 1968), pp. 96-100.

[11]Donahue, Gaston, Juel, Kelber.

[12]Taylor, *Mark*, p. 452, writes: "The key to the interpretation of the narrative is the strange combination within it of Messianic and non-Messianic elements."

[13]R. H. Lightfoot, *The Gospel Message of Saint Mark* (Oxford: Clarendon Press, 1958), p. 61

[14]Paul J. Achtemeier, *Invitation to Mark: A Commentary on the Gospel of Mark with Complete Text from the Jerusalem Bible*, Image Books (Garden City, New York: Doubleday, 1978), p. 162. Ambrozic, *The Hidden Kingdom*, p. 40, simply calls it "Jesus' approach to Jerusalem."

[15]Taylor, *Mark*, p. 453.

[16]Ambrozic, *The Hidden Kingdom*, p. 34.

[17]Ambrozic, *The Hidden Kingdom*, pp. 32-45, for a detailed analysis of tradition and redaction; Joseph Blenkinsopp, "The Oracle of Judah and the Messianic Entry," *JBL* 80 (1961): 56, for an analysis of form; Schenk, *Der Passionsbericht nach Markus*, pp. 166-75, for a source analysis.

[18]Dormeyer, *Die Passion Jesu als Verhaltensmodell*, p. 190; Gnilka, *Mark*, p. 117; Pesch, *Mark*, p. 179.

[19]J. Duncan M. Derret, "Law in the New Testament: The Palm Sunday Colt," *NovT* (1971): 241-58.

[20]Ibid., p. 246.

[21]Ambrozic, *The Hidden Kingdom*, p. 37. Also, F. F. Bruce, "The Book of Zechariah and the Passion Narrative," 43 *BJRL* (1961): 336-353.

[22]Blenkinsopp, "The Oracle of Judah and the Messianic Entry," pp. 55-64; Heinz-Wolfgang Kuhn, "Das Reittier Jesu in der Einzugeschichte des Markusevangeliums," *ZNW* 50 (1959): 80-91.

[23]Lohmeyer, *Mark*, p. 230, referring to Justin, would read the text as "vine."

[24]A. Dupont-Sommer, *The Essene Writings from Qumran*, trans. G. Vermes (Gloucester, Mass: Peter Smith, 1973), pp. 314-15.

[25]Samson H. Levey, *The Messiah: An Aramaic Interpretation: The Messianic Exegesis of the Targum*, Monographs of the Hebrew Union College, no. 2 (Cincinnati: Hebrew Union College-Jewish Institute of Religion, 1974), pp. 7,9.

[26]Reginald Fuller, *The Foundations of New Testament Christology* (New York: Charles Scribner's Sons, 1965), pp. 111-14, for a history of the text; Kelber, *The Kingdom in Mark*, p. 94.

[27]T. A. Burkill, *Mysterious Revelation: An Examination of the Philosophy of St. Mark's Gospel* (Ithaca: Cornell University Press, 1963), p. 196.

[28]On the messianic character of "Hosanna" see: J. Spencer Kennard, Jr., "'Hosanna' and the Purpose of Jesus," *JBL* 67 (1948): 171-76; Eduard Lohse, "Hosanna," *NovT* 6 (1963): 113-19; Erick Werner, "'Hosanna' in the Gospels," *JBL* 65 (1964): 97-122.

[29]Kelber, *The Kingdom in Mark*, p. 96.

[30]Conzelmann, "History and Theology in the Passion Narrative," p. 183; Gnilka, *Mark*, p. 120.

[31]Ambrozic, *The Hidden Kingdom*, p. 33; Best, *The Temptation and the Passion*, p. 167; but Taylor, *Mark*, p. 455, disagrees.

[32]Michael Hubaut, *La parabole des vignerons homicides*, Cahiers de la Revue Biblique, no 16 (Paris: Gabal, 1976), pp. 55-56, says that the "Lord of the Vineyard" (12:9) might refer to Jesus rather than to God. If so, we have another example of *Kyrios* employed as a surrogate for the royal title.

[33]Blenkinsopp, "The Oracle of Judah and the Messianic Entry," p. 58.

[34]Martin Hengel, "Das Gleichnis von den Weingärtnern Mc 12, 1-12 im Lichte der Zenopapyri und der rabbinischen Gleichnesse," *ZNW* 59 (1968): 1-39; Michel Hubaut, *La parabole des vignerons homicides*; Werner Georg Kümmel, "Das Gleichnis von den bösen Weingärtnern (Mark 12. 1-9) in *Aux sources de la tradition chrétienne: Mélange offerts à M. Maurice Goguel à l'occasion de son soixante-dixième anniversaire*, Bibliothèque théologique (Neuchatel: Delachaux & Niestle, 1950), pp. 120-31.

[35]C. H. Dodd, *The Parables of the Kingdom*, rev. ed. (New York: Charles Scribner's Sons, 1961), p. 96; Joachim Jeremias, *The Parables of Jesus*, trans. S. H. Hooke (New York: Charles Scribner's Sons, 1963), p. 77. These authors maintain that there was a non-allegorical parable spoken by Jesus.

[36]Kümmel, "Das Gleichnis von den bösen Weingärtnern," p. 128.

[37]Hubaut, *La parabole des vignerons homicides*, discusses the allegorical meaning in depth.

[38]*TDNT*, s.v. "*pais*" by Joachim Jeremias, 5:701.

[39]Ibid., 703.

[40]I. Howard Marshall, "Son of God or Servant of Yahweh? - A Reconsideration of Mark I.11," *NTS* 15 (1969): 329.

[41]Morna Hooker, *Jesus and the Servant: The Influence of the Servant Concept of Deutero-Isaiah on the New Testament* (London: SPCK, 1959), p. 70.

[42]Ibid., p. 71.

[43]Ibid., p. 72.

[44]Marshall, Son of God or Servant of Yahweh," p. 333.

[45]Hooker, *Jesus the Servant*, p. 71.

[46]*TDNT*, s.v. "*huios*," by Eduard Schweizer, 8:368.

[47]Evald Lövestam, *Son and Saviour: A Study of Acts 13, 32-37. With an Appendix: 'Son of God' in the Synoptic Gospels,* ConNT, no. 18 (Lund: C. W. K. Gleerup, 1961), p. 96.

[48]Lövestam, *Son and Saviour,* p. 97. However, Hooker, *Jesus the Servant,* p. 69, objects that the Western reading may not have correctly interpreted the scene.

[49]Lindars, *New Testament Apologetic,* p. 140.

[50]*Saint Justin Martyr,* trans. Thomas B. Falls, The Fathers of the Church: A New Translation (New York: Christian Heritage, Inc., 1948), p. 290.

[51]Ibid., p. 310.

[52]Lövestam, *Son and Saviour,* p. 96; and Marshall, "Son of God or Servant of Yahweh," p. 335, see such a secondary reference.

[53]*The Midrash on Psalms,* trans. William G. Braude, Yale Judaica Studies, no. 13 (New Haven: Yale University Press, 1959), vol. 1: Ps. 2, par. 9.

[54]Lövestam, *Son and Saviour,* p. 27.

[55]Kümmel, "Das Gleichnis von den bösen Weingärtnern," p. 123.

[56]Lövestam, *Son and Saviour,* p. 97.

[57]Lindars, *New Testament Apologetic,* pp. 169-74.

[58]James Rendel Harris, *Testimonies,* 2 pts. (Cambridge: Cambridge University Press, 1916-20).

[59]Lindars, *New Testament Apologetic,* p. 170.

[60]Peddinghaus, "Die Entstehung der Leidensgeschichte," p. 132.

[61]John H. Eaton, *Kingship and the Psalms,* SBT, 2d series, no. 32 (Naperville, Illinois: Alec R. Allenson Inc., 1975), pp. 1-20, summarizes the debate. In what follows I have drawn from him.

[62]Ibid., p. 3.

[63]Ibid., p. 6.

[64]Aubrey R. Johnson, *Sacral Kingship in Ancient Israel,* 2d ed. (Cardiff: University of Wales Press, 1967).

[65]Eaton, *Kingship and the Psalms,* pp. 12-13.

[66]Aage Bentzen, *King and Messiah,* ed. C. W. Anderson, 2d ed. (Oxford: Basil Blackwell, 1970); Ivan Engnell, "The Book

of Psalms," in *Critical Essays on the Old Testament*, trans. &
ed. John T. Willis (London: SPCK, 1970), pp. 68-122; Helmer
Ringgren, *The Messiah in the Old Testament*, SBT (Chicago: Alec
R. Allenson, 1956).

[67] John Gray, *The Biblical Doctrine of the Reign of God*
(Edinburgh: T & T Clark, 1979).

[68] Eaton, *Kingship and the Psalms*, p. 73.

[69] Lothar Ruppert, *Jesus als der leidende Gerechte? Der
Weg Jesu im Lichte eines alt- und zwischentestamentlichen Mo-
tivs*, *SB*, Bd. 59 (Stuttgart: Verlag Katholisches Bibelwerk,
1972), pp. 32-36.

[70] Eaton, *Kingship and the Psalms*, p. 73.

[71] J. A. Sanders, *The Dead Sea Psalms Scroll*, (Ithaca: Cornell University Press, 1967), p. 13.

[72] Ibid., p. 97.   Moreover, the superscription to the Greek
of Ps. 151 reads, "This psalm, though supernumerary, is truly
written by David when he single-handedly fought Goliath."

[73] Hermann Gunkel, *Die Psalmen*, 5 Aufl. (Göttingen: Vandenhoeck & Ruprecht, 1968), p. 505.

[74] Ibid., p. 506.   Gunkel recognizes the royal imagery here
but does not accept it.

[75] Eaton, *Kingship and the Psalms*, p. 62; Hans-Joachim Kraus,
Psalmen, BKAT, Bd. 15, Teilband 1-2:   *Psalmen*; Teilband 3:
Theologie der Psalmen; 3 Teilband (Neukirchen-Vluyn: Neukirchener Verlag, 1960-1979), T. 2: 803, does not support the royal
interpretation of Ps. 118 but recognizes the problem raised by
H. Schmidt.   "Wie ist es möglich, dass das Danklied eines ein-
zelnen in die Liturgie der einziehenden Gemeinde hineinverankert
ist?   Es is ja doch sehr merkwürdig, dass ein grosses und feier-
liches Aufgebot als Rahmen das individuelle Danklied umgibt."

[76] Matthew Black, "The Christological Use of the Old Testament in the New Testament," *NTS* 18 (1971), p. 12.

[77] Ibid., p. 12; *TDNT*, s.v. *"lithos,"* by Joachim Jeremias,
4:260; Hermann L. Strack und Paul Billerbeck, *Kommentar zum
Neuen Testament aus Talmud und Midrasch*, 4 Bde. (Munich: C. H.
Beck'sche Verlagsbuchhandlung, 1922-56), 1:876.

[78] Strack & Billerbeck, *Kommentar zum Neuen Testament aus
Talmud und Midrasch*, 1:876.   In the dialogue I have used the
RSV translation of Ps. 118:23-29 in order to show how the targum
distributes verses among different characters.   Except for the
manner in which the targum distributes various verses, there is
general agreement between it and the MT at this point.   The
point of my argument is the Davidic (and to that extent royal)
interpretation of the psalm.

[79]*The Midrash on Psalms*, 2: Ps. 118, par. 21.

[80]J. Duncan M. Derrett, "The Stone that the Builders Rejected," in *Studies in the New Testament*, vol. 1: *Midrash in Action and as a Literary Device;* vol. 2: *Glimpses of the Legal and Social Presuppositions of the Authors;* 2 vols. (Leiden: E. J. Brill, 1977-1978), 2:   64-65.

[81]John Gray, *The Biblical Doctrine of the Reign of God*, p. 102, writes: "This of course might refer figuratively to Israel, but the use of *pinnōt* of 'chief men' in Judg. 20:1, I Sam. 14:38 and Isa. 19:13 indicates that it had a more personal reference, which we consider more appropriate to the King." So, Artur Weiser, *The Psalms*, trans. Herbert Hartwell, 5th rev. ed., The Old Testament Library (Philadelphia: The Westminster Press, 1962), p. 728, when he writes: "They express what has happened to the king, in the now famous parable of the stone which, rejected by the builders, has become the chief cornerstone."   Lindars, *New Testament Apologetic*, pp. 169-70, cautiously offers a similar royal interpretation of Ps. 118:22. Also, supporting a royal interpretation of the verse: Derrett, "The Stone that the Builders Rejected," p. 65; Hubaut, *La parabole des vignerons homicides*, p. 62; Johnson, *Sacral Kingship in Ancient Israel*, p. 123, who calls this psalm an obvious companion piece to Ps. 18 which speaks of a suffering David.

[82]Hubaut, *La parabole des vignerons homicides*, p. 63.

[83]A review of the literature from K. L. Schmidt to approximately 1972 can be found in Schneider, "Die Davidssohnfrage (Mk 12,35-37)."   Important contributions since then include: Achtemeier, "'And He Followed Him' Miracles and Discipleship in Mark 10:46-52"; Berger, "Die königlichen Messiastraditionen des Neuen Testament"; and"Zum Problem der Messianität Jesu"; Dennis C. Duling, "The Promises to David and their Entrance into Christianity - Nailing Down a Likely Hypotheses," *NTS* 68 (1973): 55-77; and "Solomon, Exorcism, and the Son of David," *HTR* 68 (1975): 235-52; Gnilka, *Mark*, pp. 168-72; Evald Lövestam, "Jésus Fils de David chez les Synoptiques," *ST* 28 (1974): 97-109; Neugebauer, "Die Davidssohnfrage (Mark XII 35-37 Parr.) und der Menschensohn"; Pesch, *Mark*, pp. 249-57; Kelber, *The Kingdom in Mark*, pp. 92-107.

[84]The majority of scholars tend to accept this position.

[85]Achtemeier, "'And He Followed Him' Miracles and Discipleship in Mark 10:46-52," p. 130; Kelber, *The Kingdom in Mark*, pp. 95-6; Alfred Suhl, *Die Funktion der alttestamentlichen Zitate und Anspielungen im Markusevangelium* (Gerd Mohn: Gütersloher Verlagshaus, 1965), p. 91

[86]Daube, *The New Testament and Rabbinic Judaism*, pp. 158-69, for a different view.

[87]Pesch, *Mark*, p. 250.

[88]Taylor, *Mark*, p. 491.

[89]Neugebauer, "Die Davidssohnfrage (Mark XII 35-37 Parr.) und der Menschensohn," p. 89, writes: "Er hört im Geist, was Gott, der Herr, zu seinem Herrn spricht, und damit ist dieser Herr ein Herr in den unmittelbaren Nähe Gottes, der sich an Gottes rechte Seite setzt . . ."; Pesch, *Mark*, p. 253.

[90]Achtemeier, "'And He Followed Them' Miracles and Discipleship in Mark 10:46-52," pp. 128-30; Nineham, *Mark*, p. 330.

[91]Ferdinand Hahn, *The Titles of Jesus in Christology: Their History in Early Christianity*, trans. Harold Knight and George Ogg (New York: The World Publishing Co., 1969), pp. 252-53; but Achtemeier, "'And He Followed them' Miracles and Discipleship in Mark 10:46-52," p. 129, argues against this.

[92]Daube, *The New Testament and Rabbinic Judaism*, p. 163.

[93]The debate surrounding the interpretation of this response is summarized in the positions of Donahue, *Are You the Christ?*, pp. 139-187, and Juel, *Messiah and Temple*, pp. 77-107. The former sees the Son of Man saying as qualifying and correcting the messianic title while the latter interprets it in terms of Jesus' future vindication.

[94]David M. Hay, *Glory at the Right Hand: Psalm 110 in Early Christianity*, SBL Monograph Series, no. 18 (Nashville: Abingdon Press, 1973), pp. 113-14.

[95]We shall develop this point in the next chapter.

[96]Lucien Cerfaux, "Le titre et la dignité royale de Jésus," in *Recueil Lucien Cerfaux: Études d'exégèse et d'histoire religieuse réunies à l'occasion de son soixante-dixième anniversaire*, BETL, vol. 6-7 (Gembloux: Éditions J. Duculot, 1954), pp. 40-42; Joseph A. Fitzmyer, "The Semitic Background of the New Testament *Kyrios*-title," in *A Wandering Aramean: Collected Aramaic Essays*, SBL Monograph Series, no. 25 (Missoula, Montana: Scholars Press, 1979), p. 131.

[97]Cerfaux, "Le titre *Kyrios* et la dignité royale de Jésus," in *Recueil Lucien Cerfaux*, p. 9.

[98]Cerfaux, "Le titre et la dignité royale de Jésus," p. 36.

[99]*Psalmoi Solomōntos. Psalms of the Pharisees, Commonly Called The Psalms of Solomon. The Text Newly Revised from all the Mss.* ed., with Introduction, English Translation, Notes, Appendix, and Indices, Herbert Edward Ryle and Montague Rhodes James (Cambridge: Cambridge University Press, 1891). All quotations of the Psalms of Solomon have been taken from this edition.

[100]Ibid., Ryle and James note that *Christou Kyriou* may be translated either as "the Lord's Messiah" or as "Lord Messiah." They give arguments pro and con on pages 141-43.

[101]Schneider, "Die Davidssohnfrage (Mk 12, 35-37)," pp. 87-90.

[102]Gaston, *No Stone on Another*, pp. 81-88, 112-19; C. K. Barrett, "The House of Prayer and the Den of Thieves," in *Jesus und Paulus: Festschrift für Werner Georg Kümmel zum 70. Geburtstag* (Göttingen: Vandenhoeck & Ruprecht, 1975), p. 14. For an opposing view see Richard H. Hiers, "Purification of the Temple: Preparation for the Kingdom of God," *JBL* 90 (1971): 82-90.

[103]Gaston, *No Stone on Another*, p. 117.

[104]Schneider, "Die Davidssohnfrage (Mk 12, 35-37)," p. 88.

[105]Lightfoot, *The Gospel Message of St. Mark*, p. 63.

[106]Heinz Giesen, "Der verdorte Feigenbaum - Eine symbolische Aussage? Zum Mk 11,12-24:20f.," *BZ* 20 (1976): 110.

[107]The hiatus between 11:16 and 11:17 shows that Jesus is condemned for his teaching more than for his activity in the temple. Also, note that in 11:18 the leaders react to what they "hear," not to what they "see."

[108]Peddinghaus, "Die Entstehung der Leidensgeschichte," pp. 161-62, points out that these are the only two instances where the word is used in Mark. He sees the usage in both cases as favorable.

[109]The full verse applies to Jerusalem, but may have the temple in mind.

[1]Ruppert, *Jesus als der leidende Gerechte?*, p. 56. Rudolf Pesch, "Die Passion des Menschensohnes: Eine Studie zu den Menschensohnworten der vormarkinischen Passionsgeschichte," in *Jesus und der Menschensohn*, ed. Rudolf Pesch, und Rudolf Schnackenburg in zusammenarbeit mit Odilo Kaiser (Freiburg: Herder, 1975), p. 195.

[2]Joachim Jeremias, *New Testament Theology: The Proclamation of Jesus*, trans. John Bowden (New York: Charles Scribner's Sons, 1971), p. 277, writes: " . . . there can be no doubt that this passion prediction is a summary of the passion formulated after the event." Lohse, *History of the Suffering and Death of Jesus Christ*, p. 16, says that it " . . . presupposes a brief account of the passion." Nineham, *Mark*, p. 278, notes: "It has been described as 'reading like a printed programme of a Passion Play' and the six stages on the way to the Cross are clearly defined."

[3]The following authors see the prediction as influencing the passion narrative, especially Mk 15:15-20a: Frederick Houk Borsh, *The Son of Man in Myth and History* (Philadelphia: The Westminster Press, 1967); Ray McKinnis, "An Analysis of Mark X 32-34," *NovT* 18 (1976): 81-100. H. E. Tödt, *The Son of Man in the Synoptic Tradition*, trans. Dorothea M. Barton (Philadelphia: The Westminster Press, 1965). Authors who argue that the prediction draws its language from the passion narrative include: Hahn, *The Titles of Jesus in Christology*; Minette de Tillesse, *Le secret messianique dans L'Evangile de Marc*; Walter Schmithals, "Die Worte vom leidenden Menschensohn: Eine Schlüssel zur Lösung des Menschensohn-Problems," in *Theologia Crucis-Signum Crucis: Festschrift für Erich Dinkler zum 70. Geburtstag*, ed. Carl Andresen und Gunter Klein (Tübingen: J. C. B. Mohr [Paul Siebeck], 1979), pp. 418-445.

[4]Besides the works listed in note three, see: Norman Perrin, "Towards an Interpretation of the Gospel of Mark," in *Christology and a Modern Pilgrimage: A Discussion with Norman Perrin*, ed. Hans Dieter Betz, rev. ed. (Missoula, Montana: Scholars Press, 1974), pp. 10-21; Pesch, "Die Passion des Menschensohnes"; George Strecker, "The Passion- and Resurrection Predictions in Mark's Gospel (Mark 8:31, 9:31, 10:33-34)," *Int* 22 (1968): 421-42.

[5]Strecker, "The Passion- and Resurrection Predictions in Mark's Gospel," p. 19.

[6]Minette de Tillesse, *Le secret messianique dans L'Évangile de Marc*," pp. 378-79.

[7]Perrin, "Towards an Interpretation of the Gospel of Mark," p. 19.

[8]Schenke, *Studien zur Passionsgeschichte des Markus*, pp. 249-60.

[9]Hahn, *The Titles of Jesus in Christology*, p. 37.

[10]Matthew employs "crucify" in 20:19 but not in 16:21 or 17:23.

[11]*Anistēmi* can be used transitively (future and first aorist active), or intransitively (second aorist all middle forms). In the former case it has the same meaning as *egeirō*, in the latter it is distinctive and emphasizes the power of the Son of Man to raise himself (8:31; 9:31; 10:34). Perrin, "Towards an Interpretation of the Gospel of Mark," p. 18, thinks that Mark chose the verb because it blends together " . . . emphases upon both suffering and power."

[12]Matthew and Luke consistently change the expression to *tē tritē hēmera* (Mt. 16:21/Lk. 9:22; Mt. 17:23; Mt. 20:19/Lk. 18:33). However, we do not agree with Perrin, "Towards an Interpretation of the Gospel of Mark," p. 19, that it " . . . has to be assumed that 'after three days' is distinctively Markan." The redactor may simply be reproducing traditional language at this point which Matthew and Luke have altered.

[13]McKinnis, "An Analysis of Mark X 32-34," p. 94; *A Greek English Lexicon of the New Testament and other early Christian Literature*, sv. *mastigoō*.

[14]*A Greek English Lexicon of the New Testament and other early Christian Literature*, s.v. *phragelloō*.

[15]Hahn, *The Titles of Jesus in Christology*, p. 37, claims that Mark arranged the prediction so as to reach a climax in the act of killing, thus the difference in the order of events. Schmithals, "Die Worte vom leidenden Menschensohn," p. 420, writes that only "sklavischen Angängigkeit" would have made Mark conform the prediction to the passion in perfect order.

[16]Generally, we agree with Perrin, "Towards an Interpretation of the Gospel of Mark," p. 19, that " . . . the predictions are Markan literary productions, the individual parts being mined from early Christian tradition, especially the church's passion apologetic, but the predictions as a whole being Markan," cf. *TDNT*, s.v. *ho uios tou anthropou*, by Colpe, 8:444-45.

[17]McKinnis, "An Analysis of Mark X 32-34," p. 92; Tödt, *The Son of Man in the Synoptic Tradition*, p. 175.

[18]Schenke, *Der gekreuzigte Christus*, pp. 47-51.

[19]Donahue, *Are You the Christ?*, p. 96; McKinnis, "An Analysis of Mark X 32-34," p. 91.

[20]Ruppert, *Jesus als der leidende Gerechte?*, p. 52, does see some references to the psalms of the Suffering Just One in 15:16-20.

[21]Paul J. Achtemeier, "Mark as Interpreter of the Jesus Traditions," *Int* 32 (1978): 341-42, studies Mark's use of the Baptist traditions.

[22]Anderson, *Mark*, p. 166, writes: "Mark's narrative is a carefully constructed product which almost surely came to him in written form." So, Gnilka, *Mark*, p. 245; Lohmeyer, *Mark*, pp. 117-18; Pesch, *Mark*, p. 337.

[23]There are helpful surveys of the Son-of-Man literature in I. H. Marshall, "The Synoptic Son of Man Sayings in Recent Discussion," *NTS* 12 (1966): 327-51; and "The Son of Man in Contemporary Debate," *EvQ* 42 (1970): 67-87; for the linguistic background to the discussion see *TDNT*, s.v. *ho huios tou anthropou*, by Colpe, 8:401-45; Joseph A. Fitzmyer, "The New Testament Title "Son of Man' Philologically Considered," in *A Wandering Aramean*, pp. 143-161; Geza Vermes, "The Use of בר נשא / בר נש in Jewish Aramaic," in *An Aramaic Approach to the Gospels and Acts*, Matthew Black, 3rd ed. (Oxford: Clarendon Press, 1967), pp. 310-30; and *Jesus the Jew: A Historian's Reading of the Gospels* (London: Collins, 1973), pp. 160-90; concerning the apocalyptic nature of the Son of Man see Ragnar Leivestad, "Exit the Apocalyptic Son of Man," *NTS* (1972): 243-67; Barnabas Lindars, "Re-enter the Apocalyptic Son of Man," *NTS* (1976): 52-72.

[24]Robert Maddox, "The Function of the Son of Man according to the Synoptic Gospels," *NTS* 15 (1968): 45-74, recognizes the need for this type of study. Donahue, *Are You the Christ?*, pp. 162-87, has done this for the sayings of the coming Son of Man; Morna Hooker, *The Son of Man in Mark: A Study of the Background of the Term "Son of Man" and Its Use in St. Mark's Gospel* (London: SPCK, 1967), pp. 174-98, views the sayings as a redactional unity.

[25]Rudolf Bultmann, *Theology of the New Testament*, trans. Kendrick Grobel, 2 vols. (New York: Charles Scribner's Sons, 1951), 1:30.

[26]Bultmann sees the future sayings as most likely to be authentic. Eduard Schweizer, "The Son of Man," *JBL* 79 (1960): 119-29, reverses this position and claims that the sayings of the suffering Son of Man are most likely to be authentic.

[27]Bultmann, *Theology of the New Testament*, 1:29; A. J. B. Higgens, *Jesus and the Son of Man*, (Philadelphia: Fortress Press, 1964), p. 199; Schmithals, "Die Worte vom leidenden Menschensohn," pp. 435-37.

[28]*TDNT*, s.v. *ho huios tou anthropou*, by Colpe, 8: 441.

[29]Andre Feuillet, "L'exousia du Fils de l'homme (d'après Mc. 11,10-28 et parr)," *RSR* (1954): 174-75.

[30]Hooker, *The Son of Man*, pp. 174-78, points to this tendency in Cranfield's commentary; cf. *TWNT*, s.v. *ho huios tou theou*, 8: 453-54.

[31]Hooker, *The Son of Man*, pp. 178-79; Tödt, *The Son of Man in the Synoptic Tradition*, p. 131.

[32]In 2:10 certain witnesses (P[28]א C D L Δ) tried to emphasize the exalted nature of the Son of Man by arranging the word order to read *ho huios tou anthrōpou epi tēs gēs*. This seems to imply a parallel with the Son of Man in heaven.

[33]Minette de Tillesse, *Le secret messianique dans L'Évangile de Marc*, pp. 367-68, writes: "Ces deux mentions de Fils de l'homme sont donc une anticipation ou une 'rétro-projection,' question de point de vue- de la gloire de Pâques."

[34]Schweizer, *Mark*, p. 74; Taylor, *Mark*, p. 220. The verse should be read in light of 11:18; 12:12.

[35]There are no sayings about the suffering Son of Man in the Q material.

[36]Perrin, "Towards an Interpretation of the Gospel of Mark," p. 6.

[37]Schmithals, "Die Worte vom leidenden Menchensohn," p. 429.

[38]There is not a consensus on the background of 10:45. C. K. Barrett, "The Background of Mk. 10:45," in *New Testament Essays*, ed. A. J. B. Higgens (Manchester: Manchester University Press, 1959), pp. 1-18; and Morna Hooker, *Jesus the Servant*, reject Isa. 53 as the background. However, Karl Kertelge, "Der dienende Menschensohn (Mk. 10,45)," in *Jesus und der Menschensohn*, pp. 225-39; Gnilka, *Mark*, p. 104; and W. J. Moulder, "The Old Testament Background and the Interpretation of Mark 10:45," *NTS* (1977): 120-27, accept it.

[39]Minette de Tillesse, *Le secret messianique dans L'Évangile de Marc*, p. 370.

[40]Donahue, *Are You the Christ?*, pp. 149-77.

[41]Ibid., p. 152.

[42]Hahn, *The Titles of Jesus in Christology*, p. 33; Pesch, *Naherwartungen*, pp. 157-72. Below we shall address the question in detail.

[43]James Luther Mays, "Mark 8:27-9:1," *Int* 30 (1976): 176.

[44]Rudolf Schnackenburg, *God's Rule and Kingdom*, trans. John Murray (New York: Herder & Herder, 1968), p. 168.

[45]In the previous section we drew the insight that "authority" joins the Son-of-Man sayings in Mark from Hooker, *The Son of Man in Mark*. In this section we disagree with her that the source of that authority is rooted in the Son of Man of Daniel. Rather, we feel that the source of Jesus' authority is his divine sonship.

[46]Paul J. Achtemeier, *Mark*, p. 62; and "He Taught Them Many Things: Reflections on Marcan Christology," *CBQ* 42 (1980): 478-79.

[47]Best, *The Temptation and the Passion*, p. 168.

[48]Herman Hendrickx, *The Passion Narratives of the Synoptic Gospels* (Manila, Philippines: East Asian Pastoral Institute, 1977), p. 28.

[49]Authors who interpret the saints of the Most High as referring to the faithful men and women of Israel are: Louis F. Hartman and Alexander DiLella, *The Book of Daniel: A New Translation with Notes and Commentary on Chapters 1-9 by Louis F. Hartman, C.SS.R. Introduction, and Commentary on Chapters 10-12 by Alexander A. DiLella, O.F.M.* The Anchor Bible, vol. 23 (Garden City, New York: Doubleday & Co., 1978), p. 95; Norman W. Porteous, *Daniel: A Commentary*, Old Testament Library (London: SCM Press, 1965), p. 112; Hooker, *The Son of Man in Mark*, p. 28; Vermes, *Jesus the Jew*, p. 170. Authors who view the saints of the Most High as representing the angelic hosts or its leader, Michael, are: John J. Collins, "The Son of Man and the Saints of the Most High in the Book of Daniel," *JBL* 93 (1974): 61; and *TDNT*, s.v. *ho huios tou anthropou*, by Colpe, 8: 421.

[50]The translation is according to Hartmann and DiLella.

[51]The MT reads מלכין (kings) while the LXX and Theodotian read *basileiai* (kingdoms). The RSV translates it as "kings." Hartmann and DiLella, *The Book of Daniel*, p. 204, translate as "kingdoms." They note that it should probably be vocalized as *molkin* (kingdoms). The MT's *malkin* would ordinarily mean "kings."

[52]Collins, "The Son of Man and the Saints of the Most High in the Book of Daniel," p. 63.

[53]Lars Hartmann, *Prophecy Interpreted: The Formation of Some Jewish Apocalyptic Texts and of the Eschatological Discourse Mark 13 Par.*, trans. Neil Tomkinson with the assistance of Jean Gray, *ConBNT*, no. 1 (Lund, Sweden: CWK Gleerup, 1966), p. 157.

[54]LXX 7:13   *epi tōn nephelōn*
    Theodotian 7:13   *meta tōn nephelōn*
    MT 7:13   *ᶜim ᶜănānê šĕmayyāᵓ*
    Mk. 13:26   *en nephelais*
    Mk. 14:62   *meta tōn nephelōn tou ouranou*

[55]*TDNT*, s.v. *ho huios tou anthropou*, by Colpe, 8: 453.

[56]Donahue, *Are You the Christ?*, p. 182, reviews the debate and concludes that the reference " . . . seems resolved in favor of a parousia expectation, but not in an exclusive sense. For Mark, Jesus is the exalted one who will return." Hahn, *The Titles of Jesus in Christology*, p. 132, says that " . . . the moment of enthronement at the right hand was applied at first

to Jesus' return and his work as Consummator." But W. R. G.
Loader, "Christ at the Right Hand - Ps CXI in the New Testament,"
NTS 24 (1978): 200, contends that
> . . . the saying does not imply the enthronement at
> the time of the parousia, as Hahn suggests. . . . We
> have to reckon with imminent expectation of the par-
> ousia at the earliest stage, so that the focus is not
> on an interim period following enthronement, but on the
> imminence of his rule as the enthroned one.

Hay, *Glory at the Right Hand,* p. 66, also disagrees with Hahn.

[57]Tödt, *The Son of Man in the Synoptic Tradition,* p. 38.
In an effort to avoid the difficulty D eliminates *kai erchomenon.*

[58]Hooker, *The Son of Man in Mark,* pp. 168, says that the
most natural way of interpreting 14:62 is " . . . to understand
it as indicating the approach of the Son of man to God for
judgment and vindication." Certainly this is the meaning in
Daniel; but in Mark the Son of Man is seated "at the right hand"
indicating that the enthronement has already taken place.

[59]Hay, *Glory at the Right Hand,* p. 65.

[60]Eaton, *Kingship and the Psalms,* p. 124; Weiser, *The
Psalms,* p. 693.

[61]Loader, "Christ at the Right Hand," p. 199.

[62]Hay, *Glory at the Right Hand,* p. 28.

[63]Strack & Billerbeck, *Kommentar zum Neuen Testament aus
Talmud und Midrasch,* Bd. 4, T. 1, p. 454.

[64]Ibid., pp. 458-60; Hay, *Glory at the Right Hand,* p. 30;
Loader, "Christ at the Right Hand," p. 199.

[65]Explicit imagery of the Son of Man as a kingly figure
can be found in Mt. 25:34 (cf. 25:31), and Rev. 14:14.

[66]Pesch, *Naherwartungen,* pp. 166-72, the arguments listed
below are drawn from this section of his work.

[67]Jan Lambrecht, *Die Redaction der Markus-Apokalypse:
Literarische Analyse und Structuruntersuchung,* AnBib, Bd. 28
(Rome: Päpstliches Bibelinstitut, 1967), p. 185.

[68]Achtemeier, *Mark,* p. 103.

[69]Pesch, *Naherwartungen,* p. 168.

[70]Daniel J. Harrington, "Research on the Jewish Pseudepigrapha During the 1970s," *CBQ* 42 (1980): 152.

[71]Hartmann, *Prophecy Interpreted,* p. 157, notes that a
judgment is explicitly mentioned only in the extended form of
the discourse, in Mt. 25:31ff. Lohmeyer, *Mark,* p. 279, says
that 13:26 seems to presuppose that the judgment has already

occurred, otherwise how does one explain that the Son of Man
has come to gather his elect. Siegfried Schulz, "Die Bedeutung
des Markus für die Theologiegeschichte des Urchristentums," in
Das Markus-Evangelium, ed. Rudolf Pesch, Wege der Forschung,
Bd. 411 (Darmstadt: Wissenschaftliche Buchgesellschaft, 1979),
p. 161, says that chapter 13 knows no judgment, only the gathering of the elect; the judgment takes place on the cross.

[72]Hay, *Glory at the Right Hand*, pp. 21-22, points to this
usage. In what follows we are using *The Testament of Job: According to the SV Text*, Greek text and English trans. ed. by
Robert A. Kraft, *et al.*, Texts and Translations no. 5, Pseudepigrapha Series no. 4 (Missoula, Montana: Scholars Press, 1974).
Kraft gives an annotated bibliography (pp. 17-20) in which he
lists opinions concerning the date and origin of *The Testament
of Job*.

[73]Parentheses indicate that the enclosed material is absent
from S but supplied from another source. S equals Messina, one
of four Greek manuscripts of *The Testament of Job*.

[74]C. H. Dodd, *According to the Scriptures: The Sub-structure of New Testament Theology* (New York: Charles Scribner's
Sons, 1953), pp. 101-02.

[75]It is not entirely correct to claim that there is no
other reference to Ps. 80 in the NT. The imagery of the vineyard, found in this psalm, may be at the origin of Mk. 12:1.
LXX Ps. 79:9 speaks of an *ampelon* which the Lord planted (*ephy-
teusen*, cf. Mk. 12:1). Indeed, the imagery of the psalm fits
the parable better than does the imagery of Isa. 5. In Isa. 5
the vineyard is blamed for not producing fruit while in Ps. 80
the vineyard is abused.

[76]Brian McNeil, "The Son of Man and the Messiah," *NTS* 26
(1980): 419-21.

[77]Levey, *The Messiah: An Aramaic Interpretation*, p. 119.

[78]*TDNT*, s.v. *ho huios tou anthropou*, by Colpe, 8: 407.

[79]A. Gelston, "A Sidelight on the Son of Man," *SJT* 22
(1969): 196.

[80]David Hill, "'Son of Man' in Psalm 80 v.17," *NovT* 15
(1973): 266.

[81]Ibid., p. 268.

[82]Kraus, *Psalmen*: 1:559 writes:
Verbunden mit der Bitte um Überwindung der Feinde ist
eine Fürbitte für den König. אִישׁ יְמִינֶךָ (18) ist keine
"Anspielung auf Benjamin" (so H Gunkel), sondern ein
Gedenken an den König der zur Rechten Jahwes sitz
(vgl. Ps 110:1). . . . Hier klingt eine Bezeichnung
an, die in Dn 7:13ff. den ihr zugehörigen Vorstellungs-
komplex hervortreten lässt.

In a similar vein Hartmann & DiLella, *The Book of Daniel*, pp.
98-99, write:
> The author of Daniel 7 also had at hand Ps 80:18-20 which
> describes the plea of oppressed Israel for deliver-
> ance and restoration: . . . It is probable that Daniel
> 7:13 was composed in the light of Ps 80 because the
> distress of Israel in the psalm is similar to the
> plight of the Jews in Daniel.

And C. H. Dodd, *According to the Scriptures*, p. 117, says:
"There is a clear analogy with the 'Son of Man' of Ps. lxxx
and Dan. vii, which speaks of Israel, under the similitude
of a human figure, humiliated into insignificance until visited
by God and raised to glory."

[83] We are not advocating the Royal Man concept defended by
Bentzen, Borsch and others.

[84] Gnilka, *Mark*, p. 271; Pesch, *Mark*, p. 79; Schenke, *Stu-
dien zur Passionsgeschichte des Markus*, p. 262. But Suhl, *Die
Funktion der alttestamentlichen Zitate und Anspielungen im
Markusevangelium*, p. 42, suggests that it may refer to 14:27.
There Jesus prophesied that the disciples would be scattered.
Here, because Jesus accepts arrest, they are scattered.

[85] *A Greek-English Lexicon of the New Testament and Other
Early Christian Literature*, s.v. *hypagō*, says " . . . it is
rather a euphemism for death *the Son of Man is to go away* = he
must die."

[86] Suhl, *Die Funktion der alttestamentlichen Zitate und
Anspielungen im Markusevangelium*, p. 52, sees it only as a
secondary reference; Schenke, *Studien zur Passionsgeschichte
des Markus*, p. 211, does not see it as a clear reference; Ellen
Flesseman-van Leer, "Die Interpretation der Passionsgeschichte
vom Alten Testament aus," in *Zur Bedeutung des Todes Jesu:
Exegetische Beiträge*, ed. Fritz Viering (Gerd Mohn: Gütersloher
Verlaghaus, 1967), p. 83, however, does see it as a conscious
reference by the evangelist.

[87] Tödt, *The Son of Man in the Synoptic Tradition*, pp. 168-
69.

[88] Hahn, *The Titles of Jesus in Christology*, p. 40, writes:
"Now the *dei* must be regarded as a typically Hellenic transcrip-
tion of *gegraptai*."

[89] W. J. Bennett, Jr., "The Son of Man Must . . . ," *NovT*
17 (1975): 113-29, opposes Tödt's view.

[90] Ibid., p. 118.

[91] Gnilka, *Mark*, p. 16, recognizes the importance of Bennett's contribution but writes: "Die Anspeilung auf Ps. 118,22
aber legt es näher, die Notwendigkeit mit dem in der Schrift
verfügten Gotteswillen zusammenzubringen."

[92] Perrin, "Towards an Interpretation of the Gospel of
Mark," p. 17; Pesch, *Mark*, p. 79.

[93] Suhl, *Die Funktion der alttestamentlichen Zitate und Anspielungen im Markusevangelium*, p. 62.

[94] Schenke, *Studien zur Passionsgeschichte des Markus*, p. 384.

[95] Ibid., p. 383, points out that the reference to Zech. 13:7 does not refer to a known version.

[96] Pesch, *Mark*, p. 380.

[97] Jeremias, *New Testament Theology*, p. 282.

NOTES - CHAPTER VII

[1]Schreiber, *Theologie des Vertrauens*, pp. 48-9.

[2]Harmut Gese, "Psalm 22 und das Neue Testament: Der älteste Bericht vom Tode Jesu und die Entstehung des Herrenmahles," *ZTK* 65 (1968): 15; Linnemann, *Studien zur Passionsgeschichte*, pp. 149-51. Also, Grundmann, *Mark*, pp. 315-16; Lohmeyer, *Mark*, p. 356.

[3]Cranfield, *Mark*, p. 458; Joachim Gnilka, "Mein Gott, mein Gott, warum hast du mich verlassen (Mk 15,34 par)," *BZ* 3 (1959): 294-97; Taylor, *Mark*, p. 593.

[4]A. Guillaume, "Mt XXVII,46 in the Light of the Dead Sea Scroll of Isaiah," *PEQ* 83 (1951): 78-80.

[5]M. Rehn, "Eli, Eli lamma sabacthani," *BZ* n.F. 2 (1958): 275-78.

[6]Xavier Léon-Dufour, "Le dernier cri de Jésus," *Et* 348 (1978): 667-68; Harald Sahlin, "Zum Verständnis der christologischen Anschauung des Markusevangeliums," *ST* 31 (1977): 4.

[7]Luke has broken up the incident and taken only the reference to the sour wine. Moreover, he places it in a new setting which is also one of mockery (23:35-37). This alone throws doubt on the historical order of the events as recorded by Mark.

[8]Linnemann, *Studien zur Passionsgeschichte*, p. 151.

[9]Schreiber, *Theologie des Vertrauens*, p. 49.

[10]Linnemann, *Studien zur Passionsgeschichte*, p. 151.

[11]Martinez, *The Gospel Accounts of the Death of Jesus*, p. 44.

[12]Taylor, *Mark*, p. 595; Martinez, *The Gospel Accounts of the Death of Jesus*, p. 55.

[13]Peddinghaus, "Die Entstehung der Leidensgeschichte," p. 123, says that the entire section was built around Ps. 22 and that there is no reference to Ps. 69 here. While the incident may not have been inspired by the psalm, we suspect that the presence of *ochous* certainly drew attention to the psalm and the situation of mockery therein.

[14]*TDNT*, s.v. *Ēl(e)ias*, by Jeremias, 2:935; Strack & Billerbeck, *Kommentar zum Neuen Testament aus Talmud und Midrasch*, Bd. 4, T. 1, p. 770, for the tradition that Elijah comes to the aid of the just man.

[15]Martinez, *The Gospel Accounts of the Death of Jesus*, p. 43.

[16]Frederick Danker, "The Demonic Secret in Mark: A Reexamination of the Cry of Dereliction (15:34)," *ZNW* 61 (1970): 60, observes:

>   In view of the connection Mark makes between Jesus'
>   death and the Baptist's fate, the mockery about Elijah
>   finds still further clarification. Elijah cannot in
>   fact rescue Jesus, for John is Elijah and has already
>   come. What happened to his predecessor must also be
>   Jesus' own fate.

cf. Paul Lamarche, "La Mort du Christ et le voile du temple: Selon Marc," *NRT* 96 (1974): 592-93.

[17]Bultmann, *The History of the Synoptic Tradition*, p. 273.

[18]Cranfield, *Mark*, p. 458.

[19]See ch. 2, p. 30.

[20]Neirynck, *Duality in Mark*, p. 46.

[21]Martinez, *The Gospel Accounts of the Death of Jesus*, p. 39, argues for two cries. He writes:

>   However, the context that Mk leaves us can hardly
>   support such an interpretation. Mt has interpreted
>   Mk correctly by adding "again." The reason is that
>   the persons involved in the intervening incident of
>   the sour wine treat Jesus as still alive and do not
>   think he died immediately after the first shout as
>   supposed by the interpretation that there was only
>   one cry.

At this point Martinez seems to read the account as an historical report. Mark, however, is more intent on the theological meaning of the events. That is, the bystanders and the centurion stand on different sides of Jesus' death. It is this difference in perspective which leads to different reactions to the one cry.

[22]Senior, *The Passion Narrative According to Matthew*, p. 173, n. 4; p. 304.

[23]Ibid., p. 304.

[24]Ibid., p. 305.

[25]Kraus, *Psalmen*, 1: 176.

[26]Ibid., p. 183, attributes this to the Jerusalem cult tradition. Gese, "Psalm 22 und das Neue Testament," p. 13, sees these verses as a unity within the psalm.

[27]Hans Heinrich Schmid, "'Mein Gott, mein Gott, warum hast du mich verlassen?' Psalm 22 als Beispiel alttestamentlicher Rede von Krankheit und Tod." in *Wort und Dienst: Jahrbuch der kirchlichen Hochschule Bethel*, ed. Hans Heinrich Schmid, n.F., Bd. 11 (Bethel bei Bielefeld: Verlagshandlung der Anstatt Bethel, 1972), p. 124.

[28]Gese, "Psalm 22 in das Neue Testament," p. 10.

[29]Eaton, *Kingship and the Psalms*, p. 34.

[30]Gese, "Psalm 22 in das Neue Testament," p. 7.

[31]Julius Oswald, "Die Beziehungen-zwischen Psalm 22 und dem vormarkinischen Passionsbericht," *ZKT* 101 (1979): 53-66; Peddinghaus, "Die Entstehung der Leidensgeschichte," pp. 147-150.

[32]Peddinghaus, "Die Entstehung der Leidensgeschichte," p. 142.

[33]Ibid., p. 150.

[34]Oswald, "Die Beziehungen zwischen Psalm 22 und dem vormarkinischen Passionsbericht," p. 56.

[35]Ibid., p. 58.

[36]Kraus, *Theologie der Psalmen*, 15/3:238-41, discusses the use of the psalm in the NT: John H. Reumann, "Psalm 22 at the Cross, Lament and Thanksgiving for Jesus Christ," *Int* 28 (1974): 41-42, supplies a helpful chart of the quotations, allusions and influences of the psalm in and upon the NT.

[37]F. F. Bruce, *The Epistle to the Hebrews: The English Text with Introduction, Exposition and Notes*, NICNT (Grand Rapids: Wm. B. Eerdmans Publishing Co., 1964), pp. 46-47.

[38]Peddinghaus, "Die Entstehung der Leidensgeschichte," p. 147, points to the similarity between Ps. 22:28-30 and Isa. 2:2-4; Mi. 4:1-5. In each of these texts there is a picture of eschatological victory.

[39]Jean Daniélou, "Le psaume 21 dans la catéchèse patristique," *MD* 49 (1957): 17-34, provides a helpful orientation to the use of the psalm among the Fathers.

[40]Cranfield, *Mark*, p. 458; Grundmann, *Mark*, p. 315; William L. Lane, *The Gospel of Mark, The English Text with Introduction, Exposition and Notes*, NICNT (Wm. B. Eerdmans Publishing Co., 1974), pp. 572-73; Schweizer, *Mark*, p. 353.

[41]Alan Culpepper, "The Passion and Resurrection in Mark," *Rev Exp* 75 (1978): 588.

[42]Ruppert, *Jesus als der leidende Gerechte?*, p. 28.

[43]Fritz Stolz, "Psalm 22: alttestamentliches Reden vom Menschen und neutestamentliches Reden von Jesus," *ZTK* 77 (1980): 138.

[44]Ibid., p. 148.

[45]Martinez, *The Gospel Accounts of the Death of Jesus*, p. 57.

[46]Kenneth Graystone, "The Darkness of the Cosmic Sea: A Study of Symbolism in St. Mark's Narrative of the Crucifixion," *Theo* 55 (1952); 122-27, traces the darkness to the theme of chaos *via* Pss. 18,74,88,105; Jb. 34.   Mark, however, does not allude to any of these texts.
            Philo, *De Providentia*, in *Philo*, trans. F. H. Colson, The Loeb Classical Library, 10 vols. (Cambridge: Harvard University Press, 1941), 9:2,50, writes:
            The sun and moon are natural divinities, and so these
            eclipses are concomitant circumstances, yet eclipses
            announce the death of kings and the destruction of
            cities as is clearly indicated by Pindar on the
            occurrence of an eclipse in the passage quoted above.
The text supports the royal theme but it is difficult to draw a direct line between it and the gospel.
            Lagrange, *Mark*, 432, speculates about a sirocco.   Anderson, *Mark*, p. 345, is probably correct when he says that parallels from pagan records and such natural phenomena as duststorms are beside the point.   The evangelist envisioned a supernatural darkness.

[47]Lohmeyer, *Mark*, p. 345; Robert H. Smith, "Darkness at Noon in Mark's Passion Narrative," *CTM* 44 (1973): 333.

[48]Lohmeyer, *Mark*, p. 345; Loisy, *Mark*, pp. 467-68; Martinez, *The Gospel Accounts of the Death of Jesus*, p. 64; Nineham, *Mark*, p. 428.

[49]Anderson, *Mark*, pp. 345-46; and Cranfield, *Mark*, p. 458, believe that such an approach lessens the depth of Jesus' cry.

[50]Léon-Dufour, "Le dernier cri de Jésus," p. 672.

[51]It is understandable that the references to Ps. 22 come primarily from the section of complaint since Mark is describing the sufferings of Jesus.   Therefore, we find unconvincing the argument of Schmid, "Mein Gott, mein Gott, warum hast du mich verlassen?" p. 140, against Gese, i.e., Mark does not quote from the entire psalm.

[52]Gese, "Psalm 22 und das Neue Testament," p. 13.

[53]Eaton, *Kingship and the Psalms*, p. 34.

[54]Brevard Childs, "Psalm Titles and Midrashic Exegesis," *JSS* 16 (1971): 140, writes about the psalm titles: "David's inner life was now unlocked to the reader, who was allowed to hear his intimate thoughts and reflections."

[55]Heribert Schützeichel, "Der Todeschrei Jesu: Bemerkungen zu einer Theologie des Kreuzes," *TTZ* 83 (1974): 3; Sahlin, "Zum Verständnis der christologischen Anschauung des Markusevangeli- ums," p. 5.

[56]Klemens Stock, "Das Bekenntnis des Centurio: Mk 15, 39 im Rahmen des Markusevangeliums," *ZKT* 100 (1978): 290.

[57]Ibid., pp. 298-99.

[58]Gese, "Psalm 22 und das Neue Testament," p. 17.

[59]Culpepper, "The Passion and Resurrection in Mark," p. 584, has a similar outline except that he makes the third event the death of Jesus (15:33-37) and the response to the event the tearing of the curtain and the confession of the centurion (15: 38-39). Hillmann, *Aufbau und Deutung der synoptischen Leidens-berichte*, p. 127, arranges the third part under the headings, "The Son of God dies with women as witnesses" (15:33-41) and "The Son of God is buried with women as witnesses" (15:42-47). We feel that both of these outlines miss the importance of the great cry and the final mockery.

[60]A wide spread of witnesses (A C W θ f^1 ^{13}) read *kraxas exepneusen*. However, *kraxas* is probably an interpolation from Mt. 27:50, according to Metzger, *A Textual Commentary on the Greek New Testament*, p. 121.

[61]Stock, "Das Bekenntnis des Centurio," p. 292, also sees the confession as resulting from the cry. However, for him it is the second, wordless cry which functions as an "Epiphanievor-gang." Also, *TDNT*, s.v. *phōnē*, by Betz, 9: 294.

[62]Lamarche, "La mort du Christ et le voile du temple," pp. 583-86, provides a survey of opinions.

[63]Authors who favor, or lean toward an inner curtain hy-pothesis: Anderson, *Mark*, p. 347; Cranfield, *Mark*, pp. 459-60; Linnemann, *Studien zur Passionsgeschichte*, pp. 158-63; Loisy, *Mark*, p. 470; Pesch, *Mark*, p. 497; *TDNT*, s.v. *katapetasma*, by Schneider, 3:628.
    Authors who favor or lean toward an outer curtain hypothe-sis: Best, *The Temptation and the Passion*, p. 99; Donahue, *Are You the Christ?*, pp. 202-03; Dormeyer, *Die Passion Jesu als Verhaltensmodell*, p. 205; Juel, *Messiah and Temple*, pp. 140-42; Klostermann, *Mark*, p. 167; Lohmeyer, *Mark*, p. 347.
    Authors who do not make a final judgment: Nineham, *Mark*, p. 430; Schneider, *Die Passion Jesu nach den drei älteren Evangelien*, p. 128.
    Authors who see the curtain as referring to both inner and outer: Gnilka, *Mark*, p. 324; Lamarche, "La mort du Christ et le voile du temple," pp. 586-87, R. J. McKelvey, *The New Temple: The Church in the New Testament.* Oxford Theological Monographs (Oxford: Oxford University Press, 1969), p. 73.
    Authors who see the curtain as referring to the flesh of Christ: Genest, *Le Christ de la passion perspective structurale*, p. 104; Gösta Lindeskop, "The Veil of the Temple," *ConN*, vo. 11 (Lund: CWK Gleerup, 1947), p. 137.

[64]Lagrange, *Mark*, p. 436; *TDNT*, s.v. *katapetasma*, by Schneider, 3: 628.

[65]Lindeskop, "The Veil of the Temple," pp. 132-37; *TDNT*, s.v. *katapetasma*, by Schneider, 3: 630.

[66]Donahue, *Are You the Christ?*, p. 203.

[67]Ibid., pp. 113-135; Juel, *Messiah and Temple*, pp. 127-39.

[68]Juel, *Messiah and Temple*, pp. 140-42, points to " . . . miraculous portents signaling the impending doom of the temple." He suggests that the tearing of the curtain may somehow be related to these portents. In that case Mark would be referring to the outer veil.

[69]Ibid., p. 128.

[70]Lamarche, "La Mort du Christ et le voile du temple," p. 587; McKelvey, *The New Temple*, pp. 72-74.

[71]Linnemann, *Studien zur Passionsgeschichte*, p. 162.

[72]Genest, *Le Christ de la passion perspective structurale*, p. 107.

[73]Fredrick Janssen, "Die synoptischen Passionsberichte: Ihre theologische Konzeption und literarische Komposition," *Bib Leb* 14 (1973): 55.

[74]Most commentators recognize the employment of Colwell's rule here, that definite predicate nouns which precede the verb usually lack the article, so that Son of God can be translated with the definite article. See, C. F. D. Moule, *An Idiom Book of New Testament Greek* (Cambridge: Cambridge University Press, 1953), pp. 115-16. However, Philip B. Harner, "Qualitative Anarthrous Predicate Nouns: Mark 15:39 and John 1:1," *JBL* 92 (1973): 75-87, claims that the situation is more complex and argues that where an anarthrous predicate precedes the verb " . . . the question of definiteness or indefiniteness is secondary to the qualitative significance of the predicate." (p. 80) Therefore, he maintains that the word order in 15:39

> . . . suggests that Mark was primarily concerned to say something about the meaning of Jesus' sonship rather than simply to designate or define him as *the* Son of God at this point. . . . Mark may wish to emphasize . . . that Jesus' sonship to God involves suffering and death." (p. 80)

[75]Vielhauer, "Erwägungen zur Christologie des Markusevangeliums," has capitalized upon these three occurrences of the title. However, his thesis overruns the evidence when he interprets them against an Egyptian background of accession to the throne (p. 167).

[76]Metzger, *A Textual Commentary on the Greek New Testament*, p. 73; Minette de Tillesse, *Le secret messianique dans L'Evangile de Marc*, pp. 353-54, suggests that the double title "Christ" and "Son of God" may correspond to the division of the gospel which finds its first climax in Peter's confession (8:29) and its second climax in the centurion's confession (15:39).

[77]Ulrich B. Müller, "Die christologische Absicht des Markusevangeliums und die Verklärungsgeschichte," *ZNW* 64 (1973):

159-93; Schreiber, *Theologie des Vertrauens*; Theodore J. Weeden, Mark, *Traditions in Conflict* (Philadelphia: Fortress Press, 1971), represent the latter view.

[78]Oscar Cullmann, *The Christology of the New Testament*, trans. Shirley C. Guthrie (London: SCM Press, 1959), pp. 270-305; Christian Mauer, "Knecht Gottes und Sohn Gottes im Passionsbericht des Markusevangeliums," *ZTK* 58 (1953): 1-38; Minette de Tillesse, *Le secret messianique dans L'Évangile de Marc*, pp. 342,63, represent this view.

[79]Berger, "Zum Problem der Messianität Jesu," and "Die königlichen Messiastraditionen des Neuen Testaments," represents this view.

[80]Juel, *Messiah and Temple*; Lövestam, *Son and Saviour*, represent this view.

[81]Schreiber, *Theologie des Vertrauens*, p. 47, writes: "Alle Spottworte hingegen, in denen die Feinde Jesu nur ihre ungläubigen Wünsche aussprechen, sind in ihrem Wortsinn genau entgegengesetzt zu verstehen, also in dieser Weise umzukehren."

[82]*TDNT*, s.v. *huios*, by Schweizer, 8:347.

[83]Ibid., p. 351.

[84]Albert Descamps, "Pour une histoire du titre 'Fils de Dieu': Les antécédents par rapport à Marc," in *L'Évangile selon Marc*, p. 57.

[85]Ibid., p. 535, "Ces derniers mots se prêteraient mal à une interpretation messianique, et c'est pourquoi le Chroniste les omettra."

[86]Joseph Coppens, *Le messianisme royal: Ses origines. Son développement. Son accomplissement*, Lectio Divina, no 54 (Paris: Les Éditions du Cerf, 1968), p. 57.

[87]Descamps, "Pour une histoire du titre 'Fils de Dieu,'" p. 536.

[88]Gerald Cook, "The Israelite King as Son of God," *ZAW* 73 (1961): 216-17.

[89]*The Apocrypha and Pseudepigrapha of the Old Testament*, ed. R. H. Charles, 2 vols. (Oxford: Clarendon Press, 1913). For a detailed presentation of this text see, Brendan Byrne, *'Son of God' - 'Seed of Abraham': A Study of the Idea of the Sonship of God and of All Christians in Paul against the Jewish Background*, *AnBib*, no. 83 (Rome: Biblical Institute Press, 1979), pp. 23-59.

[90]It appears that Wis. 2:18 has influenced Mt. 27:43. However, there is no such allusion in the Markan parallel.

[91]Gustaf Dalman, *The Words of Jesus: Considered in the Light of Post-Biblical Jewish Writings and the Aramaic Language*, trans. D. M. Kay (Edinburgh: T & T Clark, 1909), p. 270, notes the reference to Ps. 2 in Ps. Sol. 17:26 but judges that " . . . Ps. 2 was not of decisive importance in the Jewish conception of the Messiah, and that 'Son of God' was not a common Messianic title." (p. 72)

[92]Hengel, *The Son of God*, p. 44.

[93]Vermes, *Jesus the Jew*, pp. 198-99, says that the passage is too problematic to indicate more than that "Son of God" can accompany the title Messiah.

[94]Joseph Fitzmyer, "The Contribution of Qumran Aramaic to the Study of the New Testament," in *A Wandering Aramean*, pp. 92-93, gives the following translation of the fragment:
[But your son] (7) shall be great upon the earth,
(8) [O King! All (men) shall] make [peace], and all
shall serve (9) [him. He shall be called the son of]
the [G]reat [God], and by his name shall he be named.
(Col.2) (1) He shall be hailed (as) the Son of God, and
they shall call him Son of the Most High. As comets
(flash) (2) to the sight, so shall be their kingdom.
(For some year[s] they shall rule upon (3) the earth
and shall trample everything (under foot); people shall
trample upon people, city upon ci[t]y. (4) (*vacat*)
until there arises the people of God, and everyone
rests from the sword.

[95]Fitzmyer, "Addendum: Implications of the 4Q 'Son of God' Text," in *A Wandering Aramean*, p. 106.

[96]Hengel, *The Son of God*, p. 45.

[97]Otto Betz, "Die Frage nach dem messianischen Bewusststein Jesu," *NovT* 6 (1963): 20-48.

[98]Lovestam, *Son and Saviour*, p. 14, writes: "It is impossible to resist the conclusion that the proclamation of Jesus as God's Son with quotations from Ps. 2:7 and 2 Sam 7:14, and the conception *prōtokos*, stand in an immediate exegetical connection with one another." And again, " . . . there is clear and distinct evidence that Ps. 2:7 and 2 Sam 7:14 were coupled together in the Primitive Church with this very reference to the promise of David."

[99]*TDNT*, s.v. *huios*, by Schweizer, 8: 368.

[100]Hahn, *The Titles of Jesus in Christology*, p. 285, writes: "There is no doubt that the question of the high priest *sy ei ho Christos ho huios to eulogētou* is to be understood in the sense of hendiadys."

[101]Jn. 1:49 identifies Son of God and King of Israel.

NOTES - CONCLUSION

[1]Sherman E. Johnson, "The Davidic-Royal Motif in the Gospels, *JBL* (1968): 136, writes: "The Gospel of Mark represents the culmination of a process whereby messianism is so transformed that it is practically rejected." It is this type of position that we believe must be examined once more.

SELECTED BIBLIOGRAPHY

I. COMMENTARIES

Achtemeier, Paul J. *Invitation to Mark: A Commentary on the Gospel of Mark with Complete Text from the Jerusalem Bible.* Garden City, New York: Image Books, 1978.

_____. *Mark.* Proclamation Commentaries: The New Testament Witness for Preaching. Philadelphia: Fortress Press, 1975.

Anderson, Hugh. *The Gospel of Mark.* New Century Bible. Greenwood, South Carolina: Attic Press, 1976.

Cranfield, C. E. B. *The Gospel According to Saint Mark: An Introduction and Commentary.* Cambridge: Cambridge University Press, 1959.

Gnilka, Joachim. *Das Evangelium nach Markus: 2 Teilband Mk 8, 17-16,20.* Evangelisch-Katholischer Kommentar zum Neuen Testament, Bd. 2, T. 2. Zürich: Benziger Verlag, 1979.

Grundmann, Walter. *Das Evangelium nach Markus.* Theologischer Handkommentar zum Neuen Testament, Bd. 2. 5. Aufl. Berlin: Evangelische Verlagsanstalt, 1959.

Klostermann, Erich. *Das Markusevangelium.* Handbuch zum Neuen Testament, Bd. 3. 5. Augl. Tübingen: J. C. B. Mohr (Paul Siebeck), 1971.

Lagrange, M. J. *Évangile selon Saint Marc.* Études bibliques. Éditions corrigée et augmentée. Paris: Librairie Lecoffre, 1947.

Lane, William L. *The Gospel According to Mark: The English Text with Introduction, Exposition and Notes.* NICNT. Grand Rapids, Michigan: William B. Eerdmans Publishing Co., 1974.

Lohmeyer, Ernst. *Das Evangelium des Markus.* Kritisch-exegetischer Kommentar über das Neue Testament, Bd. 2. 12. Aufl. Göttingen: Vandenhoeck & Ruprecht, 1953.

Loisy, Alfred. *L'Évangile selon Marc.* Paris: Émile Nourry, 1912.

Nineham, D. E. *The Gospel of St. Mark.* The Pelican Gospel Commentaries. Baltimore: Penguin Books, 1963.

Pesch, Rudolf. *Das Markusevangelium II. Teil: Kommentar zu Kap. 8,27-16, 20.* Herders theologischer Kommentar zum Neuen Testament, Bd. 2, T. 1. Freiburg: Herder, 1977

Schniewind, Julius. *Das Evangelium nach Markus: Übersetz und erklärt*. Das Neue Testament Deutsch, Bd. 1. 6 Aufl. Göttingen: Vandenhoeck & Ruprecht, 1952.

Schweizer, Eduard. *The Good News According to Mark*. trans. Donald H. Madvig. Richmond: John Knox Press, 1970.

Taylor, Vincent. *The Gospel According to St. Mark: The Greek Text with Introduction, Notes, and Indexes*. 2d ed. New York: St. Martin's Press, 1966.

                        II. THE PASSION

Bajsic, A. "Pilatus, Jesus und Barabbas." *Bib* 48 (1967): 7-28.

Benoit, Pierre. *The Passion and Resurrection of Jesus Christ*. trans. Benet Weatherhead. New York: Herder & Herder, 1969.

Bertram, Georg. *Die Leidensgeschichte Jesu und der Christuskult: Eine formgeschichtliche Untersuchung*. Göttingen: Vandenhoeck & Ruprecht, 1922.

Best, Ernest. *The Temptation and the Passion: The Markan Soteriology*. SNTSMS, no. 2. Cambridge: Cambridge University Press, 1965.

Blinzler, Josef. *Der Prozess Jesu: Das jüdische und das römische Gerichtsverfahren gegen Jesus Christus auf Grund der ältesten Zeugnisse dargestellt und beurteilt*. 3. Aufl. Regensburg: Verlag Friedrich Pustet, 1960.

Braumann, Georg. "Markus 15,2-5 und Markus 14,55-64." *ZNW* 52 (1961): 273-278.

Broer, Ingo. *Die Urgemeinde und das Grab Jesu: Eine Analyse der Grablegungsgeschichte im Neuen Testament*. SANT, Bd. 31. Munich: Kösel-Verlag, 1972.

Bruce, F. F. "The Book of Zechariah and the Passion Narrative." *BJRL* 43 (1961): 336-353.

Burkill, T. A. "The Condemnation of Jesus: A Critique of Sherwin-White's Thesis." *NovT* 12 (1970): 321-42.

Conzelmann, Hans. "History and Theology in the Passion Narratives of the Synoptic Gospels," *Int* 24 (1970): 178-97.

Culpepper, R. A. "The Passion and Resurrection in Mark." *Rev Ex* 75 (1978): 583-600.

Daniélou, Jean. "Le psaume 21(22) dans la catéchèse patristique." *MD* 49 (1957): 17-34.

Danker, Frederick W. "The Demonic Secret: A Reexamination of the Cry of Dereliction (15:34)." *ZNW* 61 (1970): 48-69.

Dewar, Francis. "Chapter 13 and the Passion Narrative in St. Mark." *Theo* 64 (1961): 99-107.

Dhanis, Edouard. "L'Ensevelissement de Jésus et la visite au tombeau dans l'Évangile de Saint Marc (Mc xv. 40-xvi 8)." *Gregorianum* 39 (1958): 367-410.

Dibelius, Martin. *Botschaft und Geschichte: Gesammelte Aufsätze.* ed. Gunther Bornkamm. Bd. 1, *Zur Evangelienforschung.* Tübingen: J. C. B. Mohr (Paul Siebeck), 1953.

Donahue, John R. *Are You the Christ? The Trial Narrative in the Gospel of Mark.* SBL Dissertation Series, no. 10. Missoula, Montana: SBL, 1973.

Dormeyer, Detlev. *Die Passion Jesu als Verhaltensmodel Literarische und theologische Analyse der Traditions- und Redaktionsgeschichte der Markuspassion.* NTAbh, n. F. Bd. 11. Münster: Verlag Aschendorff, 1974.

_____. *Der Sinn des Leidens Jesu: Historischkritische und Textpragmatische Analysen zur Markuspassion.* SB, Bd. 96. Stuttgart: Katholisches Bibelwerk.

Finegan, Jack. *Die Überlieferung der Leidens-und Auferstehungsgeschichte Jesu.* Beihefte zur Zeitschrift für die neutestamentliche Wissenschaft, Beih. 15. Giessen: Verlag von Alfred Töpelmann, 1934.

Fisher, Loren R. "Betrayed by Friends: An Exposition of Psalm 22." *Int* 18 (1964): 20-38.

Genest, Olivette. *Le Christ de la passion perspective structurale: Analyse de Marc 14,53-15,47, des parallèles bibliques et extra-bibliques.* Recherches, no 21 théologie. Montréal: Bellarmin, 1978.

Gese, Hartmut. "Psalm 22 und das Neue Testament: Der älteste Bericht vom Tode Jesu und die Entstehung des Herrenmahles." *ZTK* 65 (1968): 1-22.

Gnilka, Joachim. "'Mein Gott, mein Gott, warum hast du mich verlassen?' (Mk 15,34 Par)." *BZ* n. F. 3 (1959): 294-97.

Grayston, Kenneth. "The Darkness of the Cosmic Sea: A Study of Symbolism in St. Mark's Narrative of the Crucifixion." *Theo* 55 (1952): 122-27.

Guillaume, A. "Mt. xxvii, 46 in the Light of the Dead Sea Scroll of Isaiah." *PEQ* 83 (1951): 78-80.

Hendrickx, Hermann. *The Passion Narrative of the Synoptic Gospels.* Manila, Philippines: East Asian Pastoral Institute, 1977.

Hengel, Martin. *Crucifixion in the Ancient World and the Folly of the Cross.* trans. John Bowden. Philadelphia: Fortress Press, 1977.

Hillmann, P. Willibrord. *Aufbau und Deutung der synoptischen Leidensberichte: Ein Beitrag zur Kompositionstechnik und Sinndeutung der drei älteren Evangelien.* Friburg im Breisgau: Herder & Co., 1941.

Janssen, F. "Die synoptischen Passionsberichte: Ihre theologische Konzeption und literarische Komposition." *Bib Leb* 14 (1973): 40-57.

Juel, Donald. *Messiah and Temple: The Trial of Jesus in The Gospel of Mark.* SBL Dissertation Series, no. 31. Missoula, Montana: Scholars Press, 1977.

Kelber, Werner, ed. *The Passion in Mark: Studies on Mark 14-16.* Philadelphia: Fortress Press, 1976.

Lamarche, Paul. "La mort du Christ et la voile du temple: Selon Marc." *NRT* 96 (1974): 583-99.

Lang, H. D. "The Relationship between Psalm 22 and the Passion Narrative." *CTM* 48 (1972): 610-21.

Léon-Dufour, Xavier. "Le dernier cri de Jésus." *Et* 348 (1978): 666-82.

_____. "Passion [Récits de la]." *Dictionnaire de la Bible.* Supplement 6, cols. 1419-92.

Lindeskog, Gösta. "The Veil of the Temple." *Con NT* 11 (1974): 132-37.

Linnemann, Eta. *Studien zur Passionsgeschichte.* FRLANT, Hft. 102. Göttingen: Vandenhoeck & Ruprecht, 1970.

Linton, Olof. "The Trial of Jesus and the Interpretation of Psalm CX." *NTS* 7 (1961): 258-63.

Lohse, Eduard. *History of the Suffering and Death of Jesus Christ.* trans. Martin O. Dietrich. Philadelphia: Fortress Press, 1967.

Maccoby, H. Z. "Jesus and Barabbas." *NTS* 16 (1970): 55-60.

Mahoney, Aidan. "A New Look at 'The Third Hour' of Mk 15,25." *CBQ* 28 (1966): 292-99.

Martinez, Ernesto R. *The Gospel Accounts of the Death of Jesus: A Study of the Death Accounts Made in the Light of the New Testament Tradition, The Redaction and the Theology of the Four Evangelists.* Rome, 1970.

Maurer, Christian. "Knecht Gottes und Sohn Gottes im Passionsbericht des Markusevangeliums." *ZTK* 50 (1953): 1-38.

O'Neill, J. C. "The Silence of Jesus." *NTS* 15 (1969): 153-67.

Osborne, Grant R. "Redactional Trajectories in the Crucifixion Narrative." *EvQ* 51 (1979): 80-96.

Oswald, Julius von. "Die Beziehungen zwischen Psalm 22 und dem
     vormarkinischen Passionsbericht." *ZKT* 101 (1979): 53-66.

Patte, Daniel, and Patte, Aline. *Structural Exegesis: From
     Theory to Practice: Exegesis of Mark 15 and 16 Hermeneu-
     tical Implications.* Philadelphia: Fortress Press, 1978.

Peddinghaus, Carl Daniel. "Die Entstehung der Leidensgeschichte:
     Eine traditionsgeschichtliche und historische Untersuchung
     des Werdens und Wachsens der erzählenden Passionstradition
     bis zum Entwurf des Markus." Dissertation: Heidelberg,
     1965.

Piper, Otto A. "God's Good News: The Passion Story According
     to Mark." *Int* 9 (1955): 165-82.

Ramsey, A. M. "The Narratives of the Passion." *Studia Evangel-
     ica: Texte und Untersuchungen zur Geschichte der alt-
     christlichen Literatur.* Berlin: Akademia Verlag, 1964.

Rehm, M. "Eli, Eli, lamma sabachthani." *BZ*, n. F. 2 (1958):
     275-78.

Reumann, John H. "Psalm 22 at the Cross: Lament and Thanks-
     giving for Jesus Christ." *Int* 30 (1974): 39-58.

Rose, Andre. "L'Influence des psaumes sur les announces et les
     récits de la passion et de la résurrection dans les évan-
     giles." *Le Psautier: Ses origines. Ses problèmes litter-
     aires. Son influence.* ed. Robert de Langhe. Orientalia
     et Biblica Lovaniensia, no 4. Louvain: Publications
     Universitaires, 1962, pp. 297-356.

Ruckstuhl, Eugene. *Chronology of the Last Days of Jesus: A
     Critical Study.* trans. Victor J. Drapela. New York:
     Desclée Co., 1965.

Ruppert, Lothar. *Jesus als der leidende Gerechte? Der Weg Jesu
     im Lichte eines alte- und zwischentestamentlichen Motivs.*
     SB, Bd. 59. Stuttgart: Katholisches Bibelwerk, 1972.

Schelkle, K. H. *Die Passion Jesu in der Verkündigung des Neuen
     Testaments: Ein Beitrag zur Formgeschichte und zur Theo-
     logie des Neuen Testaments.* Heidelberg: F. H. Kerle
     Verlag, 1949.

Schenk, Wolfgang. *Der Passionsbericht nach Markus: Untersuchun-
     gen zur Überlieferungsgeschichte der Passionstraditionen.*
     Leipzig: Gütersloher Verlagshaus Gerd Mohn, 1974.

Schenke, Ludger. *Auferstehungsverkündigung und leeres Grab:
     Eine traditionsgeschichtliche Untersuchung von Mk 16,1-8.*
     SB, Bd. 33. Stuttgart: Verlag Katholisches Bibelwerk,
     1968.
     _____. *Der gekreuzigte Christus: Versuch einer literar-
     kritischen und traditionsgeschichtlichen Bestimmung der
     vormarkinischen Passionsgeschichte.* SB, Bd. 69. Stuttgart:
     Verlag Katholisches Bibelwerk, 1974.

_____. *Studien zur Passionsgeschichte des Markus: Tradition und Redaktion in Markus 14:1-42.* Forschung zur Bibel, Bd. 4. Würzburg: Echter Verlag Katholisches Bibelwerk, 1971.

Schille, Gottfried. "Das Leiden des Herren. Die evangelische Passionstradition und ihr Sitz im Leben." *ZTK* 52 (1955): 161-205.

Schlier, Heinrich. *Die Markuspassion.* Einseideln: Johannes Verlag, 1974.

Schneider, Gerhard. "Gab es eine vorsynoptische Szene 'Jesus vor dem Synhedrium'?" *NovT* 12 (1970): 22-39.

_____. *Die Passion Jesu nach den drei älteren Evangelien.* Biblische Handbibliothek, Bd. 11. Munich: Kösel-Verlag, 1973.

_____. "Das Problem einer vorkanonischen Passionerzählung," *BZ* 2 (1972): 222-44.

Schreiber, Johannes. *Die Markuspassion: Wege zur Erforschung der Leidensgeschichte Jesu.* Hamburg: Furche-Verlag, 1969.

_____. *Theologie des Vertrauens: Eine redaktionsgeschichliche Untersuchung des Markusevangeliums.* Hamburg: Furche-Verlag, 1967.

Schüngel, Paul H. "Der Erzählung des Markus über den Tod Jesu: Verstehenshilfen in Mk 15." *Orientierung* 38 (1974): 62-5.

Schützeichel, Heribert. "Der Todesschrei Jesu - Bermerkungen zu einer Theologie des Kreuzes." *TTZ* 82 (1974): 1-16.

Scroggs, Robin, *et al.* "Reflections on the Question: Was there a pre-Markan Passion Narrative?" A Report Prepared for the Markan Task Force of the Society of Biblical Literature. *Seminar Papers.* vol. 2:503-85.

Senior, Donald. *The Passion Narrative According to Matthew.* BETL, no. 39 Louvain: Leuven University Press, 1975.

Smith, Robert H. "Darkness at Noon: Mark's Passion Narrative." *CTM* 44 (1973): 325-38.

Stock, Klemens. "Das Bekenntnis des Centurio: Mk 15,39 im Rahmen des Markusevangeliums." *ZKT* 100 (1978): 289-301.

Stolz, Fritz. "Psalm 22: Alttestamentliches Reden vom Menschen und neutestamentliches Reden von Jesus." *ZTK* 77 (1980): 130-48.

Vanhoye, Albert. "Structure et théologie des récits de la Passion dans les évangiles synoptiques." *NRT* 89 (1967): 135-63.

Viering, Fritz, ed. *Zur Bedeutung des Todes Jesu: Exegetische Beiträge.* Gerd Mohn: Gütersloher Verlagshaus, 1967.

Weber, Hans-Reudi. *The Cross: Tradition and Interpretation.* trans. Elke Jessett. Grand Rapids, Michigan: William B. Eerdmans, 1979.

Winter, Paul. *On the Trial of Jesus.* Studia Judaica: For-schungen zur Wissenschaft des Judentums, B. 1. Berlin: Walter de Gruyter & Co., 1961.

Taylor, Vincent. *The Passion Narrative of St. Luke: A Critical and Historical Investigation.* ed. by Owen E. Evans. SNTSMS, no. 19. Cambridge: Cambridge University Press, 1972.

III. GENERAL WORKS

Achtemeier, Paul J. "'And He Followed Him': Miracles and Dis-cipleship in Mark 10:46-52." *Semeia,* 11 (1978): 116-45.

_____. "'He Taught Them Many Things': Reflections on Marcan Christology." *CBQ* 42 (1980): 465-81.

_____. "Mark as Interpreter of the Jesus Traditions." *Int* 32 (1978): 353-68.

Ambrozic, Aloysius. *The Hidden Kingdom: A Redaction-Critical Study of the References to the Kingdom in Mark's Gospel.* The CBQ Monograph Series, no. 2. Washington: Catholic Biblical Association of America, 1972.

Andresen, Carl, and Klein, Günter, eds. *Theologia Crucis-Signum Crucis: Festschrift für Erich Dinkler zum 70. Geburtstag.* Tübingen: J. C. B. Mohr (Paul Siebeck), 1979.

Aux sources de la tradition chrétienne: Mélanges offerts à M. Maurice Goguel à l'occasion de son soixante-dixième anni-versaire. Bibliothèque théologique. Paris: Delachaux & Niestlé, 1950.

Bennett, W. J., Jr. "The Son of Man Must . . ." *NovT* (1975): 113-129.

Bentzen, Aage. *King and Messiah.* ed. by G. W. Anderson. 2d ed. Oxford: Basil Blackwell, 1979.

Berger, Klaus. "Die königlichen Messiastraditionen des Neuen Testaments." *NTS* 20 (1973): 1-44.

_____. "Zum Problem der Messianität Jesu." *ZTK* 71 (1974): 1-30.

Betz, Otto. "Die Frage nach dem messianischen Bewusstsein Jesu." *NovT* 6 (1963): 20-48.

Betz, Otto. ed. *Christology and a Modern Pilgrim: A Discussion with Norman Perrin.* rev. ed. Missoula, Montana: Scholars Press, 1974.

Betz, Otto; Hengel, Martin; and Schmidt, Peter, ed. *Abraham unser Vater: Juden und Christen im Gespräch über die Bibel: Festschrift für Otto Michael zum 60. Geburtstag.* Leiden: E. J. Brill, 1963.

Black, Matthew. *An Aramaic Approach to the Gospel and Acts.* 3d ed. with an appendix on The Son of Man by Geza Vermes. Oxford: Clarendon Press, 1967.

_____. "The Christological Use of the Old Testament in the New Testament." *NTS* 18 (1971): 1-14.

Blenkinsopp, Joseph. "The Oracle of Judah and the Messianic Entry." *JBL* 80 (1961): 55-64.

Blinzler, Josef. *Die Brüder und Schwestern Jesu.* SB, Bd. 21. Stuttgart: Verlag Katholisches Bibelwerk, 1967.

Borsch, Frederick Houk. *The Son of Man in Myth and History.* The New Testament Library. Philadelphia: The Westminster Press, 1967.

Brown, Raymond E. *The Gospel According to John.* The Anchor Bible, vols. 29-29a. Garden City, New York: Doubleday & Co., 1966-70.

Bultmann, Rudolf. *The History of the Synoptic Tradition.* trans. John Marsh. rev. ed. New York: Harper & Row, 1963.

_____. *Theology of the New Testament.* trans. Kendrick Grobel. London: SCM Press, 1952. 2 vols.

Burger, Christoph. *Jesus als Davidssohn: Eine Traditionsgeschichtliche Untersuchung.* FRLANT, Hft. 98. Göttingen: Vandenhoeck & Ruprecht, 1970.

Burkill, T. A. *Mysterious Revelation: An Examination of the Philosophy of St. Mark's Gospel.* Ithaca: Cornell University Press, 1963.

Bryne, Brendan. *'Sons of God' - 'Seed of Abraham': A Study of the Idea of the Sonship of God of All Christians in Paul Against the Jewish Background.* AnBib, no. 83. Rome: Biblical Institute Press, 1979.

Cerfaux, Lucien. *Recueil Lucien Cerfaux: Études d'exégèse et d'histoire religieuse réunies à l'occasion de son soixante-dixième anniversaire.* BETL, vols. 6-7. Gembloux: Editions J. Dulculot, 1954.

Childs, Brevard S. "Psalm Titles and Midrashic Exegesis." *JSS* 16 (1971): 137-50.

Collins, John J. "The Son of Man and the Saints of the Most
    High in the Book of Daniel." *JBL* 93 (1974): 50-66.

Cook, Gerald. "The Israelite King as Son of God." *ZAW* 73
    (1961): 202-225.

Cook, Michael J. *Mark's Treatment of the Jewish Leaders.* Sup-
    plements to Novum Testamentum, no 51. Leiden: E. J.
    Brill, 1978.

Coppens, Joseph. *Le messianisme royal: Ses origines. Son
    développement. Son accomplissement.* Lectio Divina, no
    54. Paris: Les Éditions du Cerf, 1968.

Cullmann, Oscar. *The Christology of the New Testament.* trans.
    Shirley C. Guthrie and Charles A. M. Hall. London: SCM
    Press, 1959.

Dahl, Nils Alstrup. *The Crucified Messiah: And Other Essays.*
    Minneapolis, Minnesota: Augsburg Publishing House, 1974.

Dalman, Gustaf. *The Words of Jesus: Considered in the Light
    of Post-Biblical Jewish Writings and the Aramaic Language.*
    trans. D. M. Kay. vol. 1, *Introduction and Fundamental
    Ideas.* Edinburgh: T & T Clark, 1909.

Daube, David. *The New Testament and Rabbinic Judaism.* Jordan
    Lectures, 1952. London: University of London Press, 1956.

Derrett, J. Duncan M. *Studies in the New Testament.* vol. 2,
    Midrash in Action and as a Literary Device. Leiden: E.
    J. Brill, 1978.

_____. "Law in the New Testament: The Palm Sunday Colt."
    NovT 13 (1971): 241-58.

Dibelius, Martin. *From Tradition to Gospel.* trans. Bertram Lee
    Woolf. New York: Charles Scribner's Sons, n.d.

Dodd, Charles H. *According to the Scriptures: The Sub-structure
    of the New Testament Theology.* New York: Charles Scrib-
    ner's Sons, 1953.

Doudna, John Charles. *The Greek of the Gospel of Mark.* JBL
    Monograph Series, vol. 12. Philadelphia: Society of Bib-
    lical Literature and Exegesis, 1961.

Duling, Dennis C. "The Promises to David and Their Entrance in-
    to Christianity - Nailing Down a Likely Hypothesis." *NTS*
    20 (1973): 55-77.

_____. "Solomon, Exorcism, and the Son of David." *HTR* 68
    (1975): 235-52.

Eaton, John H. *Kingship and the Psalms.* SBT 2d Series, no. 32.
    Naperville, Illinois: Alec R. Allenson, n.d.

Ellis, E. Earle, and Grässer, Erich. *Jesus und Paulus: Festschrift für Werner Georg Kümmel zum 70. Geburtstag.* Göttingen: Vandenhoeck & Ruprecht, 1975.

Engnell, Ivan. *Critical Essays on the Old Testament.* trans. and ed. by John T. Willis with Helmer Ringgren. London: S.P.C.K., 1970.

Feuillel, André. "L'Exousia du Fils de l'homme (d'après Mc. II, 10-28 et parr.)." *RSR* (1954): 161-92.

Fitzmyer, Joseph A. *A Wandering Aramean: Collected Essays.* SBL Monograph Series, no. 25. Missoula, Montana: Scholars Press, 1979.

Fuller, Reginald H. *The Foundations of New Testament Christology.* New York: Charles Scribner's Sons, 1965.

Gagg, Robert Paul. "Jesus und die Davidssohnfrage: Zur Exegese von Markus 12,35-37." *Theologische Zeitschrift* 7 (1951): 18-30.

Gaston, Lloyd. *No Stone on Another: Studies in the Significance of the Fall of Jerusalem in the Synoptic Gospels.* Supplements to Novum Testamentum, no. 23. Leiden: E. J. Brill, 1970.

Gelston, A. "A Sidelight on the 'Son of Man,'" *SJT* 22 (1969): 189-96.

Giesen, Heinz. "Der verdorrte Feigenbaum - Eine symbolische Aussage? Zu Mk 11,12-14. 20f." *BZ* 20 (1976): 95-111.

Gray, John. *The Biblical Doctrine of the Reign of God.* Edinburgh: T & T Clark, 1979.

Gunkel, Hermann. *Die Psalmen,* 5. Aufl. Göttingen: Vandenhoeck & Ruprecht, 1968.

Hahn, Ferdinand. *The Titles of Jesus in Christology: Their History in Early Christianity.* trans. Harold Knight and George Ogg. New York: The World Publishing Co., 1969.

Harner, Philip B. "Qualitative Anarthrous Predicate Nouns: Mark 15:39 and John 1:1." *JBL* 92 (1973): 75-87.

Harrington, Daniel J. "Research on the Jewish Pseudepigrapha during the 1970s." *CBQ* 42 (1980): 147-59.

Harris, James Rendel. *Testimonies.* Cambridge: Cambridge University Press, 1916-20.

Hartmann, Lars. *Prophecy Interpreted: The Formation of Some Jewish Apocalyptic Texts and of the Eschatological Discourse Mark 13 Par.* Trans. by Neil Tomkinson with the assistance of Jean Gray. *ConBNT,* no. 1. Lund, Sweden: CWK Gleerup, 1966.

Hawkins, John C. *Horae Synopticae: Contributions to the Synoptic Problem.* 2d ed. rev. and supp. Oxford: Clarendon Press, 1909.

Hay, David M. *Glory at the Right Hand: Psalm 110 in Early Christianity.* SBL Monograph Series, no. 18. Nashville: Abingdon Press, 1973.

Hengel, Martin. "Das Gleichnis von den Weingärtnern Mc 12,1-12 im Liche der Zenopapyri und der rabbinischen Gleichnisse." *ZNW* 59 (1968): 1-39.

_____. *The Son of God: The Origin of Christology and the History of Jewish-Hellenistic Religion.* trans. John Bowden. Philadelphia: Fortress Press, 1976.

Higgins, A. J. B. *Jesus and the Son of Man.* Philadelphia: Fortress Press, 1964.

Hill, David. "Son of Man in Psalm 80 v. 17." *NovT* (1973): 261-69.

Hooker, Morna. *Jesus and the Servant: The Influence of the Servant Concept of Deutero-Isaiah in the New Testament.* London: S.P.C.K., 1959.

_____. *The Son of Man in Mark: A Study of the Background of the Term "Son of Man" and its Use in St. Mark's Gospel.* London: S.P.C.K., 1967.

Hubaut, Michel. *La parabole des vignerons homicides.* Cahiers de la Revue Biblique, no 16. Paris: J. Gabalda, 1976.

Jeremias, Joachim. *The Eucharistic Words of Jesus.* trans. Norman Perrin. New York: Charles Scribner's Sons, 1966.

_____. *New Testament Theology: The Proclamation of Jesus.* trans. John Bowden. New York: Charles Scribner's Sons, 1971.

Johnson, Aubrey. *Sacral Kingship in Ancient Israel.* 2d ed. Cardiff: University of Wales Press, 1967.

Johnson, Sherman E. "The Davidic-Royal Motif in the Gospels." *JBL* 87 (1968): 136-50.

Kee, Howard Clark. *Community of the New Age: Studies in Mark's Gospel.* Philadelphia: The Westminster Press, 1977.

Kelber, Werner H. *The Kingdom in Mark.* Philadelphia: Fortress Press, 1974.

Kennard, J. Spencer. "Hosanna and the Purpose of Jesus." *JBL* 67 (1948): 171-76.

Kraus, Hans-Joachim. *Psalmen.* BKAT, Bd. 15. Teilband 1-2, *Psalmen.* Teilband 3, *Theologie der Psalmen.* Neukirchen-Vluyn: Neukirchener Verlag, 1960-79.

Kuhn, Heinz Wolfgang. "Das Reittier Jesu in der Einzugsges-
chichte des Markusevangeliums." *ZNW* 50 (1959): 82-91.

Lambrecht, Jan. "The Christology of Mark." *BTB* 3 (1973): 256-
73.

_____. *Die Redaktion der Markus - Apokalypse: Literarische
Analyse und Structuruntersuchung*. AnBib, Bd. 28. Rome:
Päpsliche Bibelinstitut, 1967.

Leivestad, Ragnar. "Exit the Apocalyptic Son of Man." *NTS* 18
(1972): 243-67.

Lightfoot, Robert H. *The Gospel Message of St. Mark*. Oxford:
Clarendon Press, 1950.

Lindars, Barnabbas. *New Testament Apologetic: The Doctrinal
Significance of the Old Testament Quotations*. Philadelphia:
The Westminster Press, 1961.

_____. "Re-Enter the Apocalyptic Son of Man." *NTS* 22 (1976):
52-72.

Loader, W. R. G. "Christ at the Right Hand - Ps CX.1 in the New
Testament." *NovT* 24 (1978): 199-217.

Lohmeyer, Ernst. *Lord of the Temple: A Study of the Relationship between Cult and Gospel*. trans. Stewart Todd. Richmond: John Knox Press, 1962.

Lövestam, Evald. "Jésus Fils de David chez les synoptics."
ST 28 (1974): 97-109.

_____. *Son and Saviour: A Study of Acts 13,32-37. With An
Appendix: "Son of God" in the Synoptic Gospels*. ConNT,
no. 18. Lund, Sweden: C. W. K. Gleerup, 1961.

McKelvey, R. J. *The New Temple: The Church in the New Testament*. Oxford Theological Monographs. Oxford: Oxford
University Press, 1969.

McKinnis, Ray. "An Analysis of Mark X 32-34." *NovT* 18 (1976):
81-100.

McNeil, Brian. "The Son of Man and the Messiah: A Footnote."
NTS 26 (1980): 419-21.

Maddox, Robert. "The Function of the Son of Man According to
the Synoptic Gospels." *NTS* 15 (1968): 45-74.

Marshall, I. Howard. "Son of God or Servant of Yahweh? - A Reconsideration of Mark 1:11." *NTS* 15 (1969): 326-36.

_____. "The Son of Man in Contemporary Debate." *EvQ* 42
(1978): 67-87.

_____. "The Synoptic Son of Man Sayings in Recent Discus-
sion." *NTS* 12 (1965-56): 327-51.

Marxsen, Willi. *Mark the Evangelist: Studies on the Redaction History of the Gospel.* trans. James Boyce *et al.* Nashville: Abingdon Press, 1969.

Massaux, Édouard *et al. La venue du Messie: Messianisme et eschatologie.* Recherches bibliques, no. 6. Brugges: Desclée de Brouwer, 1962.

Mays, James Luther. "Mark 8:27-9:1." *Int* 30 (1976): 174-78.

Meeks, Wayne. *The Prophet-King: Moses Traditions and the Johannine Christology.* Supplements to Novum Testamentum, vol. 14. Leiden: E. J. Brill, 1976.

Moulder, W. J. "The Old Testament Background and the Interpretation of Mark X. 45." *NTS* 24 (1977): 120-27.

Müller, U. B. "Die christologische Absicht des Markusevangeliums und die Verklärungsgeschichte." *ZNW* 64 (1973): 159-93.

Münderlein, Gerhard. "Die Verfluchung des Feigenbaums." *NTS* 10 (1963): 89-104.

Neirynck, Franz. "ANATEILANTOS TOU H̄ELIOU (Mc 16,2)." *ETL* 54 (1978): 70-103.

_____. *Duality in Mark: Contributions to the Study of the Markan Redaction.* BETL, no. 31. Louvain: Leuven University Press, 1972.

_____. "L'Évangile de Marc (II). À propos de R. Pesch, *Das Markusevangelium, 2 Teil.*" *ETL* 55 (1979): 1-42.

Neugebauer, Fritz. "Die Davidssohnfrage (Mark XII, 35-37, Par.) und der Menschensohn." *NTS* 21 (1974): 81-108.

Nolan, Brian M. *The Royal Son of God: The Christology of Matthew 1-2 in the Setting of the Gospel.* Orbis Biblicus et Orientalis, no. 23. Göttingen: Vandenhoeck & Ruprecht, 1979.

Norden, Eduard. *Agnostos Theos: Untersuchungen zur Formgeschichte religiöser Rede.* Leipzig: Verlag B. G. Teubner, 1913.

Patsch, Hermann. "Der Einzug Jesu in Jerusalem: Eine historischer Versuch." *ZTK* 68 (1971): 1-26.

Perrin, Norman. "The Composition of Mark IX,1." *NovT* 11 (1969): 67-70.

_____. "The Creative Use of the Son of Man Traditions by Mark." *Union Seminary Quarterly Review* 23 (1968): 357-65.

_____. "Mark 14:62: End Product of a Christian Pesher Tradition?" *NTS* 12 (1965): 150-55.

Pesch, Rudolf. *Naherwartungen: Tradition und Redaktion in Mk 13*. Kommentare und Beiträge zum Alten und Neuen Testament. Düsseldorf: Patmos-Verlag, 1968.

_____. ed. *Das Markus-Evangelium*. Wege der Forschung, Bd. 411. Darmstadt: Wissenschaftliche Buchgesellschaft, 1979.

Pesch, Rudolf; Schnackenburg, Rudolf; in zusammenarbeit mit Kaiser, Odilo, eds. *Jesus und der Menschensohn: Für Anton Vögtle*. Freiburg: Herder, 1975.

Pryke, E. J. *Redactional Style in the Marcan Gospel: A Study of Syntax and Vocabulary as Guides to Redaction in Mark*. SNTSMS, no. 33. Cambridge: Cambridge University Press, 1978.

Ringgren, Helmer. *The Messiah in the Old Testament*. SBT. Chicago: Alec R. Allenson, 1956.

Sabbé, M. ed. *L'Évangile selon Marc: Tradition et rédaction*. BETL, no 34. Louvain: Leuven University Press, 1974.

Sahlin, Harald. "Zum Verständnis der christologischen Anschauung des Markusevangeliums." *ST* 31 (1977): 1-19.

Schmid, Hans Heinrich. "'Mein Gott, mein Gott, warum hast du mich verlassen?' Psalm 22 als Beispeil alttestamentlicher Rede von Krankheit und Tod." *Wort und Dienst: Jahrbuch der Kirchlichen Hochschule*. ed. Hans Heinrich Schmidt. n.F. Bd. 11. Bethel bei Bielefeld: Verlagshandlung der Anstalt, 1971. pp. 119-40.

Schmidt, Karl Ludwig. *Der Rahmen der Geschichte Jesu: Literarkritische Untersuchungen zur ältesten Jesusüberlieferuung*. Berlin: Trowitzsch & Sohn, 1919.

Schnackenburg, Rudolf. *God's Rule and Kingdom*. trans. John Murray, 2d ed. New York: Herder & Herder, 1968.

Schneider, Gerhard. "Die Davidssohnfrage (Mk 12:35-37)." *Bib* 53 (1972): 65-90.

Schweizer, Eduard. *Neotestamentica: Deutsche und Englische Aufsätze 1951-1963*. Zurich: Zwingli Verlag, 1963.

_____. "The Son of Man." *JBL* 79 (1960): 119-129.

Stock, Klemens. "Gliederung und Zusammenhang in Mk 11-12." *Bib* 59 (1978): 481-515.

Strack, Herman L., and Billerbeck, Paul. *Kommentar zum Neuen Testament aus Talmud und Midrasch*. Munich: C. H. Beck'sche Verlagsbuchhandlung, 1922-56.

Strecker, Georg. "The Passion- and Resurrection Predictions in Mark's Gospel (Mark 8:31; 9:31; 10:32-34)." *Int* 22 (1968): 421-42.

Suhl, Alfred. *Die Funktion der alttestamentlichen Zitate und Anspielungen im Markusevangelium.* Gerd Mohn: Gutersloher Verlagshaus, 1965.

Tillesse, G. Minette de. *Le secret messianique dans L'Évangile de Marc.* Lectio Divina, no 47. Paris: Les Editions du Cerf, 1968.

Vermes, Geza. *Jesus the Jew: A Historian's Reading of the Gospels.* London: Collins, 1973.

Vielhauer, Philip. "Erwägungen zur Christologie des Markusevangeliums." *Zeit und Geschichte: Dankesgabe an Rudolf Bultman zum 80. Geburtstag.* ed. Erik Dinkler. Tübingen: J. C. B. Mohr (Paul Siebeck), 1964.

Weeden, Theodore J. *Mark - Traditions in Conflict.* Philadelphia: Fortress Press, 1971.

Weiser, Artur. *The Psalms: A Commentary.* trans. Herbert Hartwell. Old Testament Library. 5th rev. ed. Philadelphia: The Westminster Press.

Werner, Eric. "'Hosanna' in the Gospels." *JBL* 65 (1956): 97-122.

Wifall, Walter. "David - Prototype of Israel's Future." *BTB* 4 (1974): 92-107.

Tannehill, Robert C. "The Gospel of Mark as Narrative Christology." *Semeia* 16 (1979): 57-95.

Tödt, H. E. *The Son of Man in the Synoptic Tradition.* trans. Dorothea M. Barton. Philadelphia: The Westminster Press, 1965.

Turner, C. H. "Marcan Usage: Notes, Critical and Exegetical on the Second Gospel." *JTS* 25 (1924): 377-86; 26 (1925): 12-20, 145-156, 225-240; 27 (1926): 58-62; 28 (1927): 9-30, 349-62; 29 (1928): 275-89, 346-61.

Zerwick, Maximilian. *Untersuchungen zum Markus-Stil: Ein Beitrag zur stilistischen Durcharbeitung des Neuen Testaments.* Rome: Pontifical Biblical Institute, 1937.

IV. REFERENCE WORKS AND TRANSLATIONS

The Apocrypha and Pseudepigrapha of the Old Testament. ed. R. H. Charles. 2 vols. Oxford: Clarendon Press, 1913.

Bauer, Walter. *A Greek-English Lexicon of the New Testament and Other Early Christian Literature.* 2d ed. rev. and augmented by F. Wilbur Gingrich and Frederick W. Danker from Walter Bauer's 5th ed. 1958. Chicago: University of Chicago Press, 1979.

Blass, F., and Debrunner, A. *A Greek Grammar of the New Testament and Other Early Christian Literature.* trans. and rev. by Robert W. Funk. Chicago: University of Chicago Press, 1961.

Dupont-Sommer, A. *The Essene Writings from Qumran.* trans. G. Vermes. Gloucester, Mass.: Peter Smith, 1973.

Levey, Samson H. *The Messiah: An Aramaic Interpretation. The Messianic Exegesis of the Targum.* Monographs of the Hebrew Union College, no. 2. Cincinnati: Hebrew Union College-Jewish Institute of Religion, 1974.

Metzger, Bruce M. *A Textual Commentary on the Greek New Testament: A Companion Volume to the United Bible Societies' Greek New Testament (Third Edition).* London: United Bible Societies, 1971.

The Midrash on Psalms. trans. William G. Braude. Yale Judaica Series, no. 13. New Haven: Yale University Press, 1959.

Moule, C. F. D. *An Idiom-Book of New Testament Greek.* 2d ed. Cambridge: Cambridge University Press, 1959.

PSALMOI SOLOMŌNTOS Commonly Called the Psalms of Solomon: The Text Newly Revised from All the Mss. Edited with Introduction, English Translation, Notes, Appendix, and Indices. Ryle, Herbert Edward, and James, Montague Rhodes, eds. Cambridge: Cambridge University Press, 1891.

Saint Justin Martyr. ed. Thomas B. Falls. The Fathers of the Church: A New Translation. New York: Christian Heritage, 1948.

Sanders, J. A. *The Dead Sea Psalms Scroll.* Ithaca, New York: Cornell University Press, 1967.

The Testament of Job: According to the SV Text. ed. Robert A. Kraft *et al.* Texts and Translations, no. 5. Pseudepigrapha Series, no. 4. Missoula, Montana: Scholars Press, 1974.

The Theological Dictionary of the New Testament. trans. and ed. by Geoffrey W. Bromiley. 10 vols. vols 1-4 ed. by Gerhard Kittle; vols 5-9 ed. by Gerhard Friedrich; vol. 10 comp. by R. E. Pitkin. Grand Rapids, Michigan: William B. Eerdmans Publishing Co., 1964-76.

INDEX OF REFERENCES